# SILENT RETAIL KILLER

**10** *Survival Strategies for*
**BRICKS GROCERS**
*to Compete with*
**CLICKS GROCERS**

# EDDY W. HOLLEMAN

RoseDog Books

PITTSBURGH, PENNSYLVANIA 15238

RoseDog Books
585 Alpha Drive
Suite 103
Pittsburgh, PA 15238
Visit our website at *www.rosedogbookstore.com*

ISBN: 979-8-88729-301-1
eISBN: 979-8-88729-801-6

*I am proud to dedicate this book to my beautiful wife,
Kimberley Kay.*

*She has endured my lengthy absences at work and at home,
and generously bestowing on me her love, support, and
patience while worked on this book.*

*All my love goes to her. I would not be the man I am without
her love and support.*

*"No deadly threat was ever conquered through ignorance, fear, or inaction."*

*Eddy W. Holleman*

# CONTENTS

# PREFACE

Before the Internet, another "silent killer" threat moved into cities across the nation and forever altered the retail landscape: Walmart Supercenters. The first Supercenter opened in 1988 in Washington, Missouri. Today there are over 3,500 Walmart Supercenters in the U.S. averaging 178,000 square feet. Walmart is the largest grocery retailer in the U.S. as well. Walmart Supercenters quickly began disrupting the retail industry, including small businesses, conventional grocery stores, and even national grocery retailers. Many small businesses were forced to go out of business due to the inability to compete against Walmart's low prices and large selection. Many of these businesses succumbed to this "silent killer" because they failed to take Walmart Supercenters seriously and did not adopt different strategies that were effective to compete against the retail giant.

Walmart's success forced many business closures and significantly disrupted the retail industry. However, over time businesses adapted. Many examined Walmart's weaknesses and learned how to beat them or adapt and coexist with them. Today, online retailing is the new "silent killer." Conventional retailers need to learn how to adopt new strategies to fight and compete against them or coexist with them. Failure to do so will force many conventional retailers to go out of business, as many already have. The good news is that data reveals that conventional or "bricks" stores are fighting back and will continue to learn how to compete against and coexist with online or "clicks" retailers.

***Silent Retail Killer*** is designed to help brick-and-mortar (bricks) grocery retailers recognize the significance of the growth in online (clicks) grocery retailing. Despite bricks grocery retailing being far from extinction, failure to take the significance of clicks grocery retailing and its future growth seriously and finding strategies to minimize its impact will prove deadly to bricks retailers. This has become even truer due to the extreme rise of online grocery ordering during the COVID-19 pandemic that is projected to last after the pandemic ends. ***Silent Retail Killer*** helps bricks grocers survive and compete against clicks grocers, so they do not fail like so many local and even national retailers who failed because they did not take the threat of Walmart Supercenters seriously.

# INTRODUCTION

I always believe an individual has his or her greatest success when following a passion. Leveraging one's strengths fueled by such passion is a profound driver of success. When I began working in the grocery business as a teen, I discovered it is an industry I am passionate about and one I have innate skills with which to succeed. I have experienced great success from following this passion and developing these strengths in making the retail grocery industry a career choice. Today, I am a proud General Manager of one of the most successful grocery retailers in the U.S. I have also been serving as an adjunct professor in the business and accounting division for 16 years and counting.

While I find my work tremendously satisfying, I have also observed, with increasing concern, the challenges confronting brick-and-mortar retailers, commonly referred to as "bricks," from the juggernaut of online retailers known as "clicks." I have witnessed firsthand the rise of such online grocery retailers as Amazon, Chewy and others that continue to win market share from traditional grocery retailers.

My experience proves to me that clicks retailers are an increasingly formidable force, and bricks retailers are under attack from this threat on a daily basis. Whatever you sell in your store, you will eventually find your products will be offered online with greater convenience for customers and at a lower price. Amazon's vast selection and low-cost model, one that typically includes free shipping, has brought down major retailers and consumed thousands of smaller businesses across the world.

There are generally two camps of thought when it comes to bricks and clicks. In one camp, the thinking is that traditional retail is doomed by the increasing presence of online retailers, which will eventually consume bricks stores completely. In the other camp, the mindset is one of denial, where it is acknowledged that the bricks retail landscape is being altered, but it is one that is still growing and represents far more in sales overall than clicks retail.

As this book will demonstrate, neither of these contrasting views represents a fully accurate picture of modern retailing. The truth is more complex.

Yes, bricks grocers do have reasons to be optimistic. In 2020, dunnhumby, the global leader in customer data science, released its Retailer Preference Index (RPI), a wide-ranging and nationwide study that analyzes the $700 billion U.S. grocery market. H-E-B was rated the No. 1 U.S. grocery retailer, showing the strongest combination of financial performance and consumer emotional sentiment. Discounter Trader Joe's came in second, followed by online giant Amazon in third.

Nevertheless, bricks retailers would be foolish to think they do not have to seriously reconsider reshaping traditional retailing to successfully compete with clicks retailers in the future. The industry is evolving at warp speed: In 2020, consumers spent $861.12 billion on online purchases from U.S. merchants—a 44% increase from 2019—according to Digital Commerce 360. As I'll explain, the COVID-19 pandemic played a large role in that trend, but there's no putting the genie back in the bottle. Ignoring that reality is dangerous. History is littered with traditional retail firms that went out of business because they ignored the threat or failed to change rapidly enough when confronted with the growth of clicks retailing.

In *Retail Marketing Strategies For Brick and Mortar Businesses*, Tara Jacobsen and Rebecca Welch explained that the online retailing threat even extends to service industry companies.

"Service-based businesses are not immune to the growing online threat," Jacobsen and Welch wrote. "Lawyers are being squeezed out of small transitions by sites like Legalzoom.com and . . . Legal Shield. Doctors are less likely to see patients when they can just 'Google' their symptoms and find out what is wrong as opposed to coming into the office."

The facts of online retailing make it clear that every size, type and kind of bricks business owner needs to sleep with one eye open. Some company online is attempting to penetrate and overtake your business. Every day new retail competitors emerge online. Bricks managers need to understand how this affects their businesses and what they must do to change their businesses before it is too late for them to survive.

Many are familiar with the term "Silent Killer" as a reference to high blood pressure. If treated immediately, you have an excellent chance of survival. If treatment is delayed too long, you risk heart attack, stroke and even death. What's more, a quick fix — medication — rarely is enough to reverse this condition. You also need to change your habits of existence, such as modifying your diet, increasing your exercise and learning healthy ways to reduce stress to thrive. This is exactly the challenge facing bricks grocery retailers. Denying the threat of online grocery retailers or ignoring the imperative for change confronted with the online grocery juggernaut is almost certainly a disaster. Survivors are those who recognize the significance of the online threat and the need for rapid response, develop strategies and change early enough to thrive.

Online grocery retailers are a potential silent killer because the days of visiting your competitors to see what strategies they were employing are no longer adequate in an online world. Today's bricks grocery retailers must stay aware of traditional competitors in addition to comprehensively analyzing what strategies clicks grocery retailers are adopting online.

The point of this analogy is that if you apply treatment and make changes to improve your health, you can overcome the "silent killer" that high blood pressure can be. The same is true for traditional grocery retailers. Understanding the necessity for change in an increasingly online retail world and developing and implementing strategies designed to compete against this threat will beat the "silent killer" of clicks retail.

The good news is that writing an obituary for bricks retailers due to the threat posed by clicks retailers is unwarranted. There are a number of steps bricks retailers can adopt to minimize penetration from clicks retailers, regardless of the size, type or kind of business they own. One of the biggest lessons my experience and the continual challenge of online retailing have taught me is that when you own or manage a bricks store, you must strive daily to drive customers into your physical location. It's what pays the bills. It's what develops loyal customer relationships. It's what keeps you growing and profitable. What's more, you must leverage technologies to align customer experiences across brick and mortar and online channels. And, above all, you must lead and develop employees into teams that can deliver in-store service experiences that exceed customer expectations; this is paramount to winning new customers, retaining old customers and driving growth.

This book will focus on such strategies for bricks grocery retailers so management does not allow their stores to become victims by underestimating the threat of clicks retailers to their future existence. Most strategies will derive from the bricks retail grocery sector because of my experience in the field, but these strategies apply to almost every size, type and kind of bricks business.

When you are finished reading this book, it is my intent to equip you with a survival plan and strategies so you can pick up the gauntlet thrown down by online retailers and position your bricks business for ongoing growth and success.

# BRICKS & CLICKS: MYTHS & REALITIES

THERE IS NO DOUBT THAT CLICKS RETAILING IS MAKING SIGNIFICANT inroads on the sales of bricks retailers. Reporting for CNBC, Kate Rooney revealed in February 2019 that the total market share of sales done with "non-store retailers" was higher than general merchandise, including department stores sales, for the first time ever.

Also in 2019, market research company eMarketer was predicting double-digit growth for online retail over the next five years, as shown in the table below.

## Online Retail Growth Over the Next Five Years

| YEAR | 2019 | 2020 | 2021 | 2022 | 2023 |
|---|---|---|---|---|---|
| Total (In Billions) | $600.63 | $686.52 | $780.57 | $884.38 | $915.00 |
| Growth % | 14.80% | 14.30% | 13.70% | 13.30% | 10.50% |

*eMarketer*

Several years later, eMarketer reported that the online retail industry could expect even more rapid growth due to the COVID-19 pandemic. What's more, the surge in online shopping caused by the pandemic was unlikely to ease up, even as life gradually "returns to normal," eMarketer predicted.

"We forecast U.S. retail e-commerce sales will grow 13.7% (in 2021), reaching $908.73 billion," eMarketer reported. "Prior to the pandemic, we expected sales would grow 12.8%, reaching $761.26 billion."

Growth was expected to vary by sector. Apparel and accessories, for example, was projected to grow 18.9% while digital grocery (food/beverage) was expected to grow 18.1%.

These trends are expected to continue for several years, CNBC has reported.

"While e-commerce sales only represented 3.6% of total retail sales in the United States in 2009, according to eMarketer, following gradual growth year after year, that figure skyrocketed to 14% in 2020, as the COVID pandemic fueled online spending on everything from groceries and toilet paper to spin bikes and workout clothes," Lauren Thomas reported for CNBC. "E-commerce sales are predicted to account for 15.3% of total retail sales by the end of this year and jump to 23.5% by 2025, eMarketer said."

While bricks retail sales are still much higher across all sectors than clicks retail sales, it is clear that the days of online commerce being a fad or something bricks stores can ignore are long gone.

As for online grocery sales, analysts are watching the industry closely.

The Institute of Grocery Distribution (IGD), based in the UK, reported in 2021 that the global grocery retail market is on track to generate an additional $440 billion in sales by 2022. Stewart Samuel, Program Director at IGD Canada, said the future is a bit less concrete for the American grocery industry.

"There's a high degree of uncertainty relating to the economic outlook in the U.S., which is dependent on the level of financial support from the new administration and the vaccine roll-out," Samuel said. "We expect relatively flat growth over the next two years, but any growth we do see is likely to be driven by e-commerce and discount and value formats."

But the news wasn't all bad for bricks grocers. "The pandemic has slowed the gradual loss of share by supermarkets and hypermarkets as shoppers have consolidated their trips in larger stores, and we expect this trend to continue," Samuel noted. "Suppliers have had an unprecedented opportunity to capture new households during the pandemic. Focusing on retention and repeat purchase will help to consolidate the share gains from 2020."

Rumors about the demise of bricks retailers are especially exaggerated in the grocery market.

What's more, brick grocers can remain very much alive — if they take steps now to remain competitive.

# BRICKS & CLICKS: GROCERY RETAIL

To help you understand the challenges and opportunities facing bricks grocery retailers today, I'd like to provide a closer look at them—and their competition. Currently, Amazon and Walmart are among the leading clicks retail grocery outlets, with online grocery delivery services FreshDirect and Instacart right behind. While online grocery sales may represent a small fraction of the overall grocery retail sector, it is among the most rapidly growing segments of clicks retailing.

Bricks grocery stores are vying to gain traction in the online grocery marketplace. Among those contending for market share in addition to H-E-B and Kroger, are Trader Joe's, WinCo Foods, Sam's Club, Giant Food Stores, Publix, Target, Costco, Giant Eagle, Save Mart, PriceRite, Food 4 Less, Shop 'n Save, Wegmans, Weis Markets and newer entrants to the market such as ALDI and Lidl.

Bricks grocery retailers are also facing competition from online retailers that sell products other than food, items that traditionally have been sold only by grocery retailers. This includes such online retailers as Chewy's, which sells pet food and supplies. Customers tell me all the time that Chewy's offers prices and conveniences bricks grocery retailers cannot match. Other clicks companies that sell items traditionally purchased in bricks grocery stores, such as diapers and vitamins, are also eroding sales and revenues for bricks grocery retailers. It is difficult for bricks grocery retailers to match the price, quality and convenience of these types of clicks retailers. Difficult, but not impossible.

## Consumer Priorities

The dunnhumby, which includes both clicks and bricks grocery retailers in its retail performance index (RPI), provides insight into the qualities resilient grocers exhibit. Retailer performance is based on the "Eight Pillars" of grocery retail: brand, quality, price, operations, convenience, digital, rewards/discounts, and speed. All of these pillars impact value perception among consumers. Grocery retailers that focus on superior value perception have "the most financial success" and the "strongest emotional bond" with customers, according to dunnhumby data.

The core of value perception is the combination of price and quality. Dunnhumby has reported for multiple years that these are the pillars of grocery retail that are most important to customers. Price, however, appears to be the most important of the two. Of course, the other pillars, including relevance and convenience, are also important for success.

Regional grocery retailers like H-E-B are growing stronger and are positioned to compete successfully with traditional and nontraditional retailers because of their focus on assortment relevance and leveraging their location advantages.

H-E-B, Kroger, Fry's and Smith's, all leading regional grocers, are prepared to withstand an economic downturn as much as "industry superstar" Costco, said dunnhumby. Working in these grocers' favor, dunnhumby said, are top-notch private brands, very relevant promotions, better existing price perception and less cross-shopping by their customers than Walmart, ALDI and Dollar General customers.

## Regional Grocery Retailers

So, what can bricks retailers learn from regional chains like H-E-B, Publix, Wegmans and others? Regional bricks grocery chains are thriving because they are strongly branded in their regional or local market. They tend to adapt more quickly to ever-changing consumer tastes because they are not burdened with layers of management like national chains.

"Regional grocers tailor their offerings by neighborhood, matching the experience to that local community. It's tough for the national players to match this," Ryan Fisher, partner of consulting firm A.T. Kearney, explained.

Also working in regional grocery chains favor, they're competitive on price with national chains on similar items and carry a wide assortment of private label budget brands popular with consumers. Instead of trying to be everything to everyone like Walmart or Kroger, regional chains leverage their core strengths. Regional chains are privately held companies. They expand carefully and avoid piling up debt.

"They can invest strategically for the long-term, even if they stumble a few times in the near-term as they learn what works," said Diana Sheehan, director at data, insights and consulting firm Kantar Retail.

Another plus, regional chains typically do not cluster stores near one another, which prevents cannibalization of sales from store to store.

The next chapter will provide a closer look at the strategies bricks and clicks grocery retailers are implementing to remain competitive and grow sales, beginning with exceptional customer service.

STRATEGY 1:

# Exceptional Customer Service & Employee Training

NEARLY EVERYONE HAS HEARD THE OFT-REPEATED MANTRA OF THE real estate industry: "Location, Location, Location!" While the location for a bricks business is a highly significant consideration for success, another mantra may overtake its significance where competing against clicks retailers is concerned: "Hospitality, Hospitality, Hospitality!"

As entrepreneur and author Danny Meyer said, "Hospitality is the foundation of my business philosophy. Virtually nothing else is as important as how one is made to feel in any business transaction."

One of the best strategies bricks stores have for competing with clicks retailers is creating a high-quality experience for in-store customers, beginning with superior customer service. Acquiring new customers is one thing, whether through promotions, discounted pricing or other strategies, but getting them to return is highly dependent on the customer service they experience.

"Good customer service is all about bringing customers back and about sending them away happy — happy enough to pass positive feedback about your business along to others," hospitality author Alex Samuely explained. This level of customer service leads to invaluable word-of-mouth recommendations that not only lead to more new customers, but also more repeat customers.

I strongly agree: Cultivating superior customer service is essential for bricks retailers to survive. Developing one-on-one relationships with customers is absolutely necessary for driving growth, retaining loyalty and competing effectively with clicks retailers. Meyer, a successful entrepreneur who's opened a dozen successful bricks operations in the restaurant industry, has written about how he achieves success in his highly competitive industry. In *Setting The Table Higher: The Transforming Power of Hospitality in Business*, Meyer attributed his success to what he calls "enlightened hospitality," a total systems approach to attaining and growing success.

"I've learned how crucially important it is to put hospitality to work, first for the people who work for me and subsequently for all the other people and stakeholders who are in any way affected by our business—in descending order, our guests, community, suppliers, and investors," Meyer wrote.

## Achieving 'Flawless' Service

What does excellent customer service look like in bricks grocery stores? For one thing, service should be expedient. Today's shoppers lead busy lives and want their questions answered and their problems solved rapidly and efficiently. But more than that, customer service should be so effective, so sensitive to customers' needs, that it could be described as "flawless." To achieve this, employees must consistently go the extra mile. If a customer is having difficulty locating a product, employees should not respond by merely directing them to this or that aisle. That is not going the extra mile. An employee going the extra mile would say something like, "They are a little tricky to find; let me show you where they are located," and accompany the customer to the location. Before walking away, the employee should go a step further and inquire if the customer has any other questions about the product or any other questions in general. The customer may not comment on this level of customer service, but they will recognize it and more than likely tell their friends or coworkers—and that leads to more customers.

Unfortunately, in too many cases, the quality of bricks shopping experiences leaves much to be desired. This is primarily because bricks grocery chains tend to depend on low-skill, under-motivated and often inadequately-trained employees to fill jobs with very high turnover rates. Flawed human resources fail to deliver the flawless experiences that are critical for driving in-store traffic, and, subsequently, the profits bricks retailers need to survive.

"Traditional Brick & Mortar retailers are dying more quickly than expected because, despite all the talk, they just can't deliver consistently perfect shopping experiences," Robert Gerace wrote in *The Brick & Mortar Survival Guide.* "Every failure at the shelf, every indifferent or rude sales associate, and every failed attempt at customer service drives consumers out of stores and into their phone for their next purchase."

In today's era of social media, it just takes one less-than-perfect experience to inspire a negative customer review that could be seen by tens of thousands of people in an instant.

## *Employees: A Critical Piece of the Puzzle*

Equally important is investing time and resources into recruiting and retaining employees who will perform beyond expectations. Bricks grocery stores should follow the lead of regional chains that have had success in this area. David Livingston, founder of DJL Research, said regional chains "hire better employees, pay them more and keep their shelves stocked. Employees have some skin in the game rather than being a number." Exactly: Highly satisfied employees are more motivated to deliver exceptional customer service. They are more productive, and they tend to stay with companies longer.

In addition to recruiting and taking good care of employees, bricks grocery retailers should be providing ongoing quality training. This approach is critical for developing superior employees who have the skills to consistently provide perfect customer service experiences. I recommend using a variety of training methods and strategies.

Many retailers are trying to train employees to treat customers in ways that build a strong connection with them. I say "trying" because most retailers are not especially successful in this regard, though that could be because they're failing to allocate sufficient resources to hire the right employees in the first place. What's more, bricks grocery retails should be training workers thoroughly in superior hospitality *before* they hit the sales floor. After workers complete their initial training, I recommend monitoring imperative employee-customer interactions to ensure employees fully understand the type and level of hospitality required to create positive customer experiences, relationships and loyalties.

Part of the initial and ongoing training should be devoted to helping employees understand the importance of excellent service and the value of connecting with customers and the community in ways that create fantastic shopping experiences and inspire customers to keep coming back for more. All employees must appreciate this is a battle for survival, and everyone needs to get involved to win the fight. One of the best ways to achieve this level of buy-in goes back to what I said earlier: Stores should be treating employees like the valuable assets they are. Finding, hiring and keeping top-performing employees is much easier when a grocery retailer invests significant effort in rewarding employees and keeping them happy.

Chick-fil-A comes to mind as a company that ensures superior customer service is a priority. Chick-fil-A employees are trained in exceptional customer service and live it every day. Blake Hoogeveen, co-founder of training and consulting provider MindSet, wrote about the Chick-fil-A training process after spending time with a franchise owner. Hoogeveen said employees are taught to follow a four-part model that begins with making eye contact when serving customers. From there, employees are expected to smile and make a point of seeing if the customer returns the smile. They ask the customer how their day is going. Finally—and this is brilliant—each staff member is encouraged to offer complimentary food to make a customer's day better. "The Chick-Fil-A employee is authorized to say something like, 'Wow, sorry to hear about that. Sounds like you need some good luck to get your day going in the right direction. Your food is on Chick-Fil-A today,'" Hoogeveen wrote. I'm not suggesting that brick retails train employees to give away merchandise, but they should find creative ways to make customers feel exceptionally valued.

*Employee training should be devoted to understanding the importance of excellent service and the value of connecting with customers and the community in ways that create fantastic shopping experiences and inspire customers to keep coming back for more.*

## H-E-B's Strong Example

We have examples of exemplary customer service in the grocery industry as well. Not only is H-E-B a strong model of excellent service, but it also shows how it's done when it comes to empowering employees and inspiring them to support the company's commitment to flawless customer experiences.

*Epicurious* has written about H-E-B's "stellar customer service." This includes taking care of their most valuable asset, their partners, as they are called. Ashley Lutz and Mary Hanbury explained that H-E-B is "highly ranked" as a place to work, because of "great benefits" and a "strong company culture." Many customers report customer service at H-E-B is superior to other grocery chains. One customer wrote on H-E-B Plus! "There is no place on earth like your local #HEB. You're always guaranteed great customer service from people who enjoy their products and share recommendations."

This level of customer service requires high-performing partners who feel cared for, respected and empowered in the work setting. In fact, H-E-B President and CEO Craig Boyen actually argues that the chain's partners are a "key differentiator" for the company among consumers. A differentiator in products is commonly heard but not so much in partners. *Storebrands* writer Lawrence Aylward said that "as much as H-E-B differentiates with its outstanding private-branded products, it also does so with its partners. Texans like to shop at H-E-B because they like the experience—the human experience influenced by H-E-B's partners." This is a purpose-driven strategy at H-E-B.

In 2021, Glassdoor ranked H-E-B No. 1 on its list of the 100 best places to work, recognizing the grocer for, among other things, prioritizing the health, safety and well-being of its employees during the COVID-19 pandemic. But even before COVID-19, H-E-B has been ranked highly by Glassdoor. The company has made a significant investment in its partners, giving 55,000 of them an equity stake in the company. The privately-owned regional chain gave approximately 15% of H-E-B's shares to partners over the age of 21 who worked for the chain for at least a year and clocked at least 1,000 hours in a calendar year. Boyen said the strategy aimed to boost partner loyalty, increase long-term financial stability and recognize partners for their contribution to the success of H-E-B.

"We believe the main thing we need to do is invest in people—and better people," he said in one interview. H-E-B's actions spoke more loudly than words: The company showed its people it truly is committed to them.

## Wegmans' Two-Fold Strategy

Look at any of the major grocery retailers with exceptional customer service, and you will find that, like H-E-B, they put people first, not just customers but their workers as well. Wegmans is no exception. The family-owned chain has been on *Fortune's* list of best places to work since the list began in 1998, was ranked No. 1 in 2005, No. 4 in 2021 and typically cracks the top 10. It is almost always the highest-rated retailer in the bunch.

Wegmans adopts a two-fold strategy for delivering superior customer service, including intense and innovative training and taking great care of its people. Wegmans employee training is thorough and innovative. Cashiers are prohibited from interacting with customers until they have participated in 40 hours of training. The company develops workers who are knowledgeable about the products they sell. In fact, it sends butchers to Colorado, Uruguay and Argentina to learn about the beef they carry. Its deli managers travel to Wisconsin, Italy, Germany and France to become cheese experts.

"We empower our people to make decisions that improve their work and benefit our customers and our company," said Wegmans media relations director Jo Natale. This kind of investment in training occurs because Wegmans understands it is the key to delivering superior customer service.

*The Atlantic* wrote that the Wegmans model is simple: "A happy, knowledgeable and superbly trained employee creates a better experience for customers. Extraordinary service builds tremendous loyalty." Wegmans recognizes that its employees are a powerful extension of its brand.

Wegmans also puts its money where its mouth is where valuing its employees are concerned. Pay is above average, and benefits are generous. Every year, Wegmans awards more than $5 million in college scholarships to employees. The company has no mandatory retirement age and has never laid off workers. Wegmans reinvests all of its profits in the company or shares them with employees. Most promotions at Wegmans are inside the company. More than half of the company's store managers were employed by Wegmans when they were teenagers. Showing just how desirable Wegmans has become among potential employees, when it opened a new store in Pennsylvania, the company received 10,000 applications for 500 job openings, according to *The New York Times*.

Former vice-president for human resources at Wegmans, Kevin Stickles, explained Wegmans' unique perspective on employees: "Our employees are our No. 1 asset, period. The first question we ask is: 'Is this the best thing for the employee?' That's a totally different model. When you think about employees first, the bottom line is better."

The two-pronged approach to developing employees who deliver superior customer service shows that investing in people can be profitable. Because of its satisfied workforce, Wegmans has a remarkably low turnover rate for the retail industry. Max Nisen reported that *Fortune* puts Wegmans' turnover rate at about 17% for all employees—including part-time, hourly workers—and as low as 4% for full-time employees. Compare that to a company like Walmart with poor customer service, where the turnover rate is closer to 40%. Wegmans' low turnover rate is even more impressive when you consider that the average turnover rate for the retail industry is 66% for part-time employees and 27% for full-time employees.

Low turnover rates help drive customer loyalty at Wegmans because aside from superior customer service, low turnover results in lower grocery prices. Grocery retail analyst Julie Peirano reported that Wegmans prices are 13% lower on average than Giant and Safeway. Low turnover also supports Wegmans' consistently excellent customer service. Wegmans shows that companies can "train, innovate and profit at the same time," grocery retail analyst David Rohde said. A former senior vice-president for Wegmans, Mary Ellen Burris, explained the company's employee strategies: "What some companies believe is that you can't grow and treat your people well. We've proven that you can grow and treat your people well."

## Costco's Superior Service

Another example to follow is Costco, which sells high-quality products at reasonable prices. This is enough to win over many customers, but what puts Costco ahead of the rest is the company adds superior customer service to the mix. Costco gets high marks from consumers in this area. Not surprisingly, it uses a mix of training and satisfying employees similar to the successful practices of H-E-B, Wegmans and other grocery retailers. Costco employees are very knowledgeable about what they sell.

Retail writer Jason Rossi explained one of the reasons Costco employees are so knowledgeable about what they sell is the relatively small number of the items they offer. "A Costco will stock fewer than 4,000 items, whereas the typical grocery store will have 30,000 or more," Rossi said.

As a result, employees on the front lines of customer service know exactly what they are selling, from where items are located to details about the products themselves. This approach makes it simpler for employees to satisfy customer questions and provide informative answers.

Speaking with *CNN*, American Customer Satisfaction Index managing director David Van Amburg explained, "Costco has that model of, this is what we do, this is who we are, what we sell, and we are going to do it really well." Unlike Wegmans, which makes a profit due to high volume, with lower inventory, Costco can negotiate lower prices for what it does sell.

Costco employees are also satisfied and happy employees. Most of today's managers at Costco were once working its cash registers. Brian Woolf of the Retail Strategy Center estimates that 76% of Costco warehouse managers began their careers as hourly employees. This not only demonstrates Costco employees are content employees, but it is also a reason managers know how to manage the frontlines so well and exceed customer expectations. Self-described Customer Service Futurist and author Blake Morgan said Costco provides value to customers through its "humble servant-leadership" and "company culture." Historically, Costco pays its workers a living wage, with even cashier assistants pulling down $13-$15 an hour, according to Glassdoor. Costco is close to the top of the *Fortune 500* list, but cutting wages is not how they achieve their success. Paying their workers well develops loyal employees who are more motivated and willing to do what it takes to please customers and create success for the company. As I've been saying, people who like their job translate to happier employees—which translates to higher levels of customer service. Turnover at Costco is higher than Wegmans, but it is still lower than the retail average at 20%, about half of what it is at Walmart or Target. "Workers at Costco tend to feel they are truly a part of a team in which every member is making the entire group successful," Rossi said. In Costco stores, customers are the main focal point, and well-trained and compensated employees are happy to provide them with a superior shopping experience.

### Other End of the Spectrum

Stores like H-E-B, Wegmans and Costco contrast sharply with low-price grocery retailers, Walmart, ALDI and Lidl. The prices attract many shoppers, but all three companies leave a lot to be desired when it comes to satisfying employees and providing customer service. Walmart is the top seller of grocery items out of all grocery chains because it offers lower prices than most stores can offer across a large array of items. However, many of its employees do not like working for the chain, which is clear when looking at Walmart's high turnover rate: 40% for full- and part-time employees. Walmart consistently scores low in customer satisfaction surveys as well.

Journalist Hamilton Nolan reported the four main questions dissatisfied Walmart customers ask are: Why is it that every time I visit Walmart there's never anyone around to help me; why is there no one who knows where anything is whenever I shop at Walmart; why are most employees who work at Walmart grouchy and surly whenever I need assistance; and why can I never find what I am shopping for on the shelves at Walmart?

The answer to these questions revolves around one key factor in Walmart's human resources strategy. Unlike H-E-B, Wegmans or Costco, Walmart does not value investment in its workers as a means of enhancing the bottom line. Retail analyst Joseph Castenando believes Walmart's issues with customer service are by design: "Excellent customer service isn't part of their brand strategy. Their business model appears to be high traffic, high product count, high transaction count, and low, low prices." The very public issues with poor customer service and understaffing at Walmart relate to strategies for frontline employees. Walmart associates, department managers and other hourly employees often suffer due to the company's compensation scheme and structure. Store managers and assistant managers are salaried. The home office sets a specific number of hours and payroll compensation for scheduling hourly employees at each store. These amounts are directly allocated based on the sales per department for the previous fiscal year. Employee hours are often cut, or stores let employees go if sales are down for that period. If the number of customers and sales in a department increase in the current period, the department is typically understaffed. Adding to this issue, bonus incentives for store managers and assistant managers, ranging from $20,000 to $80,000 per year, are partially based on their ability to reduce schedule hours and payroll from the previous year. Excellent customer service costs money, and Walmart's strategic model does not provide resources for this as one of its priorities.

Aside from the understaffing issue this creates, the high rate of turnover at Walmart means that many employees have not been there enough time to be familiar with product information and where items are located. Adding to this problem is the fact that Walmart stores are required by corporate to change the layout of departments and what they stock approximately twice a year. Each department can carry as many as 6,000 or more items at any one time. Customer service further suffers because due to understaffing, associates often spend half or more of their shift serving as cashiers or unloading product from trucks. This limits the time they have available to familiarize themselves with item location and product information. Lack of training is also an issue. Hourly associates are often asked to perform service tasks such as cutting keys, mixing paint, and other similar jobs. For every customer associates help in their specific departments, they are helping another 20 up front while carrying out multiple tasks.

A former customer service manager at Walmart for a decade, Lisa Osborne, said customer service is so poor at the chain because "they literally put more on the associates than can be done. On a night shift with two cashiers, they expect associates to wait on people, sort through returns people do not want, clean the parking lot, clean 32 registers, plus help out in electronics and watch the door."

Adding to hourly worker frustration, on top of these duties, is that they're required to set up, take down or move displays, replace labels on entire aisles of product, move hundreds of boxes of merchandise to the floor and help clean up and put items away in other departments that are even more understaffed than their own.

Long lines are a frequent and common customer complaint at Walmart. In such instances, employees who are cashier trained are pulled off the sales floor from their department to help. Because of this, hourly employees are often left with the choice of assisting customers or carrying out all of their other tasks, or they risk being let go. One sales associate at Walmart, E. Clayton Rowe, explained this system leads to the concept called "the tyranny of urgency," where the task that is most urgent is executed over a task that is also necessary. Walmart employees unhappy with work conditions have started a website called "OUR Walmart," a name that stands for Organization United for Respect at Walmart. Retail analyst Diane Stafford explained the group's purpose is "to ensure that every associate, regardless of title, age, race, or sex, is respected at Walmart." Associates have posted that Walmart pays too little, should provide paid sick days for part-time employees, discriminates against women and minorities in promotions and reduces weekly hours to fewer than are necessary to pay bills.

The pressure on store managers and assistant managers to cut hours or employees to increase their chances of securing a bonus creates a vicious cycle, one that leads to high and costly turnover and notoriously poor customer service. No company can excel at everything, and few companies have the lowest prices *and* the best service. Great prices and selection make many Walmart customers focus less on superior customer service, but improving customer service is warranted, and Walmart is highly aware of this need. To that end, it has started making greater efforts to improving employee training and creating a workforce of more satisfied and happy employees. These efforts include putting store expansions on hold to remodel stores to make them more employee-friendly—and to have more resources available to invest in increasing employee pay.

Walmart also has been establishing training academies for associates. McDonald's has long operated training academies for its managers. New efforts at training are aimed at creating consistency across Walmart's enormous retail environment. Walmart headquarters' public relations representative Erica Jones explained that "retail is changing. The way customers shop at Walmart is changing. We need to provide our associates more tools to keep up with the times."

So far, Walmart has established 200 dedicated training sites in select stores across the U.S. The Shawnee Walmart Academy, for example, covers the entire Kansas City area and occupies 2,500 square feet of space. It's equipped with the latest technology, and the walls are adorned in "upbeat messages," according to Stafford. "Facilitators" train employees on such topics as ordering and restocking, while others lead classes of trainees through "replenishment cycle" exercises that focus on adjusting inventory based on specific events, such as a major snowstorm. Walmart expects to train 140,000 associates every year, but that is still a small proportion of its more than 2 million associates.

"Our goal is to be the best place for customers to shop—whether they choose to do it in stores, online, on mobile devices, or a combination of these, it will be fast and easy," said Walmart executive Doug McMillon. Employees who complete the 90-day training program automatically receive a $1-per-hour pay increase, but it is too early to tell whether these additional training efforts by Walmart will result in improved customer service.

## Hard Discount Chains

Walmart is not the only retailer focused on low prices: ALDI and Lidl are hard discount chains that are making significant inroads in the U.S. market. German-based ALDI had more than 1,800 stores in the U.S. in 2017 when it announced plans to increase its store total to 2,500, invest $5.3 billion in remodeling current stores and open 800 new locations in the U.S. by 2020, positioning itself just behind Walmart and Kroger. With heavily discounted prices, ALDI has become a major player in the U.S. grocery market. Smaller layouts, no-frills merchandise displays and competitively low prices are ALDI's core brand strategies. Still, ALDI's employee policies are not making many of them happy to work for the chain. Of the more than 2,000 employees who reviewed ALDI on Glassdoor, "only about half would recommend working there," retail analyst Debra Kelly said. While many workers say the pay, benefits and opportunities are good, they cite difficulties in balancing work life with their home life and an inability to get enough hours to make the money they need.

Retail analyst Joel Stice described similar complaints among U.S. employees who say they dislike working for ALDI because of "impossible performance expectations, a difficult work/life balance, and a lack of gratitude." Hard physical labor and unrealistic performance demands lead to poor morale and a lack of motivation among employees. The store times its employees on how many items they can scan at checkout in an hour, typically expecting 1,000 items as a target. Employees who do not meet this target participate in a performance review, and, after three times of not meeting this target, are let go. Like Walmart, one of ALDI's strategies for keeping prices lower than other chains is to staff stores with fewer employees. Employees perform multiple roles and juggle multiple tasks, which can lead to poor customer service since they have little time to spend time helping customers. One ALDI employee said, "You don't have time to talk with customers or make them smile."

ALDI's staffing policy is all about keeping prices lower than competitors. The company keeps staffing to a minimum, with only eight to 10 people being employed at each store and only two or three working during any given shift. ALDI only hires to fill four different positions at each store. These include the store manager, the manager trainee, the shift manager and store associates who are tasked with doing everything from working the cash registers and retrieving carts to restocking shelves and cleaning. ALDI employees are cross-trained to perform multiple functions. The focus is on saving on labor costs and requiring employees to serve many roles. Streamlining efficiency is also critical to the chain. Most ALDIs do not have publicly listed phone numbers, according to retail analyst Nathaniel Meyersohn, "because ALDI doesn't want its workers to spend time answering calls."

ALDI does try to make up for the typical complaints lobbed by employees that are noted here. Wages and benefits are good. ALDI pays its employees more than minimum wage with annual increases, and there are generous healthcare and other benefits, such as on-the-clock lunch breaks and an hourly pay increase for employees who work Sunday or holiday shifts. Other employees say in-house promotion is one desirable aspect of working for ALDI. If they meet the high performance expectations, ALDI employees can be promoted to a shift manager in less than a year on the job, which comes with a significant bump in pay. Despite this, many employees complain of the difficulty maintaining a work/life balance when working for ALDI, with many complaining of being called on their days off and a "business comes first" mentality that fails to consider responsibilities in the lives of employees, according to Stice. Employees also allege that ALDI management seldom lauds a job well done without some form of qualifier. Stice reported one employee's feelings on this issue: "ALDI can never say 'you did well today;' it's always 'OK, this was better but you have to do more or you will be held accountable for your efficiency.'" ALDI did receive a 3.3 satisfaction rating out of 5 among employees on Glassdoor, but if it hopes to continue to compete in the U.S. market and remain profitable, it may need to modify its employee strategies and work environment.

Also founded in Germany and operating in the U.S. market is Lidl. Currently, Lidl has a reputation for poor employee treatment and customer service rivaled only by Walmart, according to retail industry analyst Frank Ludwig. Most employee contracts are for 10-20 hours per week to spare the company from offering any form of benefits. Those who do work full time are on call 24/7 and expected to report to work on short notice after being called, which can happen at any time, day or night. Like ALDI workers, Lidl employees are judged on speed, which management expects them to increase continually. One former employee said he was expected to change bulk pallets at the rate of 15 per minute, but when he performed the task with an average rate of nine minutes, he was told to improve it to eight minutes. Ludwig reported that cashiers, who are expected to start 10 minutes before their shift, are told to scan an average of 35 items per minute, an impossible task for most people. Attendance at staff meetings is mandatory but unpaid. Needless to say, Lidl has one of the highest rates of turnover among major grocery chains. Statistica reported that Lidl's turnover in 2018 cost the firm over $621.6 million, double the amount from 2013. Demoralized, unhappy and poorly motivated employees are contributing to poor customer service.

Lidl frequently hires young people who have often never worked in grocery retail. Because little is spent on thorough training, many customers maintain Lidl employees seldom know about their products or where they are located, despite the chain's small stores. Like ALDI, Lidl does pay its employees an above-average wage, provides them with a store discount, and offers competitive benefits for those employees who are full time. Many employees benefit from overtime because of understaffing at Lidl stores. Despite this, Lidl has suffered from bad press due to its treatment of its employees. Retail analyst Zlata Rodionova explained the firm has come under fire "from staff claiming they were overworked, undervalued and stressed to the point of endangering their health and going into depression." Lack of praise and ongoing pressure to continually improve are cited as reasons for such conditions by many employees. Rodionova reported one former manager who said employees are "treated like numbers," and despite the "market-leading wages," there is great room for improvement in how workers are trained, treated and expected to achieve.

Lidl has responded to such charges by arguing that the firm provides "Personnel Welfare Consultants" to assist employees with concerns and solicit feedback from employees continuously. A spokesperson for Lidl maintained, "We actively encourage a work-life balance for all our employees through flexible rotations and working hours, as well as enhanced vacation allowance." Despite such measures, with plans for aggressive expansion in Europe and the U.S., Lidl will need to invest more in employee training and resources that make employees happy if they hope to improve current customer service levels in their stores. *Brick Meets Click* reported that Lidl is trying to learn from the mistakes it made when first entering the U.S. market: "It always had low prices and high-quality own-label products, but poor store location decisions and under-prepared store personnel blunted the impact of its discount offer in the U.S." An adage goes that a store owner once told a customer: "We have low prices, great quality, and excellent customer service. The only problem is you can only pick two." In today's competitive grocery retail chain, this adage may no longer work for firms that hope to survive and grow as more and more customers are demanding a combination of all three to remain loyal to any particular chain.

## Amazon's Approach to Service

One company that seems to be mastering this is Amazon: Along with its competitively low prices and quality items, Amazon is also known for its superior customer service. For decades, Amazon has been the leader in e-commerce with nearly unmatchable product availability and competitive pricing.

"While that would be plenty for a successful business, what's taken Amazon to a legendary brand is the combination of customer experience and products that keeps people coming back for more," retail analyst Chelsea Hunersen said. Amazon is known for going the extra mile for customers, even when they do not have to. This is because Amazon founder Jeff Bezos understands that making customers happy and exceeding their expectations is the secret to success. It is also the secret to cementing brand loyalty among customers and promoting high levels of word-of-mouth advertising. In a *Forbes* interview, Bezos described the customer-centric mentality at Amazon: "It used to be that if you made a customer happy, they would tell five friends. Now, with the megaphone of the internet, whether online customer reviews or social media, they can tell 5,000 friends." In today's retail environment, the lion's share of power has shifted to consumers, and word of mouth is even more powerful in building or crippling brands.

While superior customer service may be true for the online giant overall, Amazon's grocery retail chain Whole Foods remains to be seen. Since Amazon bought the Texas-based grocer in 2017, industry analysts have been watching the chain to see what changes the acquisition might bring about. Whole Foods' motto is "Whole Foods, Whole People, Whole Planet." For now, it appears customer service at Whole Foods remains at a high level. Employee training at Whole Foods is thorough and ongoing. It is also a company employees value as a place to work. Since the inception of *Forbes'* 100 Best Companies to Work For list in 1998, Whole Foods has made the list every year. After making the list for 20 consecutive years, former Whole Foods CEO John Mackey said, "We're grateful for our team members, who are dedicated to our core values and who have helped our business grow over the past four decades." Employees have cited perks and programs, in addition to compensation and the capacity for work/life balance, as the main reasons for their satisfaction with Whole Foods as an employer. They describe it as a place where they feel respected and appreciated for the job they do.

Whole Foods' ongoing training is another reason for its superior customer service. Training is extensive and includes fun activities and food tastings so employees are familiar with the products they offer. The company promotes from within for most positions that become available, so there is a lot of room for advancement. Training is conducted by team members, so it is accurate. Another reason Whole Foods staff members are so knowledgeable and enthusiastic about products is, aside from in-store training programs, they also attend all-access regional training events at locations where Whole Foods sources its products, such as Backyard Farms in New England, which supplies tomatoes and seafood for Whole Foods. "We were flattered by the compliments they (Whole Foods employees) had for our tomatoes and enjoyed answering their thoughtful questions about our greenhouse and how we grow," a Backyards Farms employee said after a visit. "It's clear that working at Whole Foods is more than a job for the vast majority of the team members we met." Taking thousands of employees out of the store for an entire day and paying for their travel and hotel accommodations for training is expensive. Whole Foods make these types of investments because it knows it pays off in higher levels of customer service, which it is committed to delivering.

Whole Foods engages in unique employee strategies related to hiring decisions, work structure, and even bonuses. Whole Foods' managers now involve their whole team in the interview process to make better hiring decisions. Employees at Whole Foods are known as "team members." Teams, central to the success of Whole Foods, are the building blocks of the entire chain. Each store revolves around eight to 10 teams, each specific to a department. These teams have considerable autonomy over decisions such as what to order, pricing, and what promotions to run.

Retail analyst and leadership expert David Burkus explained: "Whole Foods calls its mission statement a 'Declaration of Interdependence,' claiming that Whole Foods is first and foremost a community of people working together to create value for other people. The team focus is so strong that the company even allows teams to select who gets to join the team." New hires undergo a 60-day process that involves multiple interviews, including in-person interviews, phone interviews, one-on-one interviews with store leaders and panel interviews with recruiters, managers and select employees. When hired, new hires are placed on a team — but only for a trial period. When the trial period ends, the rest of the team votes on whether to permanently hire the new person. It takes a two-thirds vote from the team for the employee to become fully vested. Bonuses are also paid out after measuring team performance. Known as "gainsharing," Burkus explained that "the higher a team's performance gains, the more the team members gain in bonus pay." The system of hiring is based on the presumption that the most effective and successful method of judging performance is to have colleagues who will be affected by new employees' performances do the judging.

It's impossible to know whether, under Amazon's helm, Whole Foods will continue to deliver this level of customer service and performance. However, it appears likely given Bezos' mantra for customer service and positive input from Whole Foods customers so far. Two customer experience reports from Whole Foods come from a senior leadership strategy contributor to *Forbes*, Steve Denning, and the other comes from retail analyst Nils Parker, also a Whole Foods regular.

Denning reported:

> "When I shop at Whole Foods and I ask for help from any of the workers as to where I might find an obscure product like *demi-glace* sauce or frozen *pâté feuilletée* or dark *tapenade* he or she invariably stops doing the current task and helps me solve my problem. I am impressed that the worker usually knows what the obscure product is — a good start — and also where it is located. And then they walk me to the part of the store where I can find the product. Never a moment's hesitation. The same response even if they are involved in some other task. Always gracious. Never irritated at the request. Never an excuse like 'it's not my section,' or 'try aisle five.' Even when I protest, 'There is no need to walk me there; just tell me which aisle,' they insist on walking me to the exact spot and pointing to my item. Remarkable!"

Parker's experience at Whole Foods is also exemplary when it comes to customer service employees:

> "Across the board, across the country, Whole Foods' employees have been helpful, knowledgeable, and cordial. I've received phenomenal service in every department, from the beer fridge to the butcher counter to the bulk aisle. I now know everything there is to know about lentils, for instance, thanks to a guy stocking Roma tomatoes in the produce section of the downtown Milwaukee store, who took the time to explain why he used *red* lentils for his curried lentil dish a couple nights before."

Whole Foods continues to provide the level of customer service its brand offered before the Amazon acquisition. If judging the strategy and attitude of Amazon founder Jeff Bezos is worth anything, Whole Foods and Amazon's new bricks stores, Amazon Go convenience stores and Amazon Fresh grocery markets, likely will continue to deliver superior customer service. Being customer-obsessed is a central focus of Bezos' business strategy and why Amazon is so dominant in the retail market.

"There are many ways to center a business," said retail analyst Tommy Mello. "You can be competitor focused; you can be product focused; you can be technology focused; you can be business model focused; and there are more. But in my view, obsessive customer focus is by far the most protective of Day 1 vitality."

It is no surprise that part of Amazon's strategy is keeping its employees happy. Amazon offers a substantial benefits package to all of its employees, even part-time workers. This also leads to less turnover, especially among part-time employees where turnover numbers are traditionally higher than full-time employees. Most benefits also begin on an employee's first day of service.

Being customer-focused enables retailers to deliver innovative and improved products and services because they are keyed into changing customer needs and demands and strive to meet them as their core strategy for success.

Eric Karlson and Erich Kahner of *Winsight Grocery Business* maintain that different types of grocery retailers have selected different paths to appeal to customers. These three paths are price-focused, quality-focused and value-focused. Price-focused retailers focus on maintaining strong price perception and average or lower-than-average quality perception, such as Walmart and ALDI. To win on price, Walmart's size and scope enable it to negotiate lower prices from national brand suppliers and cut promotional costs. Karlson and Kahner argue ALDI wins on price by offering a limited-SKU, private brand-dominant offering to "maximize product turnover." Quality-focused retailers, such as Wegmans and H-E-B, have high-quality perception and average or below-average price perception. Such stores have "exceptional performance in nearly every area of quality underneath store experience and products offered," say Karlson and Kahner. Value-focused retailers, like Costco and Trader Joe's, have earned above-average quality and price perceptions. Such stores have a non-traditional grocery format and an exceptional private label. They typically have a limited grocery SKU that provides benefits such as maximizing inventory turns, scale, and efficiency, according to Karlson and Kahner. Their margin-friendly, private label-heavy offerings provide more cash flow to invest in other areas like store experience or new product development.

It is clear that thorough and innovative employee training and being a great employer employees love to work for are the two most critical factors for developing a team able to deliver customer service that exceeds customer expectations each and every time. Training also needs to be ongoing. "Training isn't something you did," leadership strategist Shep Hyken said. "It's something you do. You can't onboard new employees, give them a few hours of customer service training, and then expect that they will be changed forever."

Superior customer service costs, but it also enhances the bottom line. As retail analyst Chris Haroun said, "Superb customer experiences beget more loyal customers who spend more money in the long run." It can take decades to build a strong brand in the grocery industry. Yet it only takes a few awful customer service experiences to obliterate it. A company is only as good as the customer service delivered by its employees.

STRATEGY 2:

# Customer-First Relationships

DOING WHAT IT TAKES TO HAVE WELL-TRAINED EMPLOYEES WHO are courteous, knowledgeable, motivated and happy is one aspect of building strong relationships with customers. Another part is employing customer-first strategies that go beyond superior service and lead to strong relationships with shoppers. It will be important to understand, Samuely said, that "you will be judged by what you do, not what you say" as you try to win customers' loyalty. Customer-first strategies involve listening to what a shopper truly wants and providing them the right service to get it. And accomplishing that calls for leveraging personalized customer data. Customers want to feel valued, and they want their needs satisfied expediently. A study by KPMG, a global network of professional firms providing audit, tax and advisory services, found that "personalization is key to the successful delivery of a customer experience and a stalwart of loyalty and advocacy, as customers want to be known, understood, and made to feel important and unique."

Discounted prices, promotions and other enticements are effective ways to lure new customers into a store, but if customers are not put first, they probably will not return. You need to establish a relationship, a strong bond with your customers. And you need them to enjoy that relationship so much that they keep coming back. Not only will making customers happy every time they visit foster loyalty, but it also will motivate them to spread positive word-of-mouth feedback to others who, in turn, will visit your store and also become repeat customers.

Grocery retail is an art and a science. Data from financials and research are the science. "Art is in how we operate on the floor: our merchandising, our people, and, ultimately, our customers," Karlson and Kahner said. I would add that the science is key to making the art meaningful. For one thing, it helps us understand different types of customers. Loyal customers are repeat customers who influence buying and merchandising decisions. They're the ones grocery retailers communicate with often through mail, email, social media and other outlets. They also are the ones most likely to spread positive word of mouth to others. The other four types of customers include discount, impulse, needs-based, and wandering customers. Understanding the needs and behaviors of these customers and what drives their buying decisions is critical to staying competitive. It's also essential for turning discount, impulse, needs-based, and wandering customers into loyal ones.

## H-E-B's Customer-First Strategies

We can learn from grocery retailers that employ customer-first strategies now to create excellent experiences for shoppers. H-E-B continues to best other grocery retailers and even has surpassed such online giants as Amazon for customer service experience excellence. KPMG consistently ranks H-E-B highly in its Customer Experience Excellence Report.

These efforts are producing results: Spokesperson and President of H-E-B Food & Drug Scott McClelland said he's optimistic that the marketing innovations and products his company uses will continue bringing customers to H-E-B. The company's competitive advantage is a direct result of its unique approach to customer experience, Denise Lee Yohn wrote in *Extraordinary Experiences: What Great Retail and Restaurant Brands Do*. This strategy is unusual for a price-and-item retailer like a grocery retailer, but Lee Yohn said H-E-B does what other successful brands do. "Great brands avoid selling products. Instead, H-E-B seeks to form strong, emotional customer bonds that are the most effective drivers of sustained store traffic and true loyalty."

This is where customer-first strategies come into play. One way H-E-B achieves this is the use of "My H-E-B" in marketing materials. This phrase communicates the idea that customers' needs and desires come first. H-E-B lives this philosophy by aligning its internal operations with data derived from individual customers. The company "creates a strong emotional bond with customers by leveraging an intimate knowledge of what they want and its unique capabilities to deliver on them," Lee Yohn explained. Customer-first strategies are designed to extend to the individual. This requires a commitment to truly understanding what individual customers want to create strategies that put their needs first. As KPMG market researcher Julio Hernandez said, "Organizations that go beyond the consumer to the individual, with a focus on purpose and personalization, achieve greater customer loyalty—which can translate to sustainable financial gains and increased profitability." H-E-B is dedicated to building customer loyalty through these and other strategies.

Another example of a customer-first strategy at H-E-B is its Buddy Bucks, which are given to children while their parents shop at H-E-B. Once they collect Buddy Bucks, children can spend them on prizes. This effort to reduce its customers' stress illustrates H-E-B's empathy for busy parents who have their hands full, especially when shopping with their children. It shows H-E-B's commitment to understanding and caring for customers on an individual level. Children love Buddy Bucks, and so do parents. "They always give Buddy Bucks to the kids," said CTO Evan Lucas, a parent who shops at H-E-B with his children regularly. "My kids love going to H-E-B. They have a machine that you put the Buddy Buck in like a dollar bill. You press a big spin button, and you can win prizes. It's really awesome for the kids." This is a prime example of creating a deep emotional bond with shoppers by knowing what they need while shopping.

Other H-E-B customer-first strategies include offering numerous options for shoppers who have food allergies. H-E-B also leverages knowledge about trends in individual tastes and diets. It maintains different

*One of H-E-B's strategies to build customer-first relationships is its beloved Buddy Bucks, which children collect and spend on prizes.*

sections to cater to these individuals specifically. For example, one section features products for those on the Paleo diet. In some locations, shoppers planning to get married can commission a florist.

## Costco 'Gets It'

Other grocery retailers are effectively employing customer-first strategies.

Retail analyst Chris Haroun said Costco, along with Amazon and Apple, are "incredibly successful" due, in large measure, to "a material focus on the customer experience." Companies like H-E-B, Costco, Amazon and others understand that the "optimal" and "highest lifetime value" of a customer is the result of superb customer service experiences, said Haroun. While Costco does not have a massive quantity of products like Amazon, it excels in personal and convenient service that gives it the edge in customer service over competitors. Costco understands that focusing on customers and delivering value provide the dividend of satisfied and loyal customers.

Costco is one retailer that just "gets it" when it comes to all levels of customer service interaction, said retail analyst Mark Lusky. In the most recently released American Customer Satisfaction Index (ACSI) Retail and Consumer Shopping Report, Costco scored top marks for shopper customer satisfaction, besting titan Amazon — even in the online category. Morgan said Costco's high score "validates its customer-first culture and proves that consumers love Costco."

What does Costco's customer-first culture look like? For one thing, Costco's service representatives put customers first during in-store inter-actions. When they answer customer questions, for example, they take a three-pronged approach: listen closely and ask confirming questions; address the questions as truthfully and fully as possible; and ask if the response is sufficient. Rather than apologize for an issue when a customer is upset, Costco reps address the issue head-on with "a statement about doing everything possible to correct a deficiency," Lusky said. This is an effective strategy: Customers want a resolution more than an apology. At Costco you are going to get "straight talk and real answers," which equates to "transparency" and "honesty" that are a "welcome breath of fresh air" for the store's customers, Jason Rossi said.

Another customer-first program at Costco is the firm's bullet-proof return policy. Costco spends significant resources and effort to vet the quality of its products in the first place. Should there be a deficiency or issue with a product, it increases consumer confidence and loyalty by offering a top-notch return guarantee. Costco customers are motivated to purchase more because they know there will not be a major hassle or restrictive return policy if they have to return something. The return policy is a model for the retail industry, with Costco offering multi-year return policies on some items, including TVs. Customer service reps do not even have to ask for a receipt when a customer returns something because of the company's digital receipt policy.

Another creative approach to customer-first service is Costco's membership program, which includes a number of low-cost vacations and trips around the world. This membership perk adds to the Costco customer experience, and it helps demonstrate the company's commitment to bringing savings and happiness to the lives of shoppers.

Costco also offers customers the ability to trade in their old consumer devices in exchange for a "Costco Cash Card." Offering this convenience shows Costco understands busy customers' needs.

Another customer-first policy implemented by Costco is its method of advertising or, more specifically, its lack of advertising. Because of fewer items in its inventory and the low margins of its stock, Costco does not need to advertise. Other than seasonal stock, customers know what they will find in the store before they walk in the door. Because only a fraction of Costco's operating budget is allocated for advertising, "shoppers aren't bludgeoned with an onslaught of mailers and coupons that can make the head spin," retail analyst Jason Rossi said. Costco's success in driving customer loyalty stems from a customer-first culture that is simple and direct without any trappings.

"Costco has a customer-first culture and works to meet customers' needs quickly without any bells or whistles," retail analyst Blake Morgan said. From its return policy to its informed and typically pleasant customer service reps, Costco provides a shopping experience that customers plainly understand puts their needs first.

STRATEGY 3:

# Evocative In-Store Design & Customer Experience

G REAT HOSPITALITY AND LEVERAGING INDIVIDUALIZED DATA TO develop customer-first strategies are two critical factors in driving growth, growing a loyal customer base and maintaining a competitive advantage against both bricks and clicks grocery retailers. Another significant factor in achieving these goals is an in-store design that leads to a superior customer experience, one that even moves customers' emotions and creates a high level of loyalty. A strategically created in-store design aimed at providing a phenomenal customer shopping experience is fundamentally an extension of customer-first strategies. Many grocery retailers are finding ways to achieve this, from in-store dining experiences and wine tastings to on-site custom floral arrangement services and clinics dedicated to health and wellness.

## *The H-E-B Store Experience*

H-E-B, Costco and Amazon are three brands that "stand out from the rest of the pack," because they provide superior customer service and customer experience, according to KPMG. H-E-B has created a fully immersive shopping experience. The chain provides a multitude of food

*One way that H-E-B's in-store design delivers an immersive customer shopping experience is through its demonstration kitchens, where chefs prepare and serve culinary creations using H-E-B products.*

samples throughout the store and generous wine sampling stations. The grocery retailer offers extended sampling hours and a great variety of wines to sample. H-E-B's customer experience "appeals to shoppers at a neurological level by triggering a release of dopamine in people's brains as they taste the alcohol," neurological expert Roger Dooley said. Certain samples induce people to buy the product, but they also create a halo effect that makes you feel good about, well, everything." The entire store is designed to entice. Huge displays of fresh fish on ice and full-service butcher cases serve as "eye candy," while large display cases are dedicated to products that include up to 500 varieties of yogurt. Add the mouth-watering aromas that waft throughout the store from the bakery and rotisserie chicken areas, and it's easy to understand the appeal of the H-E-B store experience.

H-E-B's newer stores go a step beyond delivering an immersive customer shopping experience; they also promote H-E-B's products. They're equipped with demonstration kitchens where chefs prepare and serve culinary creations from sushi to guacamole—always promoting recipes that utilize H-E-B products. One store in Houston also offers a sit-down restaurant with a full-time professional chef, a spice-blending station for culinary enthusiasts and even a takeout barbecue station.

"All of these factors differentiate H-E-B by transforming grocery shopping from a monotonous, mundane activity focused on meeting needs into an exciting and inspiring experience filled with discovery and entertainment," author Lee Yohn said. The customer experience at H-E-B is one of delight and excitement. Unlike prices or products, such experiences are difficult for competitors to copy.

Superior customer experiences send a message to shoppers: They are highly valued. "Every time I go into H-E-B, there are always free samples of food, whether it's fresh sushi, ice cream or cookies," said H-E-B customer Raquel Guarino, a content strategist for Help.com. "I've even won free meals. Stuff like that lets me know H-E-B appreciates me as a customer."

H-E-B also offers a fresh bakery section where shoppers can have cakes custom-made for any event. Floral arrangements can be ordered online, or shoppers can browse the floral department. Grocery retail analysts Ashley Lutz and Mary Hanbury said H-E-B's café "puts others to shame," with its creative salads and artisanal sandwiches, build-your-own pizzas with ingredients from Italy and cooked BBQ selections. Shoppers can get their food boxed up or sit down and enjoy their meal in-store with a glass of wine or a beer. H-E-B has been "providing a superior shopping experience for much longer than Whole Foods and is known for its gourmet cooked food and fresh bakery section," Lutz and Hanbury added.

In-store design at H-E-B is also focused on cost-efficiency, higher quality at lower prices and margin preservation. Some of the stores adopt a "smart approach" to store operations, according to dunnhumby. Instead of an "invisible storeroom" far removed from the floor, the storeroom frames up the entire store and a narrow extra ring, with products stored as closely as possible to where they are stocked. It is this cost-efficient approach to stock-keeping that helps keep prices lower while maintaining margins.

## *How Costco Aims to Please*

Costco has its own approach to in-store design, one founded on Costco's smaller assortment and variety of products. It is generally a no-frills shopping experience where superior customer service and ease of return policies guide the way.

Even so, Costco delivers a shopping experience that aims to please shoppers while in store. To this end, Costco has kept its food court prices low. As of 2021, shoppers were paying $1.50 for a hot dog, less than $2 for a cup of soft-serve ice cream, and less than $5 for a jumbo slice of pizza. The food court at the front of every Costco is a favorite stopping place with shoppers because they know it offers them value and is a sign of customer appreciation.

The food court offers in-store shoppers "true value," and the Costco hot dog is so popular it has its own website, retail analyst Jason Rossi said. Keeping shoppers satisfied and loyal is particularly important to Costco since its business model relies on customers buying repeat memberships, which, in turn, helps them keep prices low—just above cost in many instances.

## *'Wonderful World of Wegmans'*

Wegmans, like H-E-B, is a regional chain that understands the value of in-store design and its connection to shopping experiences and superior customer service. Retail analyst Julie Peirano has referred to the shopping experience there as the "wonderful world of Wegmans," adding that those who have not shopped at the "jaw-dropping amazing" store are missing out. Shopping at Wegmans is an unrivaled experience for many shoppers:

Their in-store design mirrors an open market. Wegmans strives to deliver nothing but the best: the best quality and the best choices. Considered by many to be a "foodie's paradise," the store offers fresh produce, freshly baked bread, cured meats, fresh-caught seafood and an incredible salad bar. Wegmans' design is all about shopper experience, and it manages to keep prices reasonable.

Retail editor for *Supermarket News*, Jon Springer, discusses the shopping experience at Wegmans as if it were a Broadway show: "You can't talk about Wegmans without talking about its ongoing emphasis on the experience, on the theatricality of going to the grocery store. It's really very different in that respect."

The Wegmans in-store shopping experience is also based on employees who are highly trained experts. Employees are trained in their areas of expertise. A fish salesman can discuss the exacting standards of Wegmans' Alaska distributor. A butcher can share details of the ranch where a steak he is selling was raised. One stand-out example is Maria Benjamin, a long-time Wegmans veteran who was put in charge of a store's bakery after managers loved her homemade Italian cookies. For customers shopping in-store, Peirano said they are "more than comfortable believing an employee's word is as good as gold."

Additional factors contributing to the enhanced shopping experience at Wegmans are the stores' wide aisles, impeccable displays and super-clean appearance. Wegmans offers many enticements to enhance shopper experience as well, from fresh-baked goods to custom-ordered ones to what Peirano calls the store's "cheese caves," featuring hundreds of cheeses to choose from with expert staff to help with selection. Wegmans also offers impressive food bars, including a Mediterranean bar with a large variety of tempting options where shoppers can create their own tapas-style platters. Wegmans makes shopping fun with its DIY bars, where customers can make their own unique blend of trail mix, along with a DIY nut butter machine and a wall of self-serve bulk candy dispensers. Like a European-style market, Wegmans also offers delicacies from around the world, with each section of international groceries organized by region of origin for shopper convenience. By "offering overseas staples and traditional foreign fare, the store knows how to keep a wide array of people happy," Peirano said.

If you are hungry while shopping at Wegmans, the chain has you covered. Its stores have a Market Café where shoppers can grab a quick bite to eat, from fresh sushi and sandwiches to pizza. If you prefer a more sophisticated dining experience, some Wegmans stores have their own restaurants where expert chefs whip up gourmet creations using the freshest ingredients from the store's own aisles. These are often tailored to regional tastes, including the seafood bar inside Virginia stores and the Amore Restaurant and Wine Bar in Rochester, New York, which offers sit-down Italian fare. Wegmans' media relation coordinator Valerie Fox said some Wegmans locations feature The Burger Bar, a family-friendly casual dining experience that serves burgers, sandwiches, salads, soup, children's meals and beer and wine by the glass. The Wegmans shopping experience is rounded out with on-site florists in sections with pre-arranged displays or custom-ordered arrangements available. Some Wegmans locations will even deliver. While not all Wegmans serve alcohol, the ones that do carry a wide assortment of beers, including craft beers that are locally produced. Add this all together and it is easy to see why Wegmans customers love their shopping experience that Peirano calls "jaw-dropping" and "magical."

Wegmans' customers aren't shy about expressing their appreciation for the Wegmans shopping experience. Each year, the Wegmans website logs thousands of posts from individuals asking Wegmans to open a store in their community. Thousands more write to praise the Wegmans shopping experience or how they were treated by employees while shopping. High volume requires happy, repeat customers, especially for Wegmans, where the chain's stores are enormous, typically 80,000 to 120,000 square feet, and feature over 70,000 products, more than double the standard grocery store, according to retail analyst David Rohde.

## *ALDI Aims for Efficiency*

A sharp contrast to Wegmans is the in-store experience at ALDI, where maximining efficiency is the driving goal—even though this often leads to inconveniences for shoppers.

"New customers may be jolted at first by the experience of shopping at an ALDI, which expects its customers to endure a number of minor inconveniences not typical at other American grocery stores," said Nathaniel Meyersohn with *CNN Business*. Shoppers who expect to use a cart must bring a quarter to rent one. Their money is returned if they return the cart by themselves, saving time and labor for the chain. When customers return their own carts, employees do not have to be paid to do so. Years before other chains followed suit, plastic and paper bags were available at ALDI only for a fee. At ALDI, checkout line speed is much faster than at most chains, because ALDI cashiers hurry shoppers away to bag their own groceries away from the cash register. ALDI employees are expected to memorize prices of everything in the store, and the chain uses multiple bar codes on items so no matter how a cashier picks up an item, it can be quickly scanned. Retail analyst Xan Rice said cashiers are so fast that some shoppers experience "ALDI panic," the fear that they cannot bag their own items quickly enough. Retail analyst Debra Kelly found that ALDI's checkouts typically move 40% faster than those of other retail chains.

ALDI also shuns free tastings of any kind, because it lowers costs and goes against the store's policy of keeping things as simple as possible for itself and for shoppers. ALDI's in-store experience does not promote the types of shopper engagement witnessed by many other chains. ALDI is ruthless in its quest to minimize costs, Meyersohn wrote. "The company strips down the shopping experience in an unapologetically and brutally efficient way."

ALDI has no in-store service, either, though food service has been described as "the fastest-growing category in a traditional supermarket," by retail analyst Phil Lempert. Instead, the company focuses on foods that offer convenience for its customers, such as meats and chickens that are marinated and ready-to-cook, quinoa bowls, salad kits and other convenience items. Over and over ALDI executives express the same mantra: "keep it simple."

This philosophy is evident in ALDI's approach to stocking. Unlike other chains, which feature impressive displays of stocked items, ALDI stores stack items on top of one another. Employees simply rip open the boxes merchandise arrives in and put the boxes on the aisles. The overall atmosphere of an ALDI store is "gritty more than pretty," Rice said. This saves significant time—and money—restocking compared to other chains. Speaking of aisles, ALDI typically has just five wide aisles in its stores, and it stocks fewer products, approximately 2,000 per store, much less than the 25,000 characteristic of big supermarkets. Each store has an approximate square footage of 12,000 square feet, much smaller than most grocery chain stores. Produce is repackaged and ready for checkout. In the stores are no frills, no decorations or embellishments. ALDI also maintains reduced hours of operation, typically an average of 11 or 12 hours: another cost-saving tactic.

ALDI's streamlined, no-frills in-store environment is crafted to appeal to customers in a different way: Instead of an excellent shopping experience, ALDI offers speed of shopping and low prices. Shoppers are happy they have spent much less time at ALDI than other chains. One mother said: "I'm a busy mom. I don't have time to navigate a huge grocery store with kids begging to get out and go home. I can get in and out of ALDI in no time. I'm not sifting through 50 different varieties of salsa."

And, shoppers experience what Rice calls the "thrill at the till," where they realize the expedited, no-frills experience is pleasurable because they have saved so much money.

And they do save: When Andy Prescott of Clark.com conducted a shopping trip to both ALDI and Walmart, he compared the prices of the national name brands and the stores' brands of the exact same items. He found that Walmart's name-brand prices cost 20% more than ALDI's private brand prices. ALDI reinforces this idea with its "ALDI Savers" symbol, displayed on Specially Selected and Simply Natural private label products, to remind customers they are benefiting from "Savings on Savings on Savings."

STRATEGY 4:

# Private Label Brands & Regional/Assortment Relevance

LONG GONE ARE THE DAYS WHEN THE WORD "GENERIC" WAS USED TO describe private label brands that came in plain black and white packaging and were of inferior quality. Consumer interest in private label groceries was increasing before COVID-19, and the pandemic accelerated that trend.

"According to research from Alix Partners . . . one-fourth of consumers tried a private label brand for the first time during the pandemic, and about 30% of them said they planned to continue using those products," *Grocery Dive* reported, citing a report by e-commerce insights platform Profitero. This heightened interest represents an excellent opportunity for bricks grocery retailers to continue to differentiate themselves and drive destination through continued investment in and marketing of quality, affordable private label brands. According to Numerator, private label owned over one-quarter of U.S. market share in grocery prior to the pandemic. And annual sales continue to grow, according to *Retail Dive*.

The dunnhumby RPI reveals that regional grocery retailers are experiencing a "resurgence in customer preference by winning with relevance and convenience." Jose Gomez said that "if they can compete on price and quality—the value core for grocers—they are especially well-positioned to fend off the growing threat of non-traditional players." One way many are achieving this is through private label brands.

Convenience has grown more important to customers, and assortment relevance enables regional grocers to leverage their location advantages. Consumer perceptions of private label brands are also changing from perceptions of a decade or more ago. Nielson reports that private label brands have "surmounted stigmas of value and quality," with private label brands now growing three times faster than national brands. Part of the reason is the high quality of private label brands offered by grocery retailers such as H-E-B, Trader Joe's, Costco, Kroger and others.

Grocery retailers in the U.S. were often reluctant to invest in private label marketing. They have had their own private labels for decades, but there was a tendency for them to encourage private label manufacturing to invest in and take the risk of marketing. This has been changing, with brands like Kroger, ALDI, Lidl and Amazon investing in innovative private brand marketing to make private label products a key destination driver. Efforts like these, promoting private label brands, can be an effective way to promote your store as a worthy destination for shoppers. *Brick Meets Click* has suggested that, for some, "this may be unique packaged private label, but for others it could be signature perishable products that separate the retailer from the competition."

Strong private brands and other factors, including relevant promotions and lower cross-shopping, are positioning regional grocers like H-E-B and others to withstand an economic downturn better than others. Dunnhumby reported that "H-E-B, Fry's, Smith's and Kroger stand out as being just as prepared for the next economic downturn as industry superstar Costco, due to having excellent private brands, highly relevant promotions, better price perception and lower cross-shopping by their customers with Walmart and ALDI." H-E-B is also at the top of the list of retailers that support their private labels through significant commitment.

## *H-E-B's Private Label Strategy*
H-E-B Chief Operating Officer Martin Otto said the key to success in growing your own brand portfolio is always "making sure that quality is

top-notch and maintaining relevance across every dimension from product to packaging to marketing."

Grocery retail blogger Raquel Guarino reported that H-E-B's "high-quality private label foods" set it apart from the competition.

H-E-B maintains a strong focus on its private label brand strategy. According to a case study by V. Kasturi Rangan in the *Harvard Business Review*, the H-E-B private label brand accounted for 20% of its sales and earned gross margins 50% higher than national brands. H-E-B is well known for its excellent private label brand collection. It includes a variety of options, from lower-cost products in the Hill Country Fare brand line to organic products in the H-E-B Organic brand line and selections for children in its H-E-Buddy brand line. Private label brands include Central Market brands, H-E-B, H-E-B Select Ingredients, and H-E-B Kitchen & Table, a line of durable, high-quality cookware, bakeware and crystal glassware at a competitive, affordable price.

One H-E-B customer wrote on Facebook: "I like H-E-B brands. Most store brands I don't like BUT H-E-B brands are good."

Retail analyst Phil Fitzell said the "H-E-B brand is aimed at either matching the quality of national brands or bettering it, but with prices 10% to 20% below category leaders." H-E-B continues to increase its customer equity by maintaining its private label brands.

I would argue that H-E-B's private label brands are among the highest quality private label brands in the country. One executive from Landor Associates, who redesigned H-E-B's private label line in the 1990s, said this quality stems from H-E-B being "ruthless" in sourcing the quality it desires. For example, only one company was found worthy of providing canned pineapples to the chain; it carried the only pineapples that reflected the desired quality of H-E-B private label brands. H-E-B's focus on private label reinforces the chain's goal of offering customers the correct product selection in general. H-E-B also scores big on customer relevance. As a regional chain primarily in Texas, the store stocks lots of local products, from Texas-shaped chips to special BBQ sauces. It also offers snack products and condiments from the very popular Texas fast-food chain, Whataburger. The company

*H-E-B's private label brand collection is successful because of its high quality and competitive affordability, including the popular private label ice cream, Creamy Creations.*

focuses on selling Texas-grown produce. And, as retail analyst Nathaniel Meyersohn noted, H-E-B Plus stores offer "an expanded range of smokers, outdoor grills and other products to outfit customers 'with all they need for Texas lifestyles.'"

H-E-B's dominance in Texas is founded upon an understanding of its market and its customers. H-E-B has the "best pulse of their shopper and Texas diversity," the executive editor of *Winsight Grocery Business* said. "The chain is ferocious on price and not concerned with what's happening in Florida or California."

High quality and competitive affordability are not the only reasons for the success of H-E-B with its private label brands. Returning to a central theme addressed earlier in the book, *Storebrands* writer Lawrence Aylward said H-E-B understands that private brands are about more than products; they are about employees, too. "When a grocer's employees are affable, accessible and treat people like they want to be treated, they can wield a tremendous influence on the retailer's own brand, not unlike a delectable line of premium private label ice cream," Aylward said.

## Kroger's Expanding Private Label Efforts

Other chains have increased their investment in marketing private label brands, too, because of their capacity to drive destination. Kroger developed a promotion program known as Treasure EmporiYum, an effort to create additional value from its most popular private label products. *Brick Meets Click* wrote that the promotion is "inspired by Kroger customers who have found and celebrated their private label 'finds' on social media, and it is designed to help customers find 'hidden gems' in its extensive roster of private label products." In Kroger markets, EmporiYum employs four-sided displays and treasure-hunt-style, X-marks-the-spot shelf tags. A website and print and digital magazine are also components of the promotion, which features stories on where Kroger's store-brand products come from, recipes and other information.

Kroger's promotion is distinct from other grocery retailers because it is designed to help shoppers wade through thousands of private label items versus hundreds offered by discounters. Kroger is the second-largest food retailer in the U.S., right behind Walmart. It owns 2,764 supermarkets under several brands in 35 states in the U.S. It also maintains a significant food processing business that stocks its private label brands. After Kroger hired a global advertising firm in 2019, a first for the company, head of brand building Mandy Rassi explained, "Consumers make 221 food-related decisions a day. A standout brand and narrative will drive more customers to choose Kroger more often via any channel."

Innovative and improved Kroger private label brands, along with a number of other chain's private label brands, have helped drive traffic and increase brick grocery retailers' revenues.

"Credit has to be given where it's due," retail analyst James Brumley said. "Kroger's Simple Truth brand, as well as house brands offered by the likes of grocers ranging from ALDI to Trader Joe's, are all proving to be drivers of foot traffic, as are private labels of Walmart and, increasingly, Target."

Kroger's Simple Truth private label brand, the largest natural and organic product line in the U.S., recently exceeded $2 billion in annual sales, according to *Progressive Grocer*. The Simple Truth private label brand was launched by the national retailer in 2012 with the slogan "Eat Clean Live Simple." Since then, it has grown to more than 1,550 products across multiple categories, including grocery, meat, produce, deli, bakery, baby, household essentials, personal care and Fair Trade Certified.

"Simple Truth is a brand that has earned our customers' trust through clean labels, fantastic flavors and affordability," said Kroger SVP of Merchandizing Robert Clark

Many grocers have worked to improve and innovate their private label brand products and Kroger is no different in this respect. The chain also offers a Simple Truth plant-based food line that includes fresh, meatless burgers, according to *Supermarket News*.

"As more of our customers embrace a flexitarian lifestyle, choosing to prioritize healthier food choices and reduce their environmental footprint, we are excited to meet their needs," said VP of Kroger Our Brands, Gil Phipps. "We are introducing our Simple Truth Plant Based collection to offer even more fresh, remarkably delicious, animal-free food to provide shoppers with a greater selection of choices that are more accessible and affordable."

Innovation did not stop with the plant-based product line. Its packaging will make it easier for customers to find the brand on store shelves. Kroger hired a team of chefs, food scientists and nutritionists to develop Simple Truth Plant Based recipes, which in addition to meatless burgers and grinds, also include 100% plant-based alternatives to chocolate chip cookie dough, pasta sauces, deli sliced meats, sour cream, queso and many other products. It was essential to Kroger that the No. 1 priority in developing the private label was a focus on taste. The fact that one of the nation's largest grocers has launched a plant-based private label shows that plant-based products are becoming mainstream. According to retail analyst Russell Redman, "besides health and wellness concerns, consumers also are considering animal welfare and environmental impact in turning to plant-based foods." Other grocers will more than likely follow Kroger's lead in this area. "Kroger is at the intersection of plant-based curiosity and culinary innovation," Phipps said.

### 'The Store is Our Brand'

Another chain with a particularly successful private brand is Trader Joe's. In fact, its private brand is a key driver of store traffic: Many customers shop at Trader Joe's specifically for its private brand products. In its *Consumer Attitudes Toward Private Label* report, research consultant Magid noted that more than half—56%—of consumers would consider purchasing private label grocery products from Trader Joe's. Shoppers were most open to purchasing private label grocery items from Trader Joe's because of the retailer's "established reputation" within the category, a *Progressive Grocer* report said. It helps that consumers consider Trader Joe's offerings "unique, trendy products that are ahead of national brands," not "mere copies of national-brand products that can lower consumers' overall evaluation of a retailer," the report added.

"Private label provides the single strongest level retailers can utilize to keep consumers engaged in an age of increased competition where differentiation matters more than ever," Magid SVP of Retail Matt Sargent said.

Trader Joe's products, like other private label items, are similar or the same as big-name national brands but sold at a much lower price. Packaging may not be as fancy, but the taste is pretty much identical to national brands and, in some cases, consumers prefer the taste of Trader Joe's products. During a blind taste test of national and virtually identical Trade Joe's brands, the panelists thought the pita chips, pretzel chips, and animal crackers were identical, but for others, they thought Trader Joe's versions were actually better tasting. On average, Trader Joe's products are approximately 37% less expensive than their name-brand versions. So Trader Joe's has locked in on the value of offering quality private label brands for a price that equates to value for shoppers. Trader Joe's purchases their products straight from the supplier, which cuts costs and leads to less expensive items on the shelves. Trader Joe's success in differentiation began when the private label specialty grocery first introduced Trader Joe's granola. Trader Joe's is often lauded for helping convince grocery shoppers that private label brands are much more than cheap, generic products with not a lot of focus on taste.

"One of the keys to Trader Joe's success has been in making private label cool," Beth Kowitt wrote in an article for *Fortune*. "While consumers for years have historically turned their noses up at grocery store brands, Trader Joe's bucked the odds by creating a highly coveted in-house label."

Over 70% of Trader Joe's products are private label, and the company takes great pains to ensure their quality. Buyers for Trader Joe's travel the globe seeking products that have no preservatives, artificial colors or flavors or genetically modified ingredients. All items considered for the private label brand must go through a rigorous taste-testing process. If the taste-testers are unanimous in highly recommending an item, Trader Joe's buys it and relabels it under its name brand. The company provides great value for customers that includes "taste, quality, private labeling and price," Trader Joe's CEO Don Bane said.

Writing for media research company Coleman Insights, Dan Milkman explained that Trader Joe's brands are "a totally different story" than most other private labels. "You trust them — they do their homework and find a better product."

Trader Joe's avoids selling online or wholesale because it wants to position its private label brands as connected to the in-store experience. "Our products work the best when they're sold as part of the overall customer experience within store," President of Stores Jon Basalone said. "We're not ready to give that up. For us, the brand is too important, and the store is our brand."

However, the company's "brand seems to be tied as much, if not more, to its private label products and product curation/selection," brand leadership author Denise Lee Yohn said. In many instances, Trader Joe's can focus on in-store experience without turning to online availability or delivery because its private label offerings continue to offer great quality and low cost to consumers.

John Owen, associate director of food and retail at Mintel, explained the secret of Trader Joe's ability to shun online and delivery alternatives that many bricks chains are currently employing. "Trader Joe's compelling food offerings give it flexibility that others don't have. It's a reminder to other retailers struggling to compete in a changing marketplace that some things don't change. Success in the grocery business still begins and ends with the food."

"Food retailers should be very pleased that their brands are becoming bigger factors in how consumers shop," the FMI/IRI report stated. "This gives retailers the opportunity to further drive loyalty and trips."

## Costco and Kirkland

That's not to say that establishing and maintaining a private brand is a cakewalk: The reports also addressed such challenges as marketing private label brands in ways that differentiate themselves from competitors. Costco is a great example of a grocery retailer that succeeds in that area.

Costco—which much like Trader Joe's, has built its empire on selling its own brands—differentiates itself by offering quality products shoppers cannot find anywhere else. Costco puts the brand on everything from bottled water, tuna and nuts to toilet tissue, golf balls and wine.

The American Customer Satisfaction Index (ACSI) *Retail and Consumer Shopping Report* survey indicated that customers love Costco's brand for two reasons: low prices and high quality. Costco began the Kirkland Signature line in 1995, naming the brand after the location of Costco's corporate headquarters: Kirkland, Washington. Since then, the brand went on to be responsible for one-third of the company's business. Not only does the brand draw club members to Costco, but it also is a key reason why members renew their $60 to $120 annual memberships.

"Kirkland is a brand in its own right. It is one of the reasons people go to Costco," Barclays retail analyst Karen Short said. "That's not necessarily something you can say about many private labels."

While the Kirkland Signature line has been more successful than many competitors' private brands, because of its limited selection, Costco can ill afford to make mistakes with it, or sales will be significantly impacted. "We have to be careful," Costco Chief Financial Officer Richard Galanti said. "We're not just putting it on things. Just like any branded item, any private label lives and dies based on how it performs."

The brand is so important to Costco's financial success that, on its annual securities filing, the company warns investors that the sales and profit margin will suffer if "Kirkland experiences a loss of member acceptance or confidence," retail analyst Nathan Meyersohn said. No other company issues a warning like that about its private label brand.

One reason Kirkland Signature products get high customer approval for quality is because many are merely repackaged national brands. Kirkland Signature White Albacore Tuna, for example, is supplied by Bumble Bee Foods, and Kirkland Signature batteries are made by Duracell. Kirkland Signature coffee is actually roasted by Starbucks, Kirkland Signature diapers are made by Kimberly Clark and all of Costco's Kirkland Signature dry dog and cat foods are made by Diamond Pet Foods in the U.S. These products are comparable in taste and or quality to their national counterparts, but they cost much less to consumers who shop at Costco. In 2020, for example, a 40-pound bag of Kirkland Signature Super Premium Chicken, Rice & Vegetable Dog Foods was approximately $29 at Costco, or about 72 cents per pound. A 28-pound bag of Diamond Naturals Grain-Free Dog Food sold for approximately $40 at specialty pet stores, or for about $1.43 per pound. It is not very difficult to see why Costco's loyal shoppers have made pet food one of the company's top-selling items.

Walmart's Sam's Club arm has tried to copy Costco with its own private label brand, Member's Mark, which makes up 27% of Sam's Club's total sales

"We really dialed up our focus on the Member's Mark brand," Sam's Club CEO John Furner said. "The power of having one brand has been really strong." Because of increased competition like this, Costco continually innovates the Kirkland Signature brand to stave off the competition. It has introduced such new items as razors, a Nutella product, kombucha, and sparkling water. Costco also invested $450 million in its own chicken farm in Nebraska.

In addition to making Kirkland Signature more competitive, Costco also has achieved supply chain efficiencies by continually improving its line. One example is that when Costco changed its Kirkland Signature cashews containers from round to square, it was able to ship a lot more of them on trucks and store a lot more of them on warehouse racks.

What's more, offering private brand products that cost at least 20% less than national brands allows Costco to keep prices low on other items, too. Because it typically sells around 3,800 products at its warehouses, Costco has tremendous clout with big brands. As Nathaniel Meyersohn wrote in a piece for *CNN Business*, "Big brands don't want to risk being left off Costco's shelves, so they'll usually drop their prices." One example is when Costco dropped the price of its 40-pack of Kirkland Signature half-liter water bottles to $2.99. The dramatic price decrease forced national brands, including Poland Spring, to do the same with their pricing.

"Kirkland acts as a universal club marshal," Kantar retail analyst Timothy Campbell said. "It keeps suppliers honest."

## Wegmans: Top Tier in Store Brands

Wegmans is also a leader in understanding that a quality private label brand at an affordable price is a differentiator and a destination. Most generic store brands aren't much to talk about, but "that's clearly not the case when it comes to Wegmans' in-house products," retail analyst Julie Peirano said. Wegmans' private label strategy is in the top tier among grocery retailers, and industry analysts estimate that Wegmans' sales per square foot are 50% higher than the industry average. Wegmans offers everything from locally sourced condiments to boxes of macaroni and cheese that not only provide superior taste, but also a great price point. There's no question that excellent and knowledgeable customer service and a superior in-store experience drive traffic and loyalty for Wegmans. However, according to *Storebrands,* "possibly more than any else, Wegmans' assortment of packaged goods drives people's passion for the retailer . . . and they do it with their private brands more so than any other retailer."

Private brands are a significant part of the chain's business strategy. According to *Storebrands,* private brand sales comprise 25% of the retailer's overall grocery dollar sales. Wegmans, like H-E-B and Trader Joe's, is confident enough in the quality of its private label brands to put its own name on them. "Central to Wegmans' private brands is the retailer's name," said Jim Hertel, managing partner of research and analytics firm, Willard Bishop. "It stands for something special, symbolizing the celebration of food. They put their name on the building, and that stands for something. They put the same name on their private labels."

Wegmans' private label brands include Wegmans, Wegmans Food You Feel Good About, Wegmans Italian Classics, Wegmans Asian Classics and Wegmans Delicatessen. Wegmans also seeks significant input from consumers when it comes to developing its private label products. To develop its Wegmans Food You Feel Good About, *Storebrands* reveals that "the retailer went straight to its customers, asking them to assist in development by taking a taste test." Wegmans understands that quality private labels also need to be affordable. *Storebrands* maintains the retailer offers "a very nice blend of top quality and solid prices, and private labels are a big part of that." Wegmans is also proactive about being transparent about its store-brand products. It does so through multiple communication "touchpoints," *Storebrands* said, including in-store materials, the company's website and social media. This transparency helps set Wegmans apart from the competition.

"Authenticity, trust and transparency are the keywords for retail's future—and Wegmans is hitting all three," said Carol Spieckerman, president of retail consultancy, Newmarketbuilders.

Since Wegmans introduced private label brands in 1979, they have steadily taken over more store shelf space. Wegmans' brands provide identity, context and meaning for a product, and they engage consumers. Unlike the simple and no-frills packaging of Costco's Kirkland Signature or Trader Joe's private-brand products, Wegmans' packaging is "engaging, invitingly displayed, and has a 'personality' apart from competing national brands," George said. "Glass jars, textured labels and lids using tactics such as black and gold colors and 'brand romance' copy set Wegmans' brands apart by signaling product quality and raising value." Wegmans achieves this level of packaging appeal because it collaborates with its supply chain at the earliest stages of both product and package development. Package development teams typically include a category manager and a culinary expert.

Because of the elevation of private label brands Wegmans, H-E-B, Trader Joe's, Costco and a number of others, retailers are in a prime space to introduce new, on-trend products under their own banners.

## *The ALDI Playbook*

They, however, aren't the only grocery retailers to achieve positive results with private brands. In addition to the savings it achieves through its low prices and bare-bones customer service, ALDI's success is based on strategies related to its private label brands. ALDI takes significant measures to make private label brands a key reason shoppers visit its stores. To begin with, more than 90% of the brands sold by ALDI are its own private labels. Its Specially Selected line of upscale foods includes fresh, never frozen, seafood and baked bread and rolls that shoppers can customize and have made in store. The Simply Nature line is part of the chain's healthier options for customers, which also includes the liveGfree line of gluten-free products and the Earth Grown line of vegetarian and vegan products. The ALDI Never Any! line comprises meat products that are not overly processed or loaded with chemicals, made from animals that, according to ALDI, were raised on a vegetarian diet that did not include any steroids, antibiotics or hormones. These measures do slightly raise prices, but shoppers interested in healthy meat consider it worth it.

ALDI's award-winning private label brands are the result of a strategic effort by the company to ensure both high quality and low costs.

In terms of quality, all of ALDI's private label brands undergo more than 50,000 well-controlled tests to ensure their recipes and ingredients are "strictly adhered to" by suppliers, retail analyst Phil Lempert said. ALDI's test kitchen teams follow rigid policies. "Product purchasers join the test kitchen twice a day, sample about 180 meals every week and try each product 30 times before it makes it to ALDI's shelves," retail analyst Debra Kelly writes. And those products that do make it to ALDI's shelves continue to be tested at least once a year. If a competitor offers a similar product, ALDI sends its version back to the test kitchen again. Even when an ALDI product does survive the test kitchen, it still has to meet the standards of the chain's managing directors. Only after they approve of the quality is a product is offered to consumers. ALDI continues to refine its private label brands based on changing consumer preferences. At one point, the chain embarked on a program to reformulate and remove more than 125 ingredients from its Simply Nature line after consumers demanded a clean label approach to their foods. The company removed all artificial and synthetic coloring, hydrogenated oils and MSG from its products.

ALDI continuously tests customer preferences through the "ALDI Finds" page on the company website, which introduces 80 to 100 new items into stores weekly, according to *Brick Meets Click*. ALDI also takes ownership of new product success by making category purchasers responsible for the factors that contribute to it, from taste and quality to packaging and advertising. And, ALDI harnesses close relationships with suppliers and tightly controlled retail execution processes to minimize the time needed to bring new products to market. An example is the chain's Earth Grown line of vegetarian/vegan products: After consumers responded positively to their introduction, ALDI implemented a chainwide rollout within nine months.

The increasing popularity of private label brands among consumers also works in ALDI's favor. "(A private brand product) used to be the white label knock-off that you were a little bit embarrassed to buy, but it was cheap," Mike Vu of Bain & Company said. "A Bain customer survey now shows that 85% of Americans say they're open to trying private label products. People don't care about the big brands the way they used to, and that plays right into the ALDI playbook."

Carrying mostly private label brand products helps ALDI keep prices lower than competitors. For one thing, this practice allows the chain to order large amounts of a single item to its own specifications at a low unit cost. ALDI's managing director of buying, Jonathan Neale, uses the chain's Burman ketchup line to illustrate this advantage. Big supermarkets' ketchup orders typically come from more than one supplier, and all of them have multiple pack sizes and formulations. ALDI's entire ketchup order comes from a single manufacturer that can complete the same product run all the time with zero marketing costs added to the price. "For many

SKUs (stock keeping units), we are the biggest buyer by a country mile," Neale said. Many of ALDI's private label brands are made specifically for the chain, including its Titan and Racer candy bars: the store's version of the popular Mars and Snickers brands.

If ALDI's heavy emphasis on private label brands seems reminiscent of the strategy adhered to by Trader Joe's, there is a good reason for it. In Europe, the company operates as ALDI NORD and ALDI SÜD, or ALDI NORTH and ALDI SOUTH. The brothers who own the company, Theo and Karl Albrecht, split it between them, with Theo taking the north and Karl the south. The U.S. is the only market where ALDI NORD and ALDI SUD share the same market, in the form of ALDI (ALDI SÜD) and Trader Joe's (owned by ALDI NORD)! Trader Joe's functions as a separate division of ALDI, but both chains focus on private label brands and low-cost quality products, and both invest in little to no advertising.

### Lidl Makes Inroads

Lidl, a hard discount chain comparable to ALDI, also relies heavily on private label brands to attract consumers and generate profits. Of the approximately 3,500 SKUs at Lidl, nearly 90% of these items are private label brands. Lidl entered the U.S. market in 2017 and has been rapidly growing its presence here. As of this writing, the firm has yet to reach profitability in the U.S., but its sales have been growing steadily as the company addresses some of its initial mistakes, including poor store locations and underprepared personnel.

"With the ability to charge prices 30% to 40% below supermarket prices, hard discounters make it nearly impossible for other grocers to compete on cost," Jessica Dumont wrote for *Grocery Dive*.

Lidl is well-known for offering a wide and deep assortment of private label branded goods. After analyzing the company's first print circular ads, data and tech company *Numerator* found that more than 94% of Lidl's promoted products were private label, which was 85% more than ALDI and significantly more than other regional grocers, including Kroger (37%) and Food Lion (30%). Lidl's Preferred Selection brand is part of the company's overall strategy to convince customers it offers value for price, according to Bill Bishop of *Brick Meets Click*. A survey conducted by Service Management Group on Lidl's first five months in the U.S. market showed customer satisfaction with Lidl's overall value for price and quality of products was higher than average for all stores in the market. While it will take more time for Lidl to increase brand awareness of its private labels among U.S. consumers, the company has already made inroads with younger shoppers aged 18 to 34. A survey from Oliver Wyman showed that shoppers in this age group had a particularly high awareness of Lidl and shopped there regularly, drawn by Lidl's private label product quality and its attractive prices.

In *Progressive Grocer*, Pete Killian said Lidle needed to invest even more in its private brands. "Private brands are brands," Killian wrote. "They take investment to build, sophistication to brand effectively, and time to gain traction. Lidl's packaging and branding signal 'this product is just a leading brand substitute' to shoppers, rather than trying to establish its own brand identity and its differentiated benefits." The Trader Joe's brand is what sells its products, which consumers do not really think of as private label brands. It will take Lidle time to build this kind of equity in the U.S., but moving forward, the company will also need to differentiate its brand beyond value for price.

Even so, Coresight Research has warned that hard discounters that rely primarily on private labels should not be taken lightly by the U.S. consumer packaged goods (CPG) market.

"The presence of grocery discounters such as ALDI and Lidl has a meaningful impact on private label's share of a country's overall CPG market, Coresight stated. "The strength of discounters—who predominantly sell private label products—is a major factor behind a high level of private label penetration in Germany." Companies like ALDI and Lidl were responsible for consumer acceptance of private labels in Europe, which own 70% of grocery market share there.

## Walmart's Successful Investment

It's also worthwhile to take a look at the example of Walmart: Its investment in private brands has driven significant revenue to the company. Walmart and Sam's Club both scored high on consumer consideration and private label brand awareness in research consultancy Magid's survey. Highly rated brands included Sam's Club's Member's Mark and Walmart's Great Value, at 70% likeliness to consider each. Awareness of Great Value was slightly higher, at 93%, versus 86% for Maker's Mark. Walmart's private label brands are not focused on building a new customer base or building name recognition like some grocers' strategies. Instead, the company has been focused on "doubling down on its core offering: low prices," retail analyst Cale Weissman said. Most of the products with the Walmart private label are focused on being a margin-reducer for the company. Tory Gundelach, VP of retail insights at Kantar, said Walmart's private label brands are focused on keeping its "value-oriented customers."

Walmart is not new to the private label brand arena. It was the first to popularize private label brands when, in 1983, it introduced its oldest brand. Ol' Roy is a dog food named after the bird dog of Walmart's founder, Sam Walton. Ol' Roy has "grown to be one of the top-selling brands of dog food in the U.S," retail analyst Greg Petro said. And Walmart's success with private label brands has continued: decades after the introduction of Ol' Roy, 84% of Walmart's customers purchase private label brands from the retailer. That puts Walmart on close footing with Kroger, where 83% of shoppers purchase private label brands, and far ahead of Amazon, where only 27% of customers are buying private labels, ScrapeHero reported.

That said, Walmart has room for improvement in the area of private-brand quality. While the company offers a huge selection of private label brands, 29,153 products across 319 private label brands in 20 categories, company data recently revealed that Walmart was losing customers to competitors because of inferior private-brand offerings. As a result, Walmart is following Kroger in retooling its private label brands with trendy, premium products like Unicorn Sparkle ice cream. Jack Pestello, Sr. VP of food and consumables for Walmart, said the company is getting serious about private brands. "We made it a core pillar of our strategy to say we are going to have a solid private brand program at Walmart," Pestello said.

Part of Walmart's new strategy is the creation of a 12,000-square-foot

*Walmart was the first to popularize private-label brands when it introduced its dog food brand, Ol' Roy, in 1983.*

facility where food products are tested and modified for private brands. Working together at Walmart's Culinary and Innovation Center are product developers, suppliers, buyers and packaging designers. In the past, Walmart maintained a very small team to work on its private brands, but the company has increased this number to over 100 people. "The majority of the team is solely responsible for going out and finding awesome products, finding suppliers who can make those awesome products for us, (and to) make sure we're driving cost inefficiencies out of the supply chain while still creating a quality product and a consistent experience for customers," Pestello said. The private label strategy is focused on bringing differentiated products to market at the right price. For example, Wag Dry Dog Food by Amazon was $45 for a 30-pound bag in 2020, but Walmart's Ol' Roy was priced around $20 for a 50-pound bag.

Despite some concerns about private-brand quality, all is not lost for Walmart. Its private label brands are still scoring fairly well in terms of customer satisfaction. According to ScrapeHero, 49.41% of its private label products have an average rating of between 3.5 and 4.5 out of 5 stars, while 35.53% of products have an average rating of 4.5. Walmart Chief Financial Officer Brett Biggs said the company is focusing on "really good products, good feedback from customers, better packaging and sharper pricing. Private label in the future is going to play a really important part of what we're doing." Walmart's private label brands have witnessed a significant change in the past few years and are likely to become even more competitive with other grocers' private label offerings in the future.

## Clicks and Private Labels

Traditional bricks retailers aren't the only ones leveraging private label products. We can expect click retailers, including Amazon, to continue developing and promoting their own brands, too. Amazon represents a triple threat in this arena: Not only does the company sell private label products online, but it also offers private label products in its brick and mortar Amazon Go and Amazon Go Grocery stores, and it has generated tens of millions of dollars in sales from Whole Foods' private label brand, the 365 Everyday Value brand.

So far, Amazon has bested national brands with some of its private label items. "It started with a simple battery," Julie Creswell wrote for *The New York Times*, describing Amazon's entry into the private label business when it offered a smattering of products under the AmazonBasics brand. In a short period of time, Amazon captured a third of the online market for batteries, outselling both Energizer and Duracell on its site.

Nevertheless, Amazon has yet to realize the level of private label successes that brick competitors are achieving. Its Amazon brand names perform well, but the other Amazon-owned private labels are not a hit with consumers yet. One example is Wag, Amazon's private label pet care brand. "We haven't seen too much traction with Wag," said Oweise Khazi, senior principal at research and advisory firm Gartner. "Brands like Purina enjoy consumer loyalty, and people care about what they're feeding their dogs."

All of the private brands and brands offered exclusively on Amazon are sold under the "Our Brands" moniker. They include more than 40 exclusive private label food and grocery brands, over 60 healthcare and beauty brands and over 20 household goods brands in the U.S., according to retail analyst Abhishek Biswas. The primary brands in competition with grocers, in addition to Wag, include Happy Belly (food), Amazon Elements (detergent, laundry items, baby products and supplements), Wickedly Prime (appetizers/snacks), Mama Bear (baby foods, snacks and diapers), and Vedaka (spices and seeds). Some brands, including Amazon Elements and Wickedly Prime, are only available to Amazon Prime members.

Amazon has come under fire for its approach to developing private labels. "Amazon has been able to leverage data from brands — those sold on its primary site as well as through its third-party sellers — to develop products that are good enough or close enough to the originals, usually at lower price points, and thereby gain an edge," *Retail Dive's* Daphne Howland said. Sen. Elizabeth Warren (D-Mass) has criticized Amazon for this practice and vowed to end it. "When Amazon can tilt the online marketplace in its own favor, small businesses see an immediate impact in their profits," Warren said. "That can be absolutely crushing, it's not fair, and I'm fighting to end that." However, Amazon argued its private label brands represented only 1% of its total sales. The company also denied it used third-party data to create its own private labels and compete against them. "Amazon uses data about individual sellers only to support them or enhance or protect our customers' experience," the firm said. "We prohibit the use of individual sellers' data to compete with them through our first-party offerings, including through our private label products."

Nevertheless, Amazon's private label brands most likely will continue to grow because the company has the resources to keep experimenting with numerous offerings to see what sticks with consumers. "Brands don't need to worry about the hundreds of brands that Amazon is putting out," Danny Silverman, the chief marketing officer at e-commerce data provider and advisory firm Edge by Ascential, explained. "They need to worry about the one in their category that succeeds. Amazon's willingness to try and fail is one of their greatest strengths because few, if any, brands have the resources to do the same."

*Marketplace Pulse* seems to side with Amazon on these points. "There is no empirical evidence that Amazon has been able to utilize proprietary data successfully to manufacture and launch products and brands," it said. "All of the best-selling AmazonBasics products, for example, are generic alternatives to competition in their category. The data to discover this is available to every brand selling on Amazon." Despite this, Amazon does give its own private labels an advantage over other brands on its site when it comes to search-results visibility. Amazon's private label brands appear in a separate box labeled, "Top Rated From Our Brands."

### *Cultivating Private Brands at Amazon's Brick Stores*

Amazon's efforts to cultivate popular private brands received a major boost when the company acquired Whole Foods, which gave Amazon the 365 Everyday Value, Whole Trade and Engine 2 private labels. Whole Foods already had a strong private label strategy before the acquisition, and it continues to experiment with its own products.

The 365 Everyday Value brand alone sold $10 million in products on Amazon in the first four months after the acquisition, product marketing manager Brittany Barron said. The 365 Everyday Value brand helped solve a main consumer complaint against the chain: high prices. Despite the lower prices on the 365 Everyday Value line, Whole Foods does not skimp on the quality of its private label products. All of its private label brands are certified organic or included in the Non-GMO Project's Verified Products List. The success of Whole Foods' private label brands has come at a cost for Amazon, though: the erosion of Amazon's own private label sales, including Happy Belly and Wickedly Prime, according to retail analyst Donna Boss. Happy Belly was a leading trail mix brand, but after the Whole Foods acquisition, sales dropped so sharply that

Happy Belly discontinued trail mix. Sales of Wickedly Prime, a line of snacks, condiments, soups and other grocery items also "flatlined" since the introduction of Whole Foods' 365 Everyday Value line, according to research firm One Click Retail.

Whole Foods even tried launching a line of stores with the 365 name but shut down the format after opening only 12 locations. "When we launched our Whole Foods Market 365 stores, the intention was to create a more value-focused and streamlined shopping experience that maintained the integrity of Whole Foods' quality in a convenient format that's less expensive to build and operate. We have been successful in achieving these goals," Whole Foods CEO John Mackey told employees in a memo. "However, as we have been consistently lowering prices in our core Whole Foods Market stores over the past year, the price distinction between the two brands has become less relevant. As the company continues to focus on lowering prices over time, we believe that the price gap will further diminish."

While Whole Foods won't be opening new 365 locations, it continues to fine-tune its 365 products brand by creating a more modern visual that replaces its multicolor label with a black background and drops the "Everyday Value" tagline, *Grocery Dive's* Jessica Dumont said. Whole Foods has also added Amazon meal kits at select stores. Amazon Prime has increased grocery sales across both retailers. A. C. Gallo, chief merchant and president of Whole Foods Market, said the retailer's priority is to make certain its products support ethical and sustainable growing practices. "We need to figure out a way to go beyond organic," Gallo said. "Organic is great in terms of growing safer food, but it doesn't really take into account everything that might be going on in the environment around it." The company aims to take its Whole Trade program and expand it to other parts of its supply chain, Gallo added, and is looking into such practices as regenerative agriculture, which emphasizes soil health, water management and fertilizer use, among other factors. Whole Foods also is expanding its sustainable packaging practices and will continue growing its range of private label products.

In addition to its Whole Foods stores, Amazon operates Amazon Go and Amazon Fresh Grocery stores. The first Amazon Go opened in 2018 in Seattle, followed by locations in New York, Chicago, San Francisco and Seattle. Most of the stores offer local and national food and beverage brands, along with such Amazon private label brands as Happy Belly and Whole Foods' 365 Everyday Value. Amazon Go stores are similar to convenience stores and range in size from 1,000 to 2,000 square feet. They "sell breakfast items, sandwiches and salads and snacks, and they are aimed at enticing busy working professionals in corporate districts on their way to and from work and on lunch breaks," retail analyst Jason Del Rey said. The stores also are the first "cashierless" chain in the nation: In most locations, shoppers enter, scan their Amazon app and purchase products without having to wait in line to checkout or pay. Advanced technology tracks customers in the store and what they purchase, charging them automatically when they leave. Customers have the option of paying in cash as well.

Ambitious to win an even bigger share of the food and beverage market, Amazon created a larger scale version of Amazon Go called Amazon Go Grocery. The first, full-size cashierless supermarket opened near Amazon's headquarters in Seattle in February 2020. Amazon founder and CEO Jeff Bezos said cashierless stores are aimed at delighting shoppers because waiting in line to checkout is "the worst thing about physical retail." Size-wise, Amazon Go Grocery is close to a Trader Joe's footprint at a little over 10,000 square feet. Not too big and not too small, it offers most items found in a traditional grocery store, including meat, seafood and deli departments, along with offer freshly prepared items, grab-and-go products and pizza. The stores stock approximately 5,000 items including national, local and private label brands—everything from organic fruit to grass-fed beef. Kevin Sterneckert of Symphony RetailAI wrote that he expected "Amazon to extend additional benefits and privileges to Prime members that will encourage and reward shopping behavior at the new grocery locations." The grocery stores probably will add more of Amazon's private label branded products to their stock going forward, Sterneckert added.

Some of the limitations of Amazon bricks grocery stores may provide an advantage to traditional bricks supermarkets. Amazon Go Grocery stores do not have a deli counter, butcher or bakery because they would undermine Bezos' goal for a streamlined and highly efficient shopping experience. Speed of shopping is a major feature of Amazon Go and Amazon Go Grocery store design. Produce must be sold by the unit or bundle instead of by weight, so monitors and computers know how to compute price. Even so, the technology may prove problematic for some grocery categories, business journalist Jason Del Ray said. "Shoppers typically spend more time picking up, placing down and just handling produce than they do with packaged items, which adds complexity to the computer identification process. And that's not even taking into account the physical differences from one pear to another." These challenges will make it difficult to determine specific customer preferences for certain items. "Where I think today's grocers have a slight advantage to Amazon at the moment is in the intricacies of the grocery supply chain, fulfillment and distribution infrastructure, and the unique ability to understand consumer demand between fresh and the center store," Sterneckert said. "Amazon will need seasoned experts to pull this off."

Nevertheless, retail analyst Bill Bishop said Amazon's physical retail locations could become formidable competition for traditional bricks retailers. Amazon Fresh is a digitally integrated grocery store merchandised for today's customers, and it provides a seamless shopping experience that is the fulfillment of the concept of omnichannel. "Amazon has worked hard to develop a grocery store that its affluent customers would like to shop," Bishop said. "Its Amazon Fresh store has a value proposition that appeals to today's shoppers, and it combines the flexibility to meet changing customer needs with lower operating costs. If this works as planned, it's a store format that other grocers will need to watch. These Amazon Fresh stores should be able to maintain profitability as margins compress, and sales volumes fall—which is a key to survival."

Bishop said Amazon Fresh is not intended to attack the competition, but it is designed to outlast other grocery retailers. He has identified six factors that give the store staying power.

1.  Amazon Fresh has a well-defined target customer. All Amazon Fresh stores are located in trade areas with above-average median income. The affluent shoppers there value time as well as money and spend more per week on groceries than other shopper segments. Amazon is already connected with many of these shoppers through Prime, so it can reach them easily with promotions and other targeted communications. The store offers customers money-saving benefits as well, including "consistently low prices" and 5% back when paying with the Amazon credit card or shopper card. It's easy to get in and out fast, thanks to the store's size, along with the navigation tools and Dash Cart. All these features combine to encourage customers to do more of their grocery shopping within the Amazon ecosystem — an important building block in the company's "long game" strategy.

2.  The product assortment can compete with larger grocery stores. A key to the Amazon Fresh store's broader appeal is the availability of items that surprise and delight customers. These include local brands like Rockenwagner Bakery and Groundworks Coffee, which are among the merchandising innovations that have proved popular in Amazon's smaller 365 stores. The store also offers regional brands with strong followings from around the country, like Duke's Mayonnaise from South Carolina and Ellenos Yogurt from Seattle, and it carries exclusive Amazon brands like Cursive Wine and Fresh, along with 365 brands. Amazon Fresh isn't the first grocer to expand the novelty of its assortment, but it may be the first to put ratings and reviews on shelf labels to more quickly raise awareness of what makes the products different and to tap into experience sharing and the social media community.

3.  There are plenty of time-saving, digitally-enabled customer service features. These digital offerings include the ability to download Alexa-created shopping lists into the Amazon app — or to the Dash Cart, which takes the uncertainty out of navigating the store. An "Ask Alexa" kiosk offers customers a familiar "face" to ask about meal prep and anything else that comes to mind. The Dash Cart also provides

navigation guidance, but the ability it gives customers to shop and leave the store without stopping to pay is one of the store's biggest selling points: It will encourage customers to visit the Amazon Fresh store to buy products they'd otherwise pick up someplace else.

4. The pricing strategy may drive some micro-merchandising objectives. In a guest blog for *Brick Meets Click*, retail pricing consultant Patrick Fisher wrote that he found evidence at Amazon Fresh that it is subtly using price to influence whether a customer buys certain items in-store or online. If this proves to be the case, it opens a new frontier for fine-tuning business performance.

5. The store deployment improves Amazon's capability to serve the last mile. Locating Amazon Fresh stores in the middle of its target market areas gives Amazon hyper-convenient access to its customers. This brings two "last mile" advantages: First, there is a shorter average distance between the customer's home and the store, making both pickup and delivery easier. Second is a higher density of online orders from the immediate trade area, which can translate into lower delivery costs. These are among the reasons Amazon emailed thousands of nearby customers before the opening of the first Amazon Fresh location. Add free, same-day delivery for Prime members, along with a convenient site to pick up and return Amazon.com orders, and Amazon Fresh is also a store that makes things a lot easier for Amazon's online shoppers.

6. The store's unit economics allow Amazon to operate profitably in extremely competitive environments. The low capital investment that comes with redeveloping existing stores creates a low cost of occupancy — and combined with the relatively small size of the stores, this translates into a low break-even sales volume. As competition increases, as it inevitably will, and margins are pushed down, many competitive stores will no longer be economically viable and will eventually need to close. This is where the low break-even of Amazon Fresh will make a big difference.

"Bottom line, what will be decisive is whether Amazon can run these stores to appeal to their target customers and operate them at such low a cost that it makes it difficult for other retailers to survive when competition intensifies," retail analyst Bill Bishop said. "Recent hires from Lidl suggest that they are tapping the expertise of those who know how to do this. If this turns out to be the case, this will be a winning strategy."

STRATEGY 5:

# Fresh Produce & Meat

ORDERING CANNED GOODS, BAGS OF DOG FOOD, AND WEEKLY SUPPLIES of coffee online is one thing, but when it's time to select fresh produce and meat, most customers want a more sensory experience. They want to feel their avocados to make sure they're not overly ripe, to sniff the melons they're considering and see the quality and cuts of meat they purchase.

This mindset is great news for bricks grocers: These needs are not something online grocery retailers can address. The retailers that work hard on being "fresh leaders" are the ones that win over the customers and their dollars. Recently in the U.S., for example, produce sales rose to $62 billion, up from $60.8 billion. This has not gone unnoticed by bricks grocery chains. "Grocers are expanding produce sections, stocking them with new exotic varieties, and adding such services as juice bars and precut fruit and vegetable packs," retail analyst Jaewon Kang said. Many bricks grocers also have redesigned their produce department by pushing it to the front, near the store entrance, and designing it with lower bins holding neat stacks of fresh and organic produce. The end result resembles a farmer's market more than a grocery store.

One chain to embrace this approach is H-E-B: Its focus is "Fresh, Fresh and more Fresh." The produce section at H-E-B is stocked with more than

*"Fresh leaders" are winning customers and dollars by redesigning their bricks grocery stores to resemble farmer's markets.*

1,000 items. Gorgeous fruits and fresh vegetables are impeccably stacked to entice consumers. H-E-B offers a wide selection of locally-grown Texas produce and an extensive variety of certified organic items. H-E-B also offers produce with its own brand, providing even greater value for customers. And customers love H-E-B's meat section; one Yelp reviewer described it as outstanding and reasonably priced. A number of meat items are sourced locally in Texas, too.

### Grocers Growing Produce

H-E-B has gone to great lengths to ensure its produce is the freshest available for shoppers. In 2017, the specialty food division of H-E-B delved into vertical farming, an indoor approach to growing food that allows the chain to deliver local, freshly harvested produce to customers. Initially, about a half dozen varieties of salad greens were grown at a Dallas H-E-B for customers to purchase. According to retail analyst Keith Loria, the greens were raised behind the store in a "four-level, vertical farm inside a retrofitted 53-foot long shipping container." H-E-B raised the greens under magenta and other color lights, and they did not require pesticides or sunlight.

For consumers, the cost of the produce is similar to other greens offered at H-E-B. The rise of urban gardens is a trend among consumers, who grow their own vegetables and fruits on rooftops, side lots, terraces and other locations. This is what inspired H-E-B's — and other grocers' — interest in growing greens, Loria said. "That trend has carried over to some grocers who have started growing their own produce, such as Whole Foods Market in its Gowanus Brooklyn store, which grows produce on its roof. Target is also looking into vertical farming at some of its stores."

For H-E-B, it is slightly more expensive to engage in vertical farming than purchasing greens for sale, but it saves the chain on transportation costs and plays into growing consumer demand for locally sourced items. Loria said grocers that farm their own produce will gain a leg up on bricks and clicks grocers. "In the ultra-competitive grocery space, any advantage that H-E-B or other retailers can get over their brick-and-mortar competitors, and those in the online space like Amazon, is invaluable." H-E-B also works with local chefs to grow products they need to appeal to customers, such as basil leaves that are typically found only in Italy.

## *Produce 2.0*

Walmart is very aware that produce is a critical component of its defense against Amazon. Because of this, Walmart has given its produce department a makeover dubbed "Produce 2.0," making it the first thing customers see when they enter one of the company's grocery stores. "The largest grocer in the U.S. renovated produce areas with new signs highlighting prices and shorter merchandise bins to create an 'open market feel' for customers," retail analyst Nathanial Meyersohn said. Walmart also moved all of its organic items into a single area of the produce section to make them easier to find, and it widened the aisles to prevent them from clogging up with customers and employees who pick up online grocery orders.

The executive vice president of food at Walmart's U.S. business, Charles Redfield, explained that clicks grocers made Produce 2.0 necessary.

"Online grocery shopping has changed the way we operate our food business within the store," he said. "We've always got associates in the produce area. The layout creates more space in the department to allow room for customers to shop."

For bricks grocers, redesigned produce departments are more than a strategy to compete against online grocery retailers: They also capitalize on health and wellness trends. And increasing numbers of bricks retailers, in addition to H-E-B and Walmart, are aware of this.

## Embracing Simplicity

ALDI, for example, has worked hard to revamp its produce and meat departments and bolster consumer awareness of its products. The pared-down, simplistic appearance of ALDI's meat case doesn't equate to low quality, nor does its low prices.

"ALDI meats can more than hold their own against other, larger stores that have a reputation for quality," retail analyst Jaron Pak said. ALDI's publicized sourcing and detailed labels on its meat appeal to customers, too, along with the convenient packaging in the ALDI meat case.

"From their bacon to their whole chickens and everything in between, the meat at ALDI tends to be carefully sourced and well-labeled, so you can feel confident with what you're getting," Pak said. "There are also quite a few options throughout the department, including things like Gianelli turkey sausage and convenient individually wrapped salmon filets. The best part is that all of these different products ring in at those famously low ALDI prices. Quality meat at an affordable price point? We call that one a win-win!"

ALDI still has room for improvement when it comes to presenting its produce. Customers likely take one look at the often disheveled open boxes and small selection in the produce section and start wondering if they should purchase their fruit and vegetables somewhere else. As Pak said, however, consumers shouldn't let presentation—or a lack of it—discourage them from trying ALDI's produce. "If you push past that initial impression you'll find that the presentation of an ALDI isn't an indicator of a lack of quality—it's simply a direct result of the desire to keep those prices so darn low." That said, customer first impressions are often difficult to change, and ALDI's presentation and smaller selection of produce may keep it from effectively competing with other grocers in this area.

## Luring Customers with Seasonal Produce

Many other grocers understand the power of presentation — particularly the benefits of showcasing seasonal fruits and vegetables, which they feature prominently in promotions and in-store displays. Whole Foods harnesses seasonal produce to lure customers into the store and keep them coming back.

"We put the emphasis in the front of the produce section," said Heith Banowetz, a 10-year veteran of Whole Foods' produce team. "We're looking to show what's in season. We get fresh produce in every day and feature our sale and in-season items in the front."

Whole Foods also offers customers added convenience by giving them the option of buying part of a pineapple or watermelon. "If a customer wants a quarter of a cabbage, half a watermelon or even half an apple, you know, I've never been asked for that. But I wouldn't be opposed to doing it to please a customer," Banowetz said. This convenience extends to other produce, such as grapes and cherries. Whole Foods informs customers they do not have to purchase a whole bag of fruit: They can opt for a handful of cherries or a dozen grapes in a container.

Freshness is another key with Whole Foods, which offers local selections when possible. "Apples last longer when they are in season," Banowetz said. "Apples from New Zealand or Chile in the offseason have a longer transportation time and therefore don't stay ripe as long. Apples last longer when we get them in season from California."

## Known for Freshness

Wegmans is another chain that realizes the value of fresh, quality produce for driving traffic and building customer loyalty.

"One of Wegmans' most well-known claims to fame is its produce department," retail analyst Julie Peirano said. Wegmans stocks quality, fresh, locally-sourced produce that never sits on the shelves for long, which is something few of its competitors can claim. "The average supermarket turns over its inventory between 18 and 20 times a year," *The Washington Post* wrote. "Wegmans, by contrast, goes through its produce as many as 100 times a year."

Because of these strategies and its well-known reputation for carrying the freshest produce available, Wegmans is well-positioned to gain a competitive advantage with its produce.

Wegmans also has an edge over many competitors when it comes to its meat and seafood offerings. The chain maintains exhausting standards for its meat, whether it is steak from ranches in Montana or salmon from the company's distributor in Alaska. Wegmans' employees often travel to where the meat and seafood they sell is sourced to gain expertise about the products they offer, a competitive edge that is difficult for other grocers to match.

### 'Fresh For Everyone'

Kroger is also trying to leverage the appeal of fresh produce to gain a competitive advantage. "Produce is what creates the trust between customers and neighboring retailers," Kroger Co. Vice President of Fresh Merchandising Suzy Monford said. Kroger is one of the largest organic food retailers in the U.S. Like H-E-B, Target, and other chains, Kroger is also growing herbs at a number of its stores, and it's ramping up its seasonal products offerings. The chain, which has a "Fresh For Everyone" slogan, recently announced it will begin growing some produce in hydroponic farms at its QFC stores in Washington.

Kroger also helps reduce food waste through its Zero Hunger/Zero Waste program. The company is a participant in the U.S. Food and Waste 2030 Champions initiative, a group of about two dozen grocers that aim to cut food waste in half by 2030. Other participating grocers include Weis Markets, Walmart, Sam's Club, Wegmans Food Markets and MOM's Organic Market. Currently, 40% of the food made in the U.S. is discarded even though one in eight Americans go hungry, Davis said.

It is likely more bricks grocers will continue to make over their produce and meat sections, knowing that competitors have done so or are making changes now. Grocers that make a poor impression in the areas of freshness and selection in these two departments will find it difficult to compete with those like H-E-B, Wegmans, and Walmart who understand the significance of these elements for driving traffic and building customer loyalty.

## STRATEGY 6:
# Meaningful Community Engagement

T OP GROCERY RETAILERS GO BEYOND PLEASING EMPLOYEES AND customers: They support their local communities in numerous ways, from supporting youth sports teams to providing food and necessities to individuals impacted by natural disasters. They find meaningful ways to meet communities' most pressing needs. During the COVID-19 pandemic, for example, many bricks grocers adjusted their shopping hours so that one of the populations most vulnerable to the virus, the elderly, could have stores available just to them during the first hour or two of store operations.

### A Customer Service Leader
H-E-B is one grocer that understands that nurturing the health and well-being of the community is essential for grocers to thrive.

"One of the most impactful things H-E-B does to bolster its reputation as a customer-service leader is understanding the needs of the community," H-E-B Quality Assurance Engineer Jesus Ochoa said. H-E-B is committed to helping the communities in Texas and Mexico where it operates.

An example of that commitment is the grocer's response to Hurricane Harvey, which caused catastrophic flooding and more than 100 deaths after making landfall in Texas on August 25, 2017. Harvey was ranked as the second-most costly hurricane to hit the U.S. mainland, causing more than $125 billion in damage. Days after Harvey made landfall, H-E-B announced a donation of $100,000 to hurricane relief efforts. The chain also initiated a campaign to raise money based on customer donations.

"Additionally, the Texas chain brought in mobile kitchens and disaster relief units to storm-stricken areas, serving up to 2,500 hot meals an hour to victims and first responders," retail analyst Raquel Guarino said.

Knowing the community so hard hit by Harvey is the foundation of its success, H-E-B did not stop with these efforts. A month after Harvey made landfall, the grocer donated $1 million to the Coastal Bend Disaster Recovery Relief Fund to support its Hurricane Harvey recovery efforts. Efforts like these demonstrate that H-E-B is a trustworthy store that profoundly cares about the well-being of its customers and the communities in which it operates.

The chain also came into the limelight in 2018 when it launched a limited-edition reusable bag featuring the late Tejano singer Selena. The bag sold out almost immediately. Selena was one of the most celebrated Mexican-American entertainers of the late 20th century. In 1995, at the height of her popularity, she was shot and killed by her friend and former manager, Yolanda Saldivar. Two weeks after the killing, Texas Governor George W. Bush declared the late artist's birthday Selena Day in Texas. After her death, radio stations in Texas played her music non-stop. H-E-B's commemorative bag shows its sensitivity to not only its community but also to the diversity of that community.

"H-E-B's widespread charitable and community efforts demonstrate integrity and deep commitment to the people it serves," retail analyst and author Lee Yohn said. "It's clear that H-E-B's priorities, like those of all great brands from Nike to Nordstrom, involve more than selling products."

H-E-B also is responsible for such initiatives as the H-E-B Food Bank Assistance Program, annual Feast of Sharing Holiday dinners and the Spirit of H-E-B trailer that offers on-site relief in areas hard-hit by natural disasters—which is in line with the chain's Helping Here philosophy. Every year, the H-E-B Excellence In Education Awards present $700,000 in cash awards to deserving teachers, principals and school districts. The chain's numerous community events include H-E-B Helping Heroes, which has been honoring Texas first responders on 9/11 and during the COVID-19 pandemic. H-E-B also established Operation Appreciation, a company-wide campaign designed to honor the brave men and women of the U.S. Armed Forces, including those who are H-E-B partners, customers, friends and family. Knowing the children in its communities are the community leaders of tomorrow, H-E-B established the Read 3 initiative. This effort to support early childhood literacy includes children's book drives. The initiative has a pledge for young readers: "A, B, C and 1, 2, 3, Reading is fun for me! It helps to grow my young mind. This week I pledge to read 3 times!"

H-E-B's community investment portfolio includes a number of green initiatives, too. H-E-B makes contributions to such organizations as Keep Texas Beautiful, The Nature Conservancy, Audubon Texas, EarthShare of Texas, Cibolo Nature Center & Farm, Ocean-Trust Texas, Hill Country Conservancy, National Wildlife Federation, San Antonio Botanical Gardens and many others. Some of these initiatives are designed to bolster local product sourcing, such as the partnership H-E-B maintains with Ocean-Trust. Through this partnership, H-E-B has helped restore 10,000 acres of estuarine habitat that is critical for the sustainability of coastal fisheries and migratory waterfowl along the South Texas coast. Partnerships like these are a win-win-win situation for the community, H-E-B and the environment.

More recently, H-E-B committed $3 million to support local orga-nizations working to stop the spread of COVID-19, according to retail analyst Michael Browne. H-E-B's partnerships with local nonprofits help provide relief to some of its communities' most vulnerable residents, including the elderly, children, and low-income families.

"During these trying times, H-E-B is here for Texas," Winell Herron, H-E-B group vice president of public affairs, diversity and environmental affairs, said. "Now, more than ever, H-E-B is keeping with our Spirit of Giving and Helping Here philosophies to do everything we can to

*An example of H-E-B's commitment to helping the communities in Texas is its support of food banks, providing truckloads of food and household items to those in need across the state.*

support our fellow Texans." As part of this commitment, H-E-B's Hunger Relief Program committed to donating $1.2 million to support 18 food banks across the state, providing over 6 million meals to those in need. In addition, H-E-B pledged to deliver 15 truckloads of food and household items to various food banks in Texas, working directly with food banks that are affiliated with Feeding Texas, a member of Feeding America, the country's top domestic hunger-relief organization. Part of this effort will also commit $500,000 to organizations that provide mobile home feeding services for seniors and low-income families, such as Meals on Wheels. H-E-B also said it would contribute $300,000 to support Texas Biomedical Research Institute, a San Antonio-based organization with a team dedicated to COVID-19 research, according to Browne. The company furthered its commitment to helping Texas communities by earmarking $1 million in financial support to its nonprofit partners who are providing critical services during the pandemic.

## Part of Being a Neighborhood Store

Most grocers are aware of the importance of supporting their local communities. Trader Joe's is another great example: Every one of its 488 locations helps its communities, whether it's buying from local produce suppliers, participating in local events, contributing products to worthy causes or featuring local artwork. They've helped protect the environment, as well, by heavily promoting the use of reusable bags long before it was commonplace.

"Contributing to our local communities is essential to being a neighborhood grocery store," the Trader Joe's website said. "We handle all requests for product donations and involvement in community events in our stores. Whether you're looking for support for a silent auction to benefit a local elementary school or a community hospital fair, your Trader Joe's store is the place to go."

Each Trader Joe's has a designated donation coordinator who is in charge of overseeing the store's community contributions. One of Trader Joe's mainstay initiatives is its Neighborhood Shares program. In this long-running program, Trader Joe's donates 100% of products that go unsold but are safe for consumption to local food banks and other nonprofit food recovery partners. In 2019 alone, Trader Joe's reported it donated almost $384 million worth of its products: the equivalent of 78 million pounds of food or 65 million meals to help fight hunger in its communities.

## A Track Record of Service

Wegmans has a similar track record of service and community support. According to retail journalist Marcia Layton Turner, Wegmans builds a strong sense of community ownership by "donating products to area charities, donating millions to area schools and colleges, sponsoring a Wegmans play area in a local museum and paying out more than $100 million in scholarships since 1984 to its workers attending college." And those are only a few examples of the chain's commitment to the communities surrounding its stores. Wegmans sponsors Little League and bowling teams, organizes employee volunteers to clean up local areas, offers economic assistance for local projects, invites scouting groups to tour Wegmans facilities and takes on a number of other projects designed to support community needs.

"Taking steps to make it easier for customers to do business with you and to recognize that you have their best interests at heart can only be good for business, as Wegmans has shown," Turner said.

Wegmans stays true to its mission of providing the very best for all people, including those most in need. The company website explained that the majority of its charitable contributions are "focused on programs that reduce hunger, help young people succeed, promote healthy eating and activity, strengthen neighborhoods and support United Way initiatives." In 2019 alone, Wegmans donated approximately 18.6 million pounds of food to local food banks and programs that feed the hungry. Like H-E-B and other grocery chains, Wegmans community initiatives also include helping in times of natural disaster. Wegmans is a strong partner with the American Red Cross and works diligently to be able to help rapidly in times of need. "We focus our efforts on disasters that directly affect the communities where we have stores," the Wegmans website says.

Founded by a veteran, Robert Wegman, the chain is also dedicated to supporting former and current military members. And through Wegmans' Passport To Family Wellness Program, the chain partners with local recreation programs, park conservancy groups, fitness programs and more to encourage community members and employees to be active, improve their lives and enjoy the beauty of nature.

### A Commitment to Outreach

Kroger has a strong outreach program, too. In addition to the Zero Hunger/Zero Waste community initiative, the chain is also committed to supporting members of the U.S. Armed Forces. Since 2009, Kroger has hired almost 45,000 veterans. Kroger also sponsors the Honoring Our Heroes 5K, maintains a Veterans Associate Resource Group and works with Warrior Homesteads, which builds and gifts tiny homes to local veterans. Kroger donates $500 to help stock the pantry and fridge of home recipients. Kroger is a proud partner with the USO as well.

Kroger's website explains its commitment to community outreach: "The Kroger Family of Companies is committed to community engagement, positive social impact and charitable giving at the national and local levels," it states. "Every community is unique, but our common goal is to partner with the neighborhoods we serve and help the people there live healthier lives."

One initiative in support of these goals is the Kroger Community Rewards program. The program supports local fundraising events, making it easy to donate to local organizations based on the shopping they do every day. Customers can link an organization to their rewards card, which tabulates a donation every time the card is swiped. Kroger donates a percentage of a shopper's spending to participating organizations annually. Kroger also makes it easy for organizations to request a charitable donation from the Kroger Co. on its website. Kroger's charitable giving extends to organizations at the national and local levels that focus on hunger relief, military personnel and their families, health and nutrition, disaster relief and more. Kroger recently donated $3 million to "rapidly deploy hunger-relief resources to communities disproportionately impacted by the coronavirus (COVID-19) pandemic," said retail analyst Michael Browne.

"Our most urgent mission is to be here for our customers when they need us most," Keith Daily, Kroger's group vice president of corporate affairs, said. "We're also mindful that the coronavirus pandemic may result in more of our neighbors struggling with food insecurity during this challenging time—and we want to help."

## Coming Together to Do Extraordinary Things
Kroger is not the only grocery retailer that has stepped in to provide community outreach during the COVID-19 pandemic. According to Browne, the Walmart Foundation committed $25 million to support organizations on the "front lines" of responding to COVID-19.

Executive Vice President and Chief Sustainability Officer for Walmart, Kathleen McLaughlin, explained, "In times of need, we see communities come together to do extraordinary things. This pandemic is no different . . . We hope these grants will help expand critical response efforts as we continue to work together to address the impact of COVID-19."

The funds committed by Walmart will be targeted to strengthening the global public health response, ramping up food security and meeting the needs of local communities in the U.S. and internationally.

Walmart also serves the communities where it operates in many other ways. Walmart is committed to providing access to healthier food, stable jobs and support in times of disaster to help create strong local economies and communities. The company supports more than 10,000 communities served by its stores, clubs and facilities. "Walmart has a long history of stepping up in times of disaster to help communities with relief and recovery," the company website says. "Since 2016, we have given nearly $50 million in cash, water, food and other products to support victims of hurricanes, wildfires and tornadoes. Additionally, during the same time period, we have raised $44 million in donations from customers to support hurricane relief." Walmart also facilitates associate volunteerism, local donations through stores and customers and support for diversity and inclusion initiatives.

Walmart provides local grants, too. "Each year, our U.S. stores and clubs award local cash grants ranging from $250 to $5,000," the Walmart website says. "These local grants are designed to address the unique needs of communities where we operate. They include a variety of organizations, such as animal shelters, elder services and community cleanup projects. In 2018, our stores and clubs provided more than $42 million in local grants." Along these lines, the company's Walmart Rise initiative is devoted to supporting the neighborhoods in which Walmart does business. To kick it off, the company committed $23 million in 2019, which amounts to a $5,000 fund for every Walmart store and distribution center in the U.S.

## *On the Front Line of Hunger Relief*

Albertsons, through its Help Feed Families During The Crisis program, is asking donors to help fight community hunger that was caused or worsened by the COVID-19 crisis. The Boise, Idaho-based chain pledged $3 million to help feed families in need during the pandemic.

"Albertsons Companies has always been on the front line of hunger relief, and our customers always stand with us," Albertsons President and CEO Vivek Sankaran said. "We are asking communities to join us in this effort to ensure that the COVID-19 crisis doesn't also become a hunger crisis." Shoppers were invited to make a donation as well during checkout at any Albertsons, Safeway, Vons, Jewel-Osco, Shaw's, Star Market, Tom Thumb, Randall's, ACME and other Albertsons Cos. stores.

## *Working Together to Make a Difference*

Many grocers have committed significant funds to the communities where they operate in response to the COVID-19 pandemic. Carlisle, Pennsylvania-based The Giant Company is one among them. It donated a quarter of a million dollars to four local hunger-relief organizations, including the Central Pennsylvania Food Bank, Philabundance, Maryland Food Bank and Meals on Wheels Pennsylvania. The pandemic has forced organizations like these to cancel their food drives, making support from the business community even more important.

"The Giant Company's purpose is to connect families for a better future, which is why we are acting with urgency and providing them with funds now so they can continue to support our most vulnerable neighbors," Company President Nicholas Bertram said, "Working together, we can truly make a difference, and it's our hope that anyone who can does join us in providing relief to these life-sustaining organizations."

## *Lidl and the Peanut Butter Challenge*

Even hard discounters like Lidl and ALDI understand the importance of visibly supporting the local communities in which they do business. Lidl fan Eric "Bean" McKay, who is autistic, is a huge fan of Lidl's private-brand peanut butter, a fact the teen shared with the chain on Twitter. In response, the grocer gave McKay 72 jars and promised McKay a lifetime supply of peanut butter if he could get 72,000 retweets on the offer. McKay took the challenge to heart, reached the Twitter goal and soon received a pallet of Lidl peanut butter. The story didn't stop there. After his father was furloughed as a result of the government shutdown in 2019, McKay announced he would award other affected families jars of his peanut butter. The move won him coverage on several local and even national news outlets.

"The story is a good example of how retailers can leverage their private brand products into marketing success," said Gina Acosta of *Storebrands*. In addition to this win-win situation, Lidl started featuring a picture of McKay on its private label peanut butter and earmarking a percentage of sales for an autism advocacy group.

Lidl, which has adopted the community service slogan, "A Better Tomorrow," also is a proud partner of Jigsaw, the National Centre for Youth Mental Health. The chain encourages customers and colleagues to become "One Good Adult" to a young person in their lives to support youth mental health. Lidl has also established what are known as Autism Aware Stores because bright lights, crowded spaces, noise, sensory overload and grocery shopping can be very stressful for many people with autism. Along the same lines, Lidl has established "Autism Aware Quiet Evenings" in each of its stores to help people and families who struggle with grocery shopping. During these Autism Aware Quiet Evenings, from 6 to 8 p.m. on Tuesdays, stores feature:

- Reduced light
- No music or announcements
- Lower till scan sounds
- Priority queuing and additional assistance
- An open door for assistance dogs

Lidl also is committed to supporting the efforts of local communities that share the values Lidl cherishes, including social inclusion, health and wellbeing and protecting the environment. "Where a local community group is hosting a community event or fundraiser which mirrors our values and pillars, we are happy to provide Lidl vouchers to support," the Lidl website said. "These vouchers have been used by hundreds of community groups and charities across the country for raffles, bake-sales, school healthy eating weeks, science projects and sports programs."

## *Offering More than Affordability*

ALDI is another hard discount chain that takes pride in supporting the communities in which it operates. It understands that being a top grocer means more than offering quality items at affordable prices: It also means supporting the growth of strong communities and helping create a better world.

"We believe support should be based on the needs of each individual community, which can range from product and monetary donations to staff volunteering to collaborations with nonprofit organizations," the ALDI website said. "We're dedicated to funding and sponsoring local and regional initiatives that support health and wellness initiatives for children and youth." Every ALDI location partners with a local Feeding America member food bank to simplify donations of overstock, short-dated items and products with lightly damaged packaging. Such partnerships help address food insecurity in local communities while supporting ALDI's goal of minimizing environmental impact by reducing waste.

ALDI also is dedicated to supporting youths in its communities. Through ALDI Smart Kids, the chain partners with nonprofit organizations that promote health and wellness for children. These activities include donating ALDI gift cards to nonprofits, schools, fire and police departments, and local churches. ALDI sponsors programs that support children through education, arts, nutrition, physical activity and other programs as well. And, ALDI partners with Action for Healthy Kids (AFHK) to promote healthy, active lifestyles for students, teachers and family members in their communities through the U.S. "Programs and projects may include refurbishing outdoor play spaces, piloting aeroponic school gardens, implementing farm-to-school programs, hosting fitness and nutrition classes, purchasing physical activity equipment and implementing before-and after- school fitness programs," the chain's website says. ALDI is a firm believer that healthy kids are kids who are better prepared to learn.

What's more, ALDI encourages and promotes employee volunteerism across a number of community events and organizations. Through its partnership with Feeding America, it provides disaster relief boxes every year to support individuals and families displaced from their homes because of natural disasters. ALDI's employees and customers are also instrumental in raising funds that go beyond product donations. "We continue to provide funding to the American Red Cross to support its efforts to provide immediate shelter and comfort to those affected by disaster," the ALDI website says. "This past year, our employees and customers donated more than $400,000 to Feeding America, and we donated an additional $250,000."

The list of bricks grocers that engage in community support and outreach is lengthy as are the number of ways in which they express that support. Not only do these efforts strengthen communities, but they're also good for business and a strong way of differentiating bricks grocers from online grocers.

STRATEGY 7:

# Seamless Omnichannel Experience

THE IRONIC PART OF BRICKS GROCERY RETAILERS COMPETING WITH clicks grocery retailers is that bricks chains must rely on digital technologies, smart devices and the Internet to succeed these days.

"The connected commerce era has arrived," said Nielsen's Chief Commercial Officer for Nielsen Global Connect, Patrick Dodd. "Consumers are no longer shopping entirely online or offline; rather, they're taking a blended approach, using whatever channel best suits their needs. The most successful retailers and manufacturers will be at the intersection of the physical and virtual worlds, leveraging technology to satisfy shoppers however, wherever and whenever they want to shop."

It requires a great deal of capital to create the seamless digital connection among different channels that is omnichannel retailing. For this reason, I believe that the smaller chains that are unable to raise or invest such capital will continue to lose sales and eventually disappear from the grocery industry.

As with the other strategies covered in this book, omnichannel is another way to focus on putting customers and their satisfaction at the top of the priorities list.

"The core element of omnichannel marketing is that it is shopper-based, not channel-based," Criteo reported. "The main goal is to make the shopper experience as easy as possible, and that means consistent engagement no matter where or how a shopper is interacting with you."

Bricks grocers that make this a priority understand the importance of differentiation when it comes to competing with clicks grocers.

Omnichannel enables bricks grocers to customize each shopper's experience. For example, mobile apps for bricks grocers offer deals and electronic coupons for customers that are data-driven based on their previous shopping trips. In-store or at-home shoppers can download these electronic deals onto their store-branded savings card so that when they check out, the deals are automatically credited to them. Or, shoppers might see a deal for saving cardholders in-store and scan the SKU with their phones to be credited for it at checkout.

Omnichannel is often referred to as multi-channel because it is a holistic process in which retailers sell across multiple channels including websites, social media and marketplaces. However, omnichannel is distinct because it defines retailers with both a physical ("bricks") and digital ("clicks") presence.

Square defines omnichannel as: "Meeting people on the channels where they are shopping and buying, whether it's in a physical store or an online store or on social media, and connecting the dots between those channels. The purpose is to keep customers moving around within the brand ecosystem, with each channel working in harmony to nurture more sales and engagement."

## Positive 'Phygital' Experiences

The goal is not to have customers choose one channel or another. It is to offer seamless integration of all three channels so that whatever combination of channels is most convenient for customers is available to them. Omnichannel appeals to all types of consumers.

"Nobody today shops exclusively through a single medium," consumer and retail analyst Tracey Wallace said. "Consumers of all generations buy online, in stores and on marketplaces."

Even so, it does appear that different generations view bricks and clicks shopping differently. *Sales & Orders* Marketing Manager Anthony Capetola said Baby Boomers and older Millennials are far fonder of bricks

*The omnichannel experience seamlessly integrates all three channels within the brand ecosystem — the physical store, online store, and social media — to make available whatever combination of channels is most convenient for customers.*

shopping, but younger Millennials almost always choose to shop online. A *Big Commerce* survey revealed that 31.9% of Baby Boomers, 27.5% of Gen X, 31.04% of Millennials, and 9.6% of Gen Z report buying items in bricks stores. Further, generational differences exist with respect to which channels each generation prefers. The top three choices for shopping among all consumers are Amazon, branded e-commerce sites and bricks retail stores.

Nick Raushenbush, co-founder of e-commerce software provider Shogun, reports that nearly 70% of Millennials shop online, but he argued this does not mean bricks retail stores should be abandoned. "Americans are still split 50/50 on whether they prefer online shopping versus in-store shopping, with in-store shopping being the dominant channel for Boomers and Seniors," he said.

Top reasons cited by consumers who prefer bricks shopping include the ability to touch and try items, in-store experience, price, convenience and the ability to make sure there is nothing wrong with an item.

Consulting company Kantar calls seamless physical and digital shopping a "phygital" experience that equates more to a lifestyle activity than a chore. Some grocers are spending significant amounts of capital to deliver positive "phygital" experiences to shoppers.

Bricks grocers can capitalize on numerous opportunities to combine and leverage the strengths of both clicks and bricks experiences. The Kantar Worldpanel has identified three key areas where bricks grocers can achieve this goal: productivity, convenience and customer experience. I agree: One of the best ways bricks grocers can add value to stave off clicks grocers is to improve productivity. Kantar Worldpanel has noted that "highly digitized" supermarkets can operate with approximately 40% fewer labor hours. This frees up staff to add greater value to stores through such activities as tasting counters and cooking classes. Robotics and AI in backrooms, warehouses and micro-fulfillment centers lead to greater efficiency, not to mention better forecasting and stock control. Enhancing sourcing and supply chain logistics will also reduce time-to-shelf. This will keep inventory fresher for longer and reduce wasted produce.

Convenience and customer experience are two other areas where bricks grocers can leverage the strengths of both clicks and bricks experiences. "Customer demand for convenience can be met through an omnichannel experience by combining in-store, local and online options, as well as providing an innovative, more efficient and quicker checkout and payment process for busy customers," Kantar said.

## Winning the 'Race to the Top'
Using omnichannel methods, bricks grocers are able to optimize their range of products. They can leverage their products and maximize the rewards of selling more "urgent" products and items customers prefer to inspect, reducing shelf space required for "stock-up" items such as toiletries and laundry products. Streamlining the checkout process should be a major goal of omnichannel strategies and leveraging technology. This is true because of the streamlined checkout process at Amazon Go and Amazon Go Stores bricks locations, and because Kantar reports that 48%

of shoppers say "slow checkout" is the most frustrating aspect of grocery shopping in bricks locations.

Ensuring elevated customer experiences, as I have discussed, is one of bricks grocers' best strategies for driving traffic and building customer loyalty, and data is an invaluable tool in achieving this. It's also readily available. Kantar reports that 50% of pre-family shoppers say they are "prepared to share data" so grocers can tailor shopping experiences to their individual needs and likes. And they're not the only ones: Customers across all generations, *Big Commerce* reports, can be incentivized to share personal data with retailers. Incentives can include product discounts, more personalization, early access to new products and faster delivery.

"Retailers who are harnessing the power of all of their data to make informed decisions on which messages and products to market are winning the race to the top," explained Alicia Thomas, former senior marketing manager for marketing software provider Klaviyo. "By understanding segments of your audience based on historical data, you have a much higher likelihood of breaking through all the noise and actually converting a browser into a buyer."

When bricks grocers know, for example, that shoppers like to inspect produce for freshness, they can act on that information, invest in fresher foods and foster positive experiences. If they offer private label produce or meat, this also is an opportunity to enhance shoppers' perceptions of those products. What's more, data-driven strategies help bricks grocers stay abreast of the latest foods and beverage trends, which also influence customer perceptions and can be used effectively in advertising and promotions.

2019 was a watershed year for omnichannel, a turning point that continues to impact the retail industry today.

"Retailers began to win or lose on consumer trust at a much more noticeable rate, specifically on their ability to win consumer trust in digital channels," said Nikki Baird, a *Forbes* retail analyst contributor.

Winning consumer trust now comes first *before* gaining consumer business, a reversal of the past when retailers gained consumer business with the intention of earning their trust and establishing long-term relationships. Winning consumer trust often occurs in social media spaces these days. Retailers, including grocers, who hope to win the trust of consumers must carry the brand appeal of such spaces through to their website and into their brick locations.

## Strategies for Success

Omnichannel helps demonstrate that we should not take an "us v. them" mentality when it comes to bricks and clicks retail. In many ways, having an online presence is complementary to bricks business. Frank Morrall of Visioncourse Media reports, "Our merchants see not only an increase in online sales but also an increase in offline retail sales due to customers looking at the site before coming into the retail store. It actually drives in-store shopping even if they do not purchase online."

How can grocers successfully implement an omnichannel strategy? *Big Commerce* interviewed 37 industry experts, agencies, consultants and enterprise brand channel managers about this process and developed a list of guidelines for retailers:

- Capture data, track conversions and target messaging for your channels.

- Capitalize upon user experience and customer experience as top priorities.

- Automate to save your sanity.

- Remember that different channels mean different devices.

- Allocate the resources, and use helpful technology.

- Conversion is only the first step: You must deliver.

Data-driven strategies are the foundation of omnichannel success. *Sales & Orders* Marketing Manager Anthony Capetola said, "Nothing is more important than taking a data-driven approach to omnichannel marketing. Data can be used at any stage (i.e., planning, execution, analysis) and is paramount in determining the value of each channel." Having the right data enables retailers to know which channels are successful and so they can focus more on them while limiting resources devoted to a less effective channel. Existing across multiple channels is effective but only when you have enough data to gauge the results from each one.

While this may come as no surprise, it is also important to remember that any great omnichannel strategy puts what the customer wants first. "Developing an omnichannel strategy is a uniquely tailored process with customer-centric goals," said Alexei Alankin, CEO of marketing company *Eventige*. "The main focus should be on how your customers want to experience shopping online."

Automation plays a large role in omnichannel success. Anything that can be automated should be automated across all channels. When automation is not an option, outsourcing omnichannel functions can be helpful. This is valuable because achieving the seamless channel integration necessary for a successful omnichannel approach can be challenging. Jenna Paton, content executive at *dotmailer*, reports that only 7% of marketers can deliver omnichannel in real-time 24/7, so to join this group, "brands need to adopt a holistic strategy that loops in every avenue of customer engagement. In theory, each channel should be able to talk to each other and leverage the necessary data to drive the next interaction in the customer journey. This level of integration promotes consistency across all touchpoints and provides customers with a seamless experience that's channel-agnostic." Bricks grocers that can deliver this experience will achieve a competitive advantage.

There are a number of additional methods to help make omnichannel successful for your bricks grocer. One of these is to incentivize loyalty. Encouraging shoppers to sign up for loyalty programs or to download apps creates a stronger relationship with shoppers. It also helps provide a higher level of data that can be used to keep customers loyal. Another method is catering to shopper preferences. For instance, by keeping track of customer purchases online or in-store, grocers can tailor promotions and discounts for them based on this data. Using such data helps create an improved shopping experience.

Another method of making omnichannel successful is to make sure that communications you send to shoppers are based on data that makes them relevant, compelling and timely. For example, a customer who buys a specific brand of coffee regularly will get an email or promotion that announces it is on sale. Today's technology also makes it possible to send promotions or coupons to shoppers through geo-targeting, which sends them a communication when they are near your bricks location.

One final strategy to make omnichannel more successful is not to forget the importance or power of leveraging your physical location. An effective omnichannel grocer will use its physical location in non-traditional ways. *Criteo* explained this includes using physical locations as "showrooms for digital sales, as shipping centers, or as a blended digital-physical interactive experience." The handheld pricing meters Kroger offers to track purchases and total sales are one example of this.

*Criteo* reminds grocers, "Incorporating new technologies into stores can make the shopping experience more enjoyable, and ultimately, get more consumers off the web and through the door."

Omnichannel services are geared toward reducing costs, creating a frictionless shopping experience, increasing convenience for shoppers, and improving productivity. Zynstra, a software provider focusing on retail, describes the store of the future in the omnichannel world: "A laser focus on store productivity and convenience needs to be accompanied by a move to viewing stores as showrooms — that drive customers online, that serve as fulfillment points for e-commerce operations, and that are the physical embodiment of the retailer's brand." A traditional bricks infrastructure is a key part of fulfilling customer needs. Zynstra maintained that with the right technical infrastructure, it "should be possible to turn bricks and mortar into a real business advantage with better distribution (and return) points, and the ability to deliver customer care with the convenience and familiarity that engenders trust." This requires an in-store foundation of technology that can respond to rapid change, offers an affordable setup and is simple to extend across new locations.

Bricks grocers must have the conviction to achieve these goals. Zynstra warned that "in an environment of massive change, a lack of conviction to change the in-store experience is a guarantee of failure."

Business writer Noreen Seebacher explained that "grocers should embrace technology without losing sight of what customers love about them today." Successfully employing the right technologies enables bricks grocers to gain a competitive advantage.

Stephen Caine and Lisa Koetter, members of Bain's Retail practice, said, "The road ahead starts by investing to protect hard-earned loyalty and market-share advantages and build on those strengths, thoughtfully expanding digital capabilities while finding new ways to reimagine physical stores to serve evolving customer needs."

## H-E-B's Ongoing Journey

When it comes to providing an omnichannel experience, not every bricks grocer does everything. Nor do they offer superior service in every area that is important to customers. Even H-E-B, known for its customer service excellence, has not been recognized for delivering a frictionless grocery e-commerce experience. The good news for H-E-B and other grocers is that this leaves room for improvement, which could lead to providing even more superior, convenient, and seamless customer shopping and service experiences.

"If you're a savvy retailer with a balance sheet and liquidity, you should have the ability to build a competitive multi-channel business," Moody's analyst Charlie O'Shea said.

This is not to say that H-E-B has not been working on this: The chain has been investing significant resources in creating a seamless digital, in-store and online experience for consumers. H-E-B customers can shop online for curbside pickup or home delivery from their computers or with the My H-E-B app on their mobile devices. With the app, customers also can use coupons and participate in promotions during in-store shopping.

"At H-E-B, we continue to evaluate and utilize innovative technologies in all parts of our business," H-E-B Group Vice President of Omnichannel and Emerging Technologies Paul Tepfenhart said. "As a leading digital retailer in Texas, we will continue to grow our partner population as well as technology presences to complement our store operations, enabling customers to choose how they shop, pay for and receive products." H-E-B has a number of omnichannel services, from Favor Delivery, an on-demand delivery service, and HEBtoyou Delivery to H-E-B Curbside and its online grocery HEB.com, which offers shoppers the ability to order and ship grocery, drugstore and general merchandise products to 48 states and military bases around the world.

The grocer also has been establishing a pilot program in partnership with Udelv, which manufactures autonomous delivery vehicles, to harness self-driving technology to make deliveries in San Antonio. The delivery vehicles, with climate-controlled compartments for the delivery of fresh, frozen and dry goods, had a human driver in the trial phase but will then become autonomous.

What's more, H-E-B hired Jag Bath, CEO of Favor Delivery, to be the chain's chief digital officer. The new position underscores H-E-B's commitment to improving and building out omnichannel service to meet customer needs and expectations.

H-E-B Chief Operating Officer Martin Otto reaffirms the independent grocer's commitment to superior customer service while building out omnichannel service. "Our primary goal is to enable our customers to shop, pay for and receive their products in whatever way they choose — all while delivering an exceptional customer experience."

H-E-B is wholly committed to capturing a greater share of the digital retail market. A prime example of this is its investment in an 81,000-square-foot, world-class tech facility and innovation lab in East Austin. "This state-of-the-art space will be a hub for creativity and innovation as we continue to develop the ultimate digital experience for our customers," Bath said. "Bringing H-E-B and Favor closer together will allow us to promote collaboration between our two companies as we strengthen our commitment to building out H-E-B's omnichannel services." Initially, the main focus of the new facility will be expanding H-E-B Delivery and H-E-B Curbside services. Retail analyst Carols Sanchez explained that prior to its acquisition, Favor already made an impact on delivery and curbside services, with a network of over 50,000 runners. The move will "make H-E-B more competitive with online retail giant Amazon, which became only the second American company to reach a $1 trillion valuation," Sanchez said.

## Kroger's Four Methods

H-E-B is not the only bricks grocer investing in creating seamless shopper experiences across multiple channels or omnichannel strategies. For several years, Kroger has been working to expand its brand across channels, unwilling to let online grocery market share be dominated by Amazon and Walmart. Retail analyst Taylor Dua explained omnichannel services at Kroger include four methods: in-store, delivery, pickup and shipping under its "Feed The Human Spirit" tagline, the main message behind its Restock Kroger initiative. The goal of Restock Kroger is to "create a flawless omnichannel experience," retail analyst Kate Dwyer said. In an outline of the grocery chain's goals for Restock America, the company maintained, "Kroger will change the way people eat in America. Redefining grocery-customer experience uniquely positions us to win with customers by accelerating our digital and e-commerce efforts."

Similar to H-E-B, one of Kroger's technology investments is a partnership with the driverless car company Nuro to automate deliveries in Houston, Texas, and Scottsdale, Arizona. Similar to H-E-B and other grocers, Kroger has also invested resources to build on its customer data so it can enhance shoppers' experiences. Kroger CEO Rodney McMullen said, "Kroger's future depends on leveraging its data and fighting for digital customers." The same is true for other grocers.

Because Kroger operates more than a dozen store brands—including Ralph's, Fred Meyer, Fry's, King Soopers, Harris Teeter, OFC Mariano's and Metro Market—it has been challenging for Kroger to differentiate itself as more than just a big box grocery retail store. Some of its store brands, like Harris Teeter, have differentiated themselves as having higher quality and local items. This has enabled Harris Teeter to become powerful and build emotional bonds with customers on the regional level. Nevertheless, investors have been concerned that despite Kroger's investment in digital and omnichannel strategies, progress is failing to meet expectations. "We realize business transformations are hard. . . What got us here won't get us to where we aspire to be," McMullen said. Many bricks retailers can relate to these views.

But Kroger is making progress. When the chain introduced a "seamless digital shopping experience" during the fourth quarter of 2018, it started by integrating its ClickList service—the grocer's online order/in-store pickup service—into Kroger's other services, including coupons, recipes, rewards and others. So far the move has been successful. "Households that participate in our seamless offerings—those who engage with our digital platforms and with our physical stores—spend more per week than households that do not," McMullen said. "And households that transact with us online spend even more."

Like many grocery retailers, Kroger has ramped up efforts to listen to customers and what they expect or want when it comes to expanding omnichannel services. "The customers tell us that they like to engage in multiple ways," McMullen said. Retail analyst James Melton explained this shows that "improving the quality of digital experiences and making online technology work seamlessly with stores is vital to winning and keeping customers." Once again, helping provide customers with what they want is data-driven. For example, Kroger improved search results on its online grocery site based on prior shopper purchasing data. Now, items that customers purchase and items they are most likely to repurchase are prioritized on the Kroger online site. Melton reports that this change, implemented in a few weeks' time, led to a 33% increase in "add to cart" clicks for items that come up under the top search results. Kroger has been at the forefront of offering customers the means of using handheld scanners to price and tally items they purchase while moving through stores. Known as Scan, Bag, Go, Melton reports the chain has expanded the program to 400 stores after testing it in 20 stores. Convenience and speed are two increasingly expected consumer expectations, and strategies like these help fulfill them.

Kroger is also leveraging its data-driven approach to components of the grocery business that are unrelated to online commerce. Melton reports the company is using data to improve store layout, price points and employee hiring and training. The Restock Kroger initiative utilizes "Internet of Things" sensors, video analytics, machine learning networks, robotics and artificial intelligence, added Melton.

Mergers and acquisitions have played a role in expanding Kroger's omnichannel services, too. When the company acquired Harris Teeter, it benefited from the grocer's buy online/pickup in-store technology, a service that was later expanded to Kroger locations. The company purchased online vitamin and health product retailer Vitacost.com in 2014. Melton reports Kroger also "made a string of pure-play technology acquisitions." These include YOU Technology—a coupon, sales and content aggregator—and Kroger-established 84.51°, a customer-analysis unit based on technology it acquired from dunnhumbyUSA. The latter acquisition, named for the longitude of Kroger's headquarters, was merged with Market6, a retail technology the company purchased.

## *Walmart's Strategy*

Walmart is one bricks retailer with the conviction to meet the challenges of clicks retailers and of successfully creating the omnichannel experience. As the largest retailer in the world, Walmart is not content to sit back and let Amazon take the lion's share of online commerce.

Retail analysts credit omnichannel success for the tremendous growth Walmart saw during the COVID-19 pandemic. The company reported online sales growth of 79% for its fiscal year 2021, and in the fourth quarter of the year, online sales grew 69%. "Over the last several years, they have: reduced spending on new stores and emphasized remodels; upped spending on digital infrastructure; re-tooled in-store communications; and developed a new loyalty program (Walmart+) that makes it easier for shoppers to access their omnichannel capabilities," Supermarket News contributor Bill Bishop wrote. "Plus, they are continuously evolving their digital infrastructure, shifting from in-store pickup to curbside, and now to expanded delivery that will include testing smart, temperature-controlled lockers and autonomous vehicles."

Walmart's omnichannel success story can be traced back to 2015 when the company hired more than 2,500 employees at its e-commerce headquarters in Silicon Valley and earmarked $1 billion annually to create a global technology platform that would support its omnichannel vision. And in 2019, after online sales were slow the previous year, Walmart purchased

Jet.com for $3.3 billion. This gave Walmart access to new customers in specific markets while affording the company better analytics capabilities.

"For Walmart, the acquisition of Jet.com will mean the company will gain access to a new platform, which will drive growth in a more cost-efficient manner than its traditional bricks-and-mortar approach," Jennifer Sherman, vice president of product and strategy at Kibo Commerce, explained at the time.

By acquiring the online discount retailer, Walmart positioned itself to gain valuable data on shopper purchasing behavior and "leverage it to enhance its own mobile offerings, such as its app and Walmart Pay mobile payments platform," retail analyst Alex Samuely said, adding that Jet.com's supply chain model would also offer valuable insights Walmart could use to maximize its bricks-and-mortar order fulfillment centers and speed up shipping.

Walmart has been proactive in realigning its organization to drive its omnichannel implementation as well. Retail analyst Russell Redman explained these changes included consolidating supply chain teams under one organization, joining the Walmart U.S. finance and e-commerce finance teams, expanding the U.S customer organization and creating the role of chief merchandising officer for the U.S. e-commerce unit.

"Our customers want one seamless Walmart experience," Walmart President and CEO Doug McMillon said. "Over time, we've been organizing our strategy, tactics and teams to serve them in that way, while preserving the focus necessary to execute on multiple initiatives in parallel. We will continue strengthening our stores while expanding our pickup and delivery capabilities."

Greater integration and a customer-centric focus are drivers for Walmart's omnichannel model.

"Our big strategic opportunity is how we use our unique physical assets in conjunction with e-commerce," Walmart spokesman Randy Hargrove said.

Retail analyst Lauran Wood wrote for *Research and Markets*: "In-store services play a role in building loyalty among customers, regardless of whether they buy online or in-store and the role physical retail locations play in building loyalty from the omnichannel purchaser." Wood said these are Walmart's strengths.

### Better Serving Digital Shoppers

Walmart also has succeeded in providing a smooth online buying-store pickup experience and implementing such omnichannel features as curbside pickup and in-app directions, according to Digital Commerce 360 writer April Berthene. In-store design investments, including changing store layouts to better serve digital shoppers, have been beneficial, too. Adding giant towers for retrieved orders and piloting pickup lockers are two examples, Berthene noted.

Walmart has also made significant improvements to its mobile technology capabilities. Retail analyst John Walton explained one of these is implementing "geo-fencing" in all stores, a technology that "links up with customers' loyalty accounts and mobile devices to alert the retailer when a customer arrives in the parking lot to pick up an online order." Walmart also launched a "wish list" that enables shoppers to add items they want from home or by scanning them in stores, according to Walton.

Additional innovations include the "endless aisle system" being tested in Walmart stores. It comprises kiosks at the end of physical aisles where customers have online access to Walmart's entire inventory. If a bricks location does not have the specific item a customer is searching for, they can use the kiosk, find it, and place their order. They can choose to return to the store to pick up the item or opt to have it delivered to their home. This demonstrates the simplicity and convenience that omnichannel technologies deliver. The system also decreases the odds of a customer switching to a competitor for an item they cannot get.

Complementing this program is the discount Walmart offers on items shoppers are willing to pick up in-store.

Walton explained that by "paying" shoppers to pick up packages in-store, "Walmart once again demonstrates it understands the value of omnichannel marketing strategies. Instead of viewing e-commerce and in-store retail as two competing revenue streams, Walmart views them as complementary."

## Top Provider

Walmart's omnichannel strategies have been highly effective. In 2019, for example, Internet Retailer's *Omnichannel Report* listed Walmart Inc., Target Corp. and the Home Depot Inc. as the top three omnichannel services providers among retail chains. Out of 200 total points possible, the three chains scored 159, 158.5 and 155, respectively.

Senior Director of Business Development at Walmart Jeff Muench explained: "Meeting customers' needs is critical as they adopt more digitally-driven lifestyles, expectations increase, and, increasingly, shopping options do not require a trip inside a store."

This is a viewpoint other bricks grocery retailers must adopt to experience a high level of success through omnichannel strategies.

## Technology-Based Conveniences

Leveraging digital engagement to enhance the overall shopping experience is part of an omnichannel strategy. However, it is important across all channels of shopping. Technology-based, in-store convenience options have strong appeal to bricks customers. Self-service checkouts are rising in popularity in brick-and-mortar grocery stores. In North America, a Nielsen survey conducted before the COVID-19 pandemic revealed that 41% of grocery customers already used self-service checkouts, while another 45% said they're willing to use this method of checking out. That interest has only increased since social distancing drove more consumers to order groceries online. Using technology to offer time-strapped customers a faster, easier and more efficient shopping experience enhances the overall shopping experience. In stores where only two or three traditional checkout lines may be staffed, and lines are long, self-service checkouts are a great option for rushed customers with a handful of items. This technology also cuts labor costs.

A number of other technological innovations will enhance overall shopping experiences for bricks grocery customers. Some grocery chains, including Kroger, are starting to allow customers to use hand-held scanners throughout the store as they shop. When customers are done with their shopping, they avoid checkout lines and simply input payment card information before leaving the store. Only 10% of North American shoppers currently use this technology, which is not prevalent in the industry yet, but a whopping 65% acknowledged in a Nielsen survey they are willing to use it once it becomes available to them. We're likely to see more stores offer hand-held scanners soon because they enhance the shopping experience by putting more control in consumers' hands, literally. The name of the game for technology is to meet consumer demands for greater convenience, speed and store experience.

Other digital engagement options, as I've mentioned, include online ordering for home delivery or pickup at the store, online and mobile coupons, online and mobile shopping lists, loyalty apps and in-store Wi-Fi that allows customers to use their mobile devices in the store to find information about products and special offers. Some chains also offer in-store computers where customers can find more details about the range of products the retailer offers or scan product codes with mobile devices to access more detailed product information. From geo-fencing to in-store kiosks, bricks grocers are creating multichannel services designed to not only create seamless experiences for shoppers no matter how they like to shop, but also to increase convenience.

Bricks grocers must continue to innovate and reimagine the role physical stores will play in the digital age and beyond. Grocers like H-E-B invest on this level to emphasize local store formats and product assortments that appeal to their regional market. Others like Wegmans do so to focus on their reputation for "retail theater" and prepared foods, while Publix has made "high-touch" customer service their main emphasis. The most successful grocers will also continue to invest in new omnichannel capabilities that are data-driven, such as the ability to generate, collect and analyze shopper data to provide tailored marketing and services.

A decade from now, Seebacher said, "stores will have expansive pickup areas, a convenience section for topping up purchases made online, and other changes we have yet to imagine."

Bain's Retail urges bricks grocers to imagine what roles they want their physical stores to serve for shoppers and start heading in that direction now. The retail consultancy also argued that where omnichannel is concerned, it is "critical" for bricks grocers to "understand profitability across channels," while warning "there is a cost of doing nothing in your analysis." It is the former that will make some bricks grocers fall prey to online retail. As with services for customers, profitability can no longer be separated from the physical location and the online realm.

"It won't be long before collective consumer expectation rises once more, and those retailers that don't bring themselves up-to-date will find themselves hopelessly stranded at the altar as the polygamous practices of mobile, web and in-store integrations become the norm," Walton said.

The constantly connected modern shopper demands omnichannel integration from retailers, including grocers. This includes the ability for their order history and customer data to follow them seamlessly across mobile, website and in-store.

STRATEGY 8:

# Convenient Online Ordering, Delivery, Store Pickup & Fulfillment

IN 1916, CLARENCE SANDERS LAUNCHED THE PIGGLY WIGGLY GROCERY chain and sparked a self-service revolution: For the first time, items displayed on a shelf were available for customers to hold and examine. Up to then, customers handed a list of the items they needed to their grocers, and they'd pick the items, bag them and ring them up.

The Piggly Wiggly business model linked marketing and fulfillment and has remained pretty much unchanged — until recently.

Now the grocery industry is evolving again, this time to meet rapidly changing customer demands for online shopping and rapid order fulfillment. Historically, retailers of all varieties could create differentiation based on the brands they offered, the assortment they carried, and the pricing of their products. Now, speed and convenience have taken on equal significance as a means of differentiation.

IAM Robotics, which provides robotic order-fulfillment systems, credits four factors for this emerging business model:

- Urbanization: Today, 54% of the world's population lives in urban areas, and this number is expected to rise to 68% by 2050.

- Instant gratification: Consumers have become increasingly impatient about waiting for their stuff to be delivered. They want it now.

- Access to anything: Consumers expect online retailers to offer a seemingly unlimited variety of products.

- Convenience: Consumers demand a fast and easy ordering process and free delivery.

Grocery shopping certainly is moving in that direction. Customers still want to buy from their local stores, but increasingly, they'd rather make their selections online.

Retail analyst Jennifer Smith reported that online orders were still a very small portion of the U.S. grocery market, about 3.5% in 2020, but food and beverage is the fastest-growing U.S. e-commerce segment, according to eMarketer. While online grocery represented just $22.63 billion in sales for U.S. grocers in 2019, this number is projected to nearly double by 2022, to $40.4 billion.

Not only are increasing numbers of shoppers opting to order groceries online, they expect speedy results.

"Our research shows that 65% of consumers would consider shopping from a different retailer if their normal grocery store didn't provide a same-day home delivery or curbside pickup option," said Steve Hornyak, Chief Commercial Officer with micro-fulfillment company Fabric.

What's more, a Fabric survey showed that not only do 92% of consumers prefer to have their online grocery orders fulfilled on the same day, but 33% said they wanted their order ready in two hours or less.

Two-hour or same-day delivery is not an unreasonable customer demand. It's necessary for many grocery items, especially perishables.

These new expectations, just like the arrival of Piggly Wiggly, are ushering in a new business model for buying groceries: Bricks grocers must provide convenience as well as positive experiences and quality. For bricks grocers, achieving this will require a comprehensive, carefully considered approach that leverages multiple solutions.

## Grocers' Responses

One strategy bricks grocery retailers have implemented, or are in the process of adopting, is offering curbside pickup.

Curbside pickup of online orders has become an extremely popular service. Of Walmart's 3,750 Supercenters in the U.S., for example, 3,000 offer this option. Yet, while curbside pickup of online grocery orders makes buying groceries quicker and easier for shoppers, the task of fulfilling orders still falls to grocery retailers, leaving them with increased labor costs. The same can be said about providing deliveries, which also comes with the challenges of providing two-hour, or at least same-day, turnarounds.

"Every order end-to-end takes about one hour of labor to pick, consolidate, stage, and prepare for delivery," Hornyak said. "That alone would be about $5 to $15 of direct costs per order, and that's not factoring in other labor costs such as added store replenishment, management overhead, increased supply chain costs, etcetera."

Grocers also face the obstacle of figuring out how to redesign their stores for more efficient order picking and packing. There needs to be space designated for online orders to be staged so that they're ready for customers to pick them up.

In some instances, grocers have been able to repurpose underperforming bricks locations to leverage their value as fulfillment centers. For example, when an H-E-B store location was not big enough to support a full-size perishables department, and local shoppers complained, H-E-B decided to turn the location into a satellite fulfillment warehouse for online orders (both for delivery and curbside pick-up) made in the Houston area, retail analyst Ryne Misso said.

Rather than remodeling the store to enlarge its capacity for perishables, H-E-B realized that in an era when omnichannel services are required to meet customer needs and expectations, turning the location into a satellite fulfillment warehouse was a more rewarding strategy than competing against bigger grocers in the area. H-E-B does have plans to build a new store near the fulfillment warehouse that will have the capacity for a full perishables department.

"One of the primary advantages enjoyed by regional and local grocery chains over Amazon is their network of store locations," Misso said. "They are now at a point where store locations may need to be re-imagined in order to maintain their advantage."

But converting "dark stores," locations with no physical customers, into manual fulfillment centers is not a perfect solution. Operating a dark store fulfillment center includes a combination of labor, real estate and other operational costs that make fulfillment too expensive to sustain in the long term.

This is why implementing automation in fulfillment and distribution centers has become so important for grocers. Bricks grocers who continue to pick orders manually will find it virtually impossible to maintain the status quo.

Some grocers are making significant investments into large, automated warehouses where merchandise is stored, and robotic systems pick and pack grocery orders. Currently, Amazon, Walmart, Target and even Kroger, the largest national supermarket in the U.S., use large, automated warehouses for order fulfillment. In fact, Kroger inked a deal with digital grocer Ocado to build automated customer fulfillment centers to facilitate home delivery of groceries. The first center in development, part of the "Restock Kroger" initiative, is a $55 million, 335,000-square-foot facility that uses robotic automation.

But large, automated warehouses are an expensive option for regional grocers, and they come with their own challenges. In most cases, large warehouses cannot support the two-hour delivery windows customers want from their grocers, or even same-day deliveries, because they are located too far away from shoppers.

Because of this, increasing numbers of bricks grocers are relying on third-party delivery services like Instacart and Shipt to perform fulfillment. This, too, has drawbacks. If a grocer outsources fulfillment to a third party, the bricks grocer loses control over customer relationships, data and delivery quality, according to Hornyak.

Despite the challenges associated with order fulfillment, bricks grocers cannot ignore consumers' interest in online grocery ordering.

That has been particularly true since March 2020, when demand for this service exploded.

## Painful Lessons

In a matter of weeks, COVID-19 brought online grocery shopping, curbside pickup and delivery activity to unheard-of levels. (Please see my COVID-19 chapter for more details). Almost overnight, grocers had to learn how to use their store aisles and backrooms to fill online orders. The process didn't always go smoothly.

"Depending on retail floors to fill orders is terrible for a pick-and-pack operation, where you have 50,000 SKUs spread across 40,000 or more square feet," Neil Stern a senior partner at retail strategy and consulting firm, McMillanDoolittle, said in 2020. "The store-centric model doesn't scale, and that's what we're learning from what's happening right now."

The surge in online shopping caused by the pandemic created a nightmare for regular grocery shoppers. Finding products became a struggle as a flood of workers, either in-store employees or third-party fulfillment service workers, grabbed up groceries to fill online orders. This caused many grocers to push back fulfillment times by days and even weeks—and even forced some services to temporarily close down.

## Micro-Fulfillment Centers: Win-Win for Grocers

The silver lining is that increasing numbers of bricks grocers discovered a new solution to effectively meet burgeoning demand for online orders: micro-fulfillment centers (MFCs). These are small facilities, usually 10,000 square feet or less, that usually feature automated technologies. Delivery orders can be fulfilled in MFCs, and retailers can also provide pick-ups there.

For grocers, micro-order fulfillment is a means of increasing profitability, collecting shopper information and taking ownership of the consumer shopping experience.

When bricks grocery customers order online, fulfillment must be completed quickly, which requires additional labor costs. If an employee is paid to fulfill online grocery orders, Hornyak explained, a grocer loses $10 or more on every order delivered. Large regional warehouses that utilize robots to pick and pack orders take years to complete and cost tens of millions of dollars. And, as I mentioned, these warehouses are usually too far away from customers to accommodate same-day delivery services.

MFCs cost much less than regional warehouses, take far less time to set up and offer considerably faster delivery. According to retail analyst Jason Goldberg, a typical MFC costs approximately $3 million, stocks 15,000 SKUs and can fulfill orders 10 times faster than a human employee.

One of the centers' strengths is the fact they place automated technologies, including robotic fulfillment, within bricks grocers' reach. And automation offers great advantages over manual pickers and packers when it comes to speed and efficiency. Human grocery pickers working inside a traditional grocery store are able to pick between 20 to 30 items per hour, but a robot-based system can pull together as many as 350 items in the same amount of time.

Compact enough to fit nearly anywhere, an MFC can have hyperlocal placement on the store level, meaning it is close enough to shoppers' homes to dramatically reduce the last-mile delivery cost, said Carol Abel, vice president of education program development at FMI (Food Marketing Institute).

The growth in online grocery sales has been forcing bricks grocers to take on tasks that grocery shoppers used to do for themselves, from gathering their merchandise to checking out. Analysts predict that MFCs will become the least expensive method for grocers to fulfill online grocery orders for delivery moving forward.

Not only that, but data compiled by Jeffries for Fabric shows that MFCs make online fulfillment profitable, generating an average of $18 per delivery order and $24 per curbside pickup order.

"Retailers can maintain the remainder of their stores for customers who still prefer in-person shopping," Jeffries said. "Both the micro-fulfillment centers and the brick-and-mortar stores would offer retailers greater profitability, positioning grocers to deliver winning customer experiences both online and offline."

Curt Avallone, Chief Business Officer of Takeoff Technologies, a builder of automated fulfillment centers, said the company's grocery business is already accelerating. As of 2020, the company was working with nine large grocery chains with six operational MFC units and another 20 under construction.

"Demand for online grocery is up 80% to over 100% at our facilities," Avallone said.

Grocers' order volume is also increasing. Where the average basket size used to be $150, that number is now pushing upwards of $200, according to Avallone.

## *Path of a Product*

MFCs help alter the path of a product for grocery retailers. Typically, a product moves from the warehouse to the grocery store's backroom and then to the store floor. But when customers order online, products must make a return trip from the store floor to the backroom where they are readied for delivery.

MFCs help simplify this process by changing product pathways: Products go directly from the micro-fulfillment center to the store's backroom and then to the consumer's door. In some instances, the trip to the backroom is not even required because, for many grocery retailers, the backroom *is* a micro-fulfillment center.

Many industry experts are predicting that MFCs and related automation are going to be directly incorporated into more and more local brick-and-mortar grocery retailers. IAM Robotics contends this trend only makes sense because:

- Grocery stores are already full of inventory that can be used for e-commerce.

- Goods-to-person fulfillment automation is more accessible than ever with low-cost picking robots that are more cost-effective and reliable than manual labor.

- Retailers can reduce last-mile delivery costs.

All of these factors are contributing to the rise of MFCs, as are emerging challenges facing grocery retailers.

According to IAM Robotics, those challenges include:

- Lack of space: Industrial and logistics real estate vacancies are at near-record lows.

- Shortage of labor: The labor crunch is trending worse every year as a result of the baby-boom generation aging out of the workforce just as the younger tech-centric generations, less interested in manual labor, enter the workforce.

- The need for speed: Retailers are under pressure to increase click-to-door speed to satisfy consumer desire for near-immediate delivery.

This brings us back to the value of MFCs for grocers. They are particularly important with respect to helping grocery retailers lower the cost and increase the efficiency of last-mile costs and delivery.

With profit margins slim in the grocery retail industry, last-mile logistics are a focus for grocers hoping to gain competitive advantage, and MFCs are a key factor in this battle.

"By building in dense urban settings where more than half the population lives, retailers can reduce the cost of last-mile delivery by simply shortening shop-to-door distance," IAM Robotics said. "Retailers who can lower last-mile related costs will be at a competitive advantage.

A number of key players in the micro-fulfillment business are working with grocery retailers to help them capitalize on these opportunities. The chart below, provided by *Grocery Drive*, displays major MFC companies with some of their retail clients, the number of weeks the company takes to build an MFC, the minimum square footage needed and the number of items that can be fulfilled in a certain amount of time. The chart illustrates MFCs' potential to empower bricks grocers to provide cost-effective fulfillment services.

## MFCs Empowering Grocery Retailers

| MFC COMPANY | EXAMPLE RETAIL PARTNERS | NO. OF U.S. GROCERS | NO. OF WEEKS TO BUILD | MIN. SQ. FOOTAGE TO BUILD | ITEMS FULFILLED & MINUTES |
|---|---|---|---|---|---|
| Alert Innovation | Walmart | 2 | 12 | 8,000 | 50 items, 6 mins. |
| Dematic | Meijer | 1 | 12 | 10,000 | 62 items, 5 mins. |
| Fabric | Undisclosed | 3 | 14-15 | 5,000 | 60 items, 10 mins. |
| Takeoff Technologies | Albertsons | 5 | 20 or less | 10,000 | 60 items, 5 mins. |

## *The Cost of Out-of-Stocks*

Offering online shopping and delivery is one thing. Actually delivering in a way that meets or exceeds customer expectations is another. One challenge relates to product availability. When customers shop in-store, they can tell immediately whether a product they want is available. That's not necessarily the case when they're making online orders.

"Finding out that a product a consumer wants from the supermarket is sold out only when a worker is in a store aisle fulfilling their order can be jarring," *Brick Meets Click* Partner David Bishop said. "All the technical stuff that goes on behind the scenes to sync online ordering systems with in-store inventories fall by the wayside to a customer. The customer just says, 'If it's not available, then tell me it's not available.'"

For instance, say a shopper orders groceries online in the morning before work and requests a 6 p.m. delivery time for when they get home. The order arrives, but a significant number of items are missing because they weren't in stock. This leaves the customer angry and wondering if the service is even worth using. This all-too-common scenario is cutting into grocers' bottom line. A *Harvard Business Review* study reports that grocery retailers lose nearly half of intended purchases, which equates to a 4% loss in total sales when consumers encounter stock-outs. Traditional bricks grocers are geared toward regional sales where customers come to the store with a written list of items to purchase. These grocers base their prices, promotions, replenishing and supply chain on this. Forecasting systems typically used by bricks grocers today are manually intensive and infrastructure-heavy and might offer category-level forecasting down to the store level.

Kerry Liu is the CEO of Rubikloud, which provides AI software for enterprise retailers. He said bricks grocers lacking store-level forecasting at the SKU level certainly need it now, but that will only take them "half the distance."

On top of this, Liu said, "grocers need to handle 200,000 plus SKUs and integrate with third-party delivery services to cover the last mile and fill the consumers' demand for time-saving shopping tactics."

## Supply Chain Strategies

Poor supply chain management has a detrimental impact on customer experience and margins. Liu suggests five strategies grocers can implement to improve in the areas of online shopping and delivery, while also making shopping across multiple channels (omnichannel) a more seamless experience:

- Recognize the opportunity and ensure that all levels of top management are aligned with the need for this level of business transformation because it's complex. That said, it's worth it. A well-developed and mature supply chain can bring real financial impact, including better margins and improved profitability.

- Develop a feedback loop between all the omnichannel delivery systems—including third-party delivery services—that captures all of the online and offline data. Trying to predict things like demand, replenishment, promotions, pricing and safety stock with only online historical data is like predicting the weather with data from inside a house.

- Implement an artificial intelligence (AI) solution that will link the supply chain gaps through predictive measurements. AI can predict shopping preferences and prices and also forecast changing foot traffic and the increasing quantities of people turning to online orders. This means last-mile delivery services can better source and retrieve ordered items and predict better substitutions. But it's critical to start slow. Test the solution in one specific category, see how it performs, and then roll it out more broadly once the results have been proven.

- Let go of legacy systems and allocate additional investment in cloud-based technologies that further bridge the gap between disparate systems, allowing for real-time inventory tracking and management. This investment alone will significantly improve inventory allocations, minimize stockouts and reduce food waste.

- Optimize change readiness and management processes so new technology can be implemented and adopted quickly and effectively.

Supply chain strategies also should include MFCs, which are designed to stock and pull the fastest-selling items in stores, leveraging stock to create more sales. The centers also reduce the number of personal shoppers on the sales floor, which provides more space for traditional customers.

### Strategic Stocking

Store design is another feature of bricks grocers that is changing due to increased online grocery ordering and the demand for same-day delivery and curbside pickup. A number of grocery chains, including Albertsons, already operate a type of MFC from their grocery aisles. Tom Custer, vice president of strategic design for FRCH Design Worldwide, said he expects to see even more retailers with insufficient back-to-house space to follow suit.

Many bricks grocers have spent years developing store design to enhance in-store shopping experience for customers, which is an important strategy for competing successfully with clicks retailers. However, Custer argued that today's new realities, increased online ordering and demand for delivery and pickup, offer a prime opportunity for brands to "rationalize their in-store inventory, stocking front-of-the-house with only the most popular lines while offering a broader catalog of products that can be ordered online or via kiosk for same-day delivery."

For example, does a bricks grocer really need to carry an entire aisle of pet food when they are already faced with competition from online pet food suppliers? Pet food is one of a number of items that could be subscription-based. Serving as fulfillment centers is a new role for bricks grocery stores that lends itself to modular retail design.

"As order volumes vary, the reallocation of front-of-house and back-of-house will be required to seamlessly flex, morphing so that stores can accommodate and support the journey of a package as much as it does the journey of the customer," said Melissa Gonzales, CEO of retail consulting firm The Lionesque Group.

## *Holistic Approach*

For grocery retailers to take full advantage of the new normal where online grocery ordering, same-day delivery and curbside pickup are concerned, they must take a holistic approach instead of relying on one strategy. Focusing on robotics, online grocery ordering, micro-fulfillment or curbside pickup individually is not the answer. Grocery retailers seeking to improve customer service, improve performance, cut costs and increase speed and sales should take a thorough look at their challenges and their resources. Retail analyst Brittain Ladd encourages grocers to ask the following questions:

1. What is the optimal supply chain and logistics strategy for meeting customer demand across our retail stores and online?

2. Should we manage our supply chain and logistics or outsource?

3. How do we leverage our supply chain to enable growth and achieve a strategic advantage?

4. What is the optimal solution for leveraging robotics and micro-fulfillment? How do we become profitable at online grocery? Are we maximizing the potential of every square foot of space in our stores?

5. What is the optimal last-mile delivery strategy? How do we increase order density?

6. What digital strategy will generate the highest levels of customer satisfaction and sales while providing a competitive advantage?

7. How do we design, manufacture and provide customers with exceptional private label products?

8. What is the optimal pricing strategy by category and product? How do we lead in quality?

9. How do we leverage data and analytics to create a better customer experience, optimize operations, increase velocity across the enterprise, increase revenue and achieve a competitive advantage?

10. What are our differentiating capabilities? How do we design and implement a capabilities-based strategy?

I would add that as grocers adopt e-commerce capabilities to meet shopper demand, they must consider the entire shopper journey to win the loyalty of repeat shoppers.

"When evaluating potential e-commerce platform providers, grocers must assess the complete ecosystem of partners and their capabilities, from digital advertising to picking and fulfillment, and the impact of those relationships," said Sylvia Perrier, president and CEO of Mercatus. "Grocers should look to partners who help them retain shoppers and increase revenue with each of these capabilities, rather than diluting their brand and bottom line at every customer touchpoint."

STRATEGY 9:

# Using Big Data as a Weapon in the Grocery Wars

I N 2017, THE WALL STREET JOURNAL TITLED A RETAIL GROCERY ARTICLE "The Future of Grocery Shopping is All about Data." Big Data, that is. Today, the McKinsey Global Institute estimates that the yearly value of Big Data (also known as advanced analytics) for the retail industry is $400 billion to $800 billion. Big Data has the potential to revolutionize the shopping experience across numerous domains by sending personalized messages to customers, analyzing customer sentiments, and encouraging in-store sales and food quality maintenance. Data helps grocery stores enhance customer loyalty and provides the ability to personalize marketing messages.

Expert360's Tim Bowen defines big data as "large or complex data sets." There are currently three primary types of data that the grocery industry relies upon. These are:

- Scan Data
- Panel Data
- Card Data

Scan data is electronic point of sale (EPOS) data. This is collected in-store when purchases are sold and scanned at checkout points. The data is primarily numeric and includes information such as the number of units purchased, sales price, time and date of purchase, method of payment, etc.

Panel data is data about the individual households making purchases and provides further insight into consumer demographics. Bowen explains,

> "Panel data adds more depth to the data as consumers join the panel and normally will take their shopping home and then scan their purchases. Panel data will then include other data such as the age of the consumer, number of people in the household, income levels etc. In Australia, this data is normally provided by agencies such as IRI and Nielsen."

The third type of big data is card data, which is data collected when shoppers scan their store loyalty or bonus card and/or their credit cards when buying items.

Grocery stores are also collecting data from social media sites and their own websites. For example, if consumers are researching popular topics such as "keto diet" or "fish taco recipes," grocery store managers can review their offerings to make sure they are keeping pace with the continually changing demands of customers.

All of these types of data are geared toward grocers gaining deeper insight and understanding into their customers so they are able to entice them with offers and items that match their needs and wants. Bowen asserts: "The ultimate objective of mining the different data sources is to increase consumer loyalty by personalizing offers." This helps grocers target customers in a more efficient and less costly manner. For example, stores know not to send fliers filled with salty snacks, candy, soda and other unhealthy items to a consumer who is known to be very health conscious in their purchasing habits.

Big Data now impacts all aspects of the food and beverage industry, from inventory optimization to transport and logistics management. Marketing manager Anirban Choudhury of Quantzig, a global analytics and advisory firm, argues that utilizing Big Data helps resolve some of the biggest challenges in the retail grocery business while also enhancing the bottom line:

> "Considering the competitive retail landscape, running a grocery chain can be challenging. There are numerous products to manage, many of which spoil quickly, often resulting in wastage of products. With the profit margin for grocery retailers typically ranging between 1% and 2%, careful planning and strong marketing are essential. There are many ways big data and the strategic use of food and beverage analytics solutions can facilitate this by contributing to the bottom line."

## *Maintaining Satisfaction*

Big Data Analytics helps grocers pinpoint insights from their business data, enabling them to analyze and integrate all of their data at the same time. This provides crucial insights for driving customer satisfaction and loyalty. Today's grocery retailers who strive to remain competitive are leveraging one of the most important weapons in their arsenal: Big Data.

The use of Big Data is one of the most important strategies for grocery retailers to gather information that keeps them ahead in the grocery wars, as stores compete not only against one another but also with online giants like Amazon. Leveraging Big Data makes it possible for grocery retailers of all forms and sizes to compete with the big guys. Writing for The Wall Street Journal, Bambi Majumdar explains:

> "The digital age has made it possible for all businesses, big or small, to compete on an equal footing. Media and marketing are no longer just the domain of those with deeper pockets. Stores have realized that the future of grocery shopping lies in reading and leveraging information about shoppers — what and how they buy products."

Augmented reality apps that permit shoppers to check out items while they shop is one example. This not only lets them view cost of items and compare options, but it also provides invaluable information for store managers. This includes what types of items are selling in each department, sales numbers, projections and even inventory data.

Large chains like Kroger have been implemented such technologies for mining data for years now, including using apps that mine consumer data on everything from customer eating habits to lifestyle preferences. This enables the chain to make suggestions to specific customers for what to purchase, where to find it in-store and even recipes to sample. Such apps and use of Big Data are also geared toward enhancing the customer shopping experience and driving loyalty and satisfaction. Majumdar discusses one application by Kroger aimed at achieving these types of goals: "Recent innovations include infrared sensors to track the number of customers in a store. It automates the checkout process and deploys clerks to the checkout stations when needed. This helps streamline resources and reduce customer wait times at once. Retailers hope that this would also make grocery shopping enjoyable for the new generation."

A host of other information is provided to store management by leveraging Big Data. This is why chains like Kroger and Walmart are investing millions in Big Data emerging technologies. This is because analyzing such data plays a significant part in managers being aware of the freshness of products, management of inventory, shelf presentation, logistics and other aspects of doing business.

Amazon is also helping drive such major investment in Big Data by other grocery retailers. Amazon spends more than 12 percent of its revenue on technology, research and innovation, compared to other food retailers that spend approximately three percent. Yet, according to Majumdar, leveraging Big Data Analytics makes it possible for such food retailers to stay competitive against Amazon and their online counterparts: "[Big Data] are making it possible for retailers to compete with Amazon. The latter has won customers over with its quick deliveries and competitive prices, and of course its robust data analytics. It has set the trend in using data successfully to target customers based on their buying and shopping habits."

One study conducted by Dinesh Gauri and his cohorts at the Sam M. Walton College of Business reveals that data-based promotions are 85 percent effective across grocery retail categories. The study gathered data from point-of-sales and millions of transactions across major retail grocery categories. Leveraging such data enables grocery retailers to forge a lean model for success that does not sacrifice the customer experience. The study also found that the impact of promotions on shoppers differs between segments like premium, economy and value. Big Data is critical in helping grocery retailers create promotions and marketing. Majumdar reports that the study found the following contributors most important for such a database:

- Store and category characteristics
- Geographical locations
- Demographics
- Logistics
- Inventory management
- Distance to competition

### *Inventory Analysis*

Grocery retailers who leverage analytics to turn Big Data into business insight will make the most informed decisions. Many areas of grocery retail, like inventory analysis and customer loyalty, are greatly enhanced and streamlined through the use of information culled from using Big Data. For example, Quantzig explains that Big Data Analytics offers more than just inventory levels of different items. It can also identify the most profitable items, which are not always the same as the higher cost or most popular items. This, in turn, enables managers to tailor marketing campaigns to the most profitable items, while also freeing them to stock fewer of the less profitable items.

Quantzig explains how Big Data Analytics is also invaluable with respect to cutting down on waste among perishable items: "Analytics determine how quickly promoted products leave the shelf and predict when they will need to be restocked, resulting in fewer empty shelves

*Using Big Data aims to forge long-term relationships with shoppers, based on keener insight and understanding into the individuals needs and demands of each. Simply relying on sales and promotions to drive traffic and sales will no longer be effective in building customer loyalty and relationships.*

and dissatisfied customers. This analysis can even be done while a sale is currently in progress: by analyzing the first several hours of sales, it is possible to get a stronger idea of how those items are moving, allowing you to more accurately predict necessary stock levels." Many grocery retailers end up with massive amounts of waste. Quantzig reported 1.3 billion tons of food from grocery stores is wasted every year. Using Big Data Analytics helps control inventory levels and increase consumer satisfaction by reducing overstock and limiting out-of-stock items.

## Consumer Loyalty and Direct Marketing

All grocery retailers are aware of the importance of enhancing shopper experience and driving customer loyalty for success against the competition.

The collection and use of Big Data are also instrumental in helping achieve these critical goals. Collecting data and using it in an effective manner leads to successful loyalty programs. Such data offers keen insight into shopper preferences and purchasing behavior. This, in turn, helps tailor more effective marketing and promotions to shoppers. Quantzig cautions that, to be most effective, such information should not be used in isolation, providing the following example:

If a customer buys a long-lasting product like peanut butter or bathroom cleaner, for example, sending them a promotion for that item next week will be useless (and frustrating to the consumer, who will wish they had this deal last week). Analytics makes it possible to determine how frequently a customer buys a particular product, and then offer them a deal for it around the time they will be wanting to purchase it again.

Loyalty program data is also useful for knowing when shoppers might be using the competition. For example, if a shopper purchases seafood weekly but abruptly stops purchasing seafood, this might mean the cost is too high or perhaps the quality is not good enough. This is a good opportunity to send such a shopper coupons for seafood or a text or email when seafood is on sale. Such information also informs management they need to examine prices and product quality to determine if change is necessary.

## Pricing

Inventory and marketing are only two aspects of retail grocery that greatly benefit from Big Data. Other aspects such as pricing help retail grocers remain competitive, acquire new customers and attract new business in an industry where such factors are critical due to low profit margins. Big Data helps grocers set prices that are appealing to customers while enabling them to stay competitive. AImazing reports: "Through examining real-time sales numbers and customer feedback, they are able to determine the right price that customers respond positively to, yet one which allows them to remain profitable. Questions retailers often ask themselves include: 'What is the right price point that will help maximize sales?' or 'What is the customer's optimal price,?' which are answered easily with data analytics." Such factors are especially important for grocery retailers due to very narrow profit margins. Big Data helps set optimal prices.

## *Kroger and Big Data*

Major bricks grocery retailers understand that leveraging Big Data is one of the most important weapons in keeping people coming into stores, especially with the enormous inroads being made online by Walmart and Amazon. Kroger, the biggest supermarket chain in the U.S., is one such grocery retailer. Kroger has spent billions over the past fifteen years luring away engineers from universities and other companies seeking talent with the same types of skills, such as data analytics, logistics and app-development.

Stuart Aiken, chief executive of Kroger's $84.51^0$ data-analytics division, maintains that "Data is the new battleground." The division is referred to as $84.51^0$ because that is the longitude of Kroger's headquarters in Cincinnati. The apps developed by the division's engineers are designed to impact all aspects of retail grocery, from apps that monitor the freshness of certain products and ones that alert managers to malfunctioning machinery to those that reduce shopper wait times and streamline the shopping process for customers. Retail analyst Heather Haddon writes: "Recent innovations developed in Kroger's labs include infrared sensors that monitor the number of customers in a store and automatically deploy checkout clerks as the number grows. This tool alone, Kroger says, has reduced wait times by several minutes across its stores."

Kroger has also developed apps that have sensors embedded on store shelves that enable the retailer to communicate on the mobile devices of specific customers, while wireless scanning is being used to streamline and revolutionize the shopping experience. Haddon says of these two developments: "The apps contain data about each customer's shopping habits, and the shelves, in response, display banner ads customized for them, for such products as gluten-free or nondairy products. Kroger also rolled out a wireless scanning device it calls Scan, Bag, Go at 400 stores. Customers will use the device to ring up groceries as they shop, then pay for their purchases through an app." Other grocery retailers are following Kroger's lead and leveraging Big Data to remain competitive against online grocery retailers, while also increasing customer loyalty and generating new business.

Increasing customer loyalty is a primary goal in using Big Data to make every shopper experience an exceptional shopping trip every time they visit a bricks grocer. This is especially important because of a reduction in the percentage of shoppers who purchase a majority of their items at a single grocery store. One survey that found only 47% of grocery shoppers shop for the majority of their food at one primary supermarket, down from 61% ten years ago. Mining shopper data is viewed as critical for maintaining market share for supermarkets. Large regional chains like Meijer Inc. and Raley's Supermarkets employ consultants to mine customer data. Knowing your customers is extremely important for keeping them loyal and generating new business. Kroger is ahead of many of its competitors in this area. Haddon explains:

Today Kroger uses 850 algorithms to personalize the coupons it mails to 12 million households. The company can use purchase data to determine whether someone has gone on a diet, had children or retired, and to market different products to those customers accordingly. Some Kroger coupons have a redemption rate of 65%, compared with a national average of about 5%, executives say.

Today's bricks grocers must see themselves more like technology firms to be competitive. Chris Hjelm, Kroger's chief information officer, maintains: "This is the obsession—the customer experience in our stores and how technology can be a part of that."

Kroger continues to be committed to Big Data analytics for the long-term. The company is ahead of many of its competitors in this commitment in the grocery industry. Muller outlines the different aspects of Kroger's long-term commitment to Big Data analytics, including its widely admired and sophisticated mailing program:

- Kroger management acknowledges Big Data as its secret weapon in the grocery wars

- Dunnhumby has 120 analysts working full time on Kroger business

- Teams sift through 300 terabytes of data from 40 billion purchases made from 4 billion shopping trips over two years by 42 million card-carrying customers

- Big Data analytics alone drives annual revenues in excess of $100 million

- Pilot stores leverage data to serve up real time coupons to consumers in different aisles in the stores

- Personalization of communications/promotions has been driving incremental sales and profitability for over a decade

- Kroger's mailing program is widely recognized in the industry as having the most sophisticated and influential retailer database in the U.S.

- 11 million households get regularly mailed coupons, and 97% of those are personalized

- Focus is on growing basket size rather than acquiring new customers

## Gaining a competitive advantage

Grocery retail by its very nature is a Big Data industry. This is true on the macro and micro levels. Muller defines Big Data in the grocery industry on both of these levels:

MACRO LEVEL
- Thousands of stores
- Hundreds of thousands of product SKUs to be sourced, shipped, sold
- Tens of millions of customers

- Billions of transactions
- 500 Petabytes of data stored as U.S. retailers alone

MICRO LEVEL (Each customer is a data generator)
- Dozens of transactions a year, online and offline
- Multiple communication channels: Web, Mobile, Email, Kiosk, Phone, Social, etc.
- Massive amounts of unstructured data generated by mobile and social in particular
- No way to capture, process, analyze these growing datasets in most organizations today

Grocery retailers that are able to analyze and leverage the insights from the above datasets into action plans will gain competitive advantage. This is true where intelligence, efficiency, speed, pricing, promotion, cost effectiveness, inventory management and logistics are concerned.

There are three types of analytical maturity, according to the McKinsey Global Institute: basic, advanced, and leading. Basic equates to an Excel culture where only reporting occurs. Advanced involved standard business intelligence, but it is separate from decision support systems. Leading is the highest level of analytical maturity, where data-driven decision making is embedded across all business processes. In contrast to analytical maturity, organizational maturity involves the breadth of use of analytical analysis. The McKinsey Global Institute provides key element s for both analytics-led and business- or organization-led analytics, shown below:

ANALYTICS-LED
- Build a small team of data scientists
- Assign a strong sponsor
- Identify and leverage quick wins to prove potential
- Systematize learning from data

## BUSINESS/ORGANIZATION-LED
- Roll out analytics products across the business
- Create new processes based on insights
- Embed organizational change
- Strong representation at board level (e.g., through a chief analytics officer)

The Institute maintains that realizing the full value of advanced analytics depends more on organizational maturity than analytical maturity. Going further, the Institute advises: "Retailers can achieve results only if organizational maturity is in place—which is still the exception in the industry rather than the rule." The Institute's analysis of both clicks and bricks grocery retail "winners" reveals five strategies that enabled them to excel, especially where organizational maturity is concerned:

1. Focus on strategic use cases instead of on data.

2. Agile, interdisciplinary product teams.

3. Investments in large-scale change management to ensure use-case adoption.

4. Development of fit-for-purpose analytics platforms to maintain and scale multiple use cases.

5. Buying existing solutions versus developing new ones in-house.

As with most aspects of change in the grocery industry, effectively leveraging Big Data Analytics requires change management and training to be most effective. Many Big Data use cases require managers or employees to alter their decision-making approach or adopt different ways of working. McKinsey advocates the following: "Deploying a use case often requires adjustments to processes, roles and responsibilities, and incentives as well as the acquisition of new capabilities. Merely giving employees access to a new tool and explaining it in a training session is not enough." For these reasons, it is strongly advised that analytic insights must be deeply embedded in existing workflows and processes. Success is also heavily dependent on significant investments in developing the necessary capabilities and understanding of those who will utilize analytics in decision making and developing actionable strategies based on them.

To be mst successful at leveraging Big Data to achieve their goals, bricks grocers require fast and efficient processing and analytic capability, along with enormous and elastic storage capability. There are challenges for grocers that can make turning effective analysis of Big Data into actionable strategies difficult. Muller reports four key challenges:

- Big Data is expensive and difficult to mine through traditional means
- Low knowledge and agility in the organization
- Avoiding extending the past to grow into the future
- Strategize what the future should look like, then fill in the pieces

Because of these challenges, it is important for bricks grocers to determine whether purchasing an existing analytics solution or developing one in-house is best for their needs. For many aspects of retail grocery, such as pricing, promotion and assortment, standardized software is available in the market. McKinsey Global Institute maintains many companies have ramped up their analytics capacity (analytical maturity) but struggled to produce analytics due to low levels of organizational maturity. The Institute argues "All grocers must master advanced analytics to remain relevant. For more analytically mature retailers, more experimental use cases, including localization of assortment or personalization of promotions, are the next frontier." To be most successful, grocers must invest in organizational capabilities aside from technical solutions. This will require considerable investment in change management that is driven from the top down.

## Keeping up with Online Grocers
With the dramatic increase in online grocery sales, Big Data plays a

valuable role in helping bricks grocery retailers compete against online retailers. AImazing argues:

> "With the rise of e-commerce, many more people are going online to purchase their groceries, effectively taking them away from brick-and-mortar grocery stores and supermarkets. With real-time data analytics, they will be able to be competitive with these e-commerce sites by making use of valuable transactional data generated in stores."

Using Big Data aims to forge long-term relationships with shoppers, based on keener insight and understanding into the individuals needs and demands of each. Simply relying on sales and promotions to drive traffic and sales will no longer be effective in building customer loyalty and relationships.

The overall goal of leveraging Big Data is not just to collect vast amounts of information. Rather, the data collected needs to be used to help grocers better understand and connect with customers so they are in a better position to fulfill their expectations and needs. Leveraging Big Data in this manner is one of the best tools to ensure grocers not only keep up with ever-changing consumer demands but also are able to compete with online grocers who used advanced analytics to understand consumer demands and target customers based on an understanding of their preferences and lifestyles. Bowen reports that nearly a decade ago McKinsey & Company released a report that foretold the significance of leveraging Big Data to keep up with consumers and the competition:

Forward-thinking retailers are leveraging the vast amounts of data they possess and building analytical muscle to enable targeted marketing, tailored assortments, and effective pricing and promotions. Gathering and analyzing data to understand the needs, preferences, and attitudes of growing consumer segments ... will be especially important, as will understanding individual consumers and customizing offers on a one-on-one basis.

Today, more Big Data is available than ever before. So are the tools for turning analysis into action plans based on the insights such data provides. Bricks grocers who are unable to take advantage of these tools will fail to build customer loyalty, as shoppers will switch to a competitor who does offer them products and prices that more specifically suit their needs. This, in turn, will lead to negative outcomes such as decreased sales, profits and market share.

STRATEGY 10:

# A Final Weapon in the Grocery Wars: Artificial Intelligence

THE SUPERMARKET INDUSTRY WAS SLOW TO ADOPT DIGITAL TECH- nologies. As an older industry, there were two many legacy systems in place and not many start-ups to push change. This has changed as some really innovative technologies—mainly Artificial Intelligence (AI) and Machine Learning (ML) tools—have been adopted in the grocery retail industry more recently due to the numerous challenges wrought by the COVID-19 Pandemic, from panic buying, delivery and curbside pickup, to supply chain disruptions and order fulfillment. Writing for Food Logistics, Pini Mandel argues that today, "AI is impacting everything in the grocery store, from pricing enhancements to product placements and online order fulfillment. For an industry that was slow to adopt digital anything, nearly every square meter in the supermarket is fair game for enhancements from AI."

Closely aligned with Big Data in the grocery wars is the increasing use of artificial intelligence (AI). Innovation analyst Nadejda Alkhaldi maintains: During the pandemic, 85% of U.S. grocery sales still occurred in physical stores. Contrary to popular assumptions, physical stores will not be replaced by their online alternatives. But they will rely on AI to tackle pandemic-induced challenges." AI is being used for a variety of aspects within the grocery retail industry. These include customer personalization, improved inventory management, theft reduction, streamlined checkout processes and enhanced customer safety. From robots that clean floors and perform warehouse duties, to innovations such as autonomous checkout, shoppers and employees are kept safer due to less human traffic and greater social distancing. The following data shows the top AI applications being used in retail by percentage.

| AI APPLICATION | PERCENTAGE |
| --- | --- |
| Customer Care | 48 |
| Quality Control | 47 |
| Inventory Management | 47 |
| Customer Personalization | 36 |
| Pricing | 29 |
| Fraud Detection | 24 |

(itrex, 2021)

The use of AI is also helping grocers tackle some of their biggest and most costly challenges, such as food waste. According to Quest, $43 billion worth of food annually in the U.S. grocery industry leaves store shelves to be put directly in the trash.

## Reducing Food Waste

There are several technologies that work together to enable grocers to reduce food waste. These include dynamic pricing, electronic shelf labels and computer vision. These technologies work in tandem to help grocers move products from their shelves before they reach their "sell by" date. In-built cameras alert management when shelves are low or empty for restocking, but they can also inform inventory systems when items are nearing the end of their shelf life. The inventory system is connected to the AI-based dynamic pricing engine. The dynamic pricing engine reports data on inventory, consumer behavior and pricing, such as the ideal sale price to make an item sell. Mandel explains: "The dynamic pricing engine assesses the situation, and typically recommends adjusting prices downward to drive sales of older products. Using ML tools, the system quickly learns the right balance between price and sales, while also considering the grocer's expenses." When prices are changed, electronic shelf labels (ESLs), connected to the dynamic pricing engine through Wi-Fi or other technology, provide shoppers with up-to-date prices. This not only helps sell the products before they are removed for waste, it also provides grocers with a chance to recoup some of their investment on inventory that would otherwise become a total loss. Mandel explains this combination of systems is known as next-gen pricing:

The beauty of using next-gen pricing to move near end-of-life products before they spoil is beneficial to both the grocery store and the consumer. Rather than simply throw out unsellable products for a total loss, grocers have the opportunity to recover some of the value in their inventory. The dynamic pricing engine uses AI tools to find the balance price point where consumers are willing to pay for products that need to be consumed within the next few days. This enables grocery stores to recover as much of their investment as possible, rather than just use a gut feeling to adjust prices. Consumers, meanwhile, have the opportunity to save money by purchasing products at a discount. Consumers who prefer fresher products always have the opportunity to buy longer-lasting products at a higher price, but those who are price sensitive can buy expiring products at a more affordable price.

### Store Maintainance

More and more grocery retailers are learning to gain competitive advantage by a combination of Big Data, AI and Machine Learning (ML). Author of Creatives on Call, Jim Lochner argues: "Artificial intelligence, machine learning, and data are transforming the grocery industry." The future is here in many grocery stores. This includes reliance on robots for a variety of tasks and areas from inventory to store maintenance. AI-driven robots help drive fulfillment in warehouses or fulfillment centers, while in-store bots do everything from clean floors to scan store shelves daily. Bots that scan store shelves also take high-definition images of items, then ML algorithms search the photos looking for out-of-stock products, misplaced items, improper labels and incorrect pricing. All of this enables grocers to improve efficiency and efficacy, while providing higher quality shopping experiences for customers.

AI-driven robots are also helping grocery stores combat the "ghost economy," according to Lochner, that costs grocers $1.7 trillion due to out-of-stocks, inaccurate price execution and lack of product location optimization. Use of AI-driven robots like Simbe Robotic's AI robot "Tally" is one weapon for combatting the ghost economy. Tally scans and tracks products and processes real-time shelf data related to inventory position, price accuracy and promotional execution. Lochner explains: "Tally roams store aisles up to three times a day and autonomously captures on-shelf data for 15,000–30,000 products an hour, freeing up as many as 100 hours per week for store teams to focus on customers. Where manual audits usually happen once a week with 65% accuracy, Tally audits 3 times a day with an average scan time of 2 hours and over 97% accuracy, resulting in a 20%–30% reduction of out-of-stock items in stores." Location data helps in-store employees and third-party fulfillment shoppers locate item and fulfill orders more rapidly. With more shoppers relying on online shopping and third-party fulfillment companies, such data is essential for great efficiency and lower costs. Tally also provides real-time reporting on in-store stock to online platforms of bricks grocers, which enables customers to know if the products they seek are available prior to visiting a bricks location. Changed consumer behaviors illustrates the growing need for real-time inventory information provided by AI.

The AI Trends staff maintains "AI is proving to be an unstoppable force in food retail, shaping the future of supermarkets and grocery stores." One of the biggest drivers of this development revolves around the COVID-19 pandemic. Many innovations implemented during the pandemic proved their value, as shoppers expanded in-store shipping with online shopping combining the two in novel ways. Milan Mahadevan, president of Kroger's data company, 84.51°, argues: "The pandemic that we've all experienced became a strategic imperative for every organization to leverage data, analytics, and artificial intelligence to make things better. Ultimately,

*There are several technologies that work together to enable grocers to reduce food waste. These include dynamic pricing, electronic shelf labels and computer vision. These technologies work in tandem to help grocers move products from their shelves before they reach their "sell by" date. In-built cameras alert management when shelves are low or empty for restocking, but they can also inform inventory systems when items are nearing the end of their shelf life. The inventory system is connected to the AI-based dynamic pricing engine.*

almost everything can be improved through leveraging data and artificial intelligence." The pandemic has been an unquestionable driving force for AI innovations and developments that are designed specifically for use in the grocery retail industry at all points in the supply chain.

Another area where AI is having a dramatic impact in grocery stores is fresh food. AI helps define what data the store workflows need to "drive algorithms to make good decisions," says Matt Schwartz, CEO of Agresh Technologies. Schwartz maintains "the benefits are immense," and include higher employee satisfaction from have more effective tools and increased profits from reduced shrinkage or loss of inventory. More in-stock food options for shoppers are another benefit. AI enables grocers to know what is working and what is not working. From this combination of information, grocers can learn how to eliminate or change what does not work and leverage what does to effect continuous improvement.

## *Accepting Substitutions*

AI greatly enhances customer satisfaction by increasing the acceptance of substitutions. The AI Trends staff reports that approximately 60% of U.S. consumers now purchase groceries online and will continue to do so. However, a sticking point with online ordering of groceries for delivery or curbside pickup is getting customers to accept substitutions when items they prefer are out-of-stock. Executive Vice President of Walmart Global Tech, Srini Venkatesan, explains: "The decision on how to substitute is complex and highly personal to each customer. If they wrong choice is made, it can negatively impact customer satisfaction and increase costs." Walmart relied on personal shoppers to make the decision on how best to substitute an item. But there are almost 100 different factors that can go into that decision, leaving plenty of room for error and unsatisfied customers. AI solutions now exist that greatly improve the methods and acceptance for substitutions. The AI Trends staff reveals: "The tech solution uses deep learning AI to consider hundreds of variables—size, type, brand, price, aggregate shopper data, individual customer preference, current inventory and more—in real time to determine the best next available item. It then preemptively asks the customer to approve the substituted item or not, a signal fed back into the learning algorithms to improve the accuracy of future recommendations."

AI Trends reports that since the AI app has been implemented, shopper acceptance of substitutions has increased to over 95% for Walmart. Yet the AI app that Walmart developed does more than increase customer acceptance and satisfaction with substitutions. It helps lower costs by saving time for personal shoppers. The AI app used for substitutions is able to make substitution suggestions to personal shoppers or order fulfillment employees in real time. Venkatesan explains: "The solution is also designed to make our associates' jobs easier. Instead of having to guess, the personal shopper can be told precisely what the customer may prefer," he said. "If our personal shoppers are preparing orders and come across an item that is not available, our system suggests the alternative product. Our tech even shows our personal shopper where the item is located in the store, simplifying the decision-making process for our team and enabling them to prepare orders quickly and efficiently."

The goal for every grocer is to never have out-of-stocks and to never have to offer substitutions. This goal is difficult to achieve in reality, so when an item is out-of-stock such AI apps as the one developed by Walmart help increase the chances that shoppers will get the next best alternative.

## Partnering technologies

A number of grocers are partnering with tech giants to help integrate grocery and technology. One such company is Albertsons. Albertsons formed a partnership with Google to "merge the grocer's broad reach and retail know-how with the tech company's capacity for customer-centric disruptive innovation," according to DateCheckPro. Among planned innovations are shoppable maps with dynamic hyperlocal features, artificial intelligence-powered conversational commerce and predictive grocery list building via Google Cloud, reports DateCheckPro. Cleaning and sanitation practices are benefiting from the application of AI-powered robotics. Giant and other grocers employ AI software to power robotic floor scrubbers. The company named their tall, slow-moving, gray robot with oversized eyes "Marty." "Marty" is not just a floor scrubber, however. He is an "autonomous robot that uses image capturing technology to report spills, debris and other potential hazards to store employees to improve your shopping experience," reports retail analyst Peter Holley. Holley reports that Marty is now roaming through all of the supermarket chain's 172 stores across Pennsylvania, Maryland, Virginia and West Virginia. The company even manufactured and started selling stuffed versions of the robot in their stores. Marty has also been rolled out by giant's parent company, Ahold Delhaize USA, to its Martin's and Stop & Shop locations as well.

Marty wears a sign that reads: "This store is monitored by Marty for your safety." The robot moves around the store scanning for any unsafe events, from spilled items to trip hazards. Once a threat is detected, Marty begins to beep and reports the hazard verbally to workers after paging them. The robot also alerts customers in the vicinity, "Caution. Hazard detected." Marty does much more than check for safety issues. The robot is also able to perform price checks and detect any discrepancies between the shelf and store's scanning system, says Patrick Maturo, manager of store optimization at Ahold USA. Marty consists of scanners to avoid collisions with customers or displays and is equipped with a number of cameras. Some customers ignore Marty, but many, especially children shopping with parents, are excited by the robot's presence and even take video or selfies with it, according to Maturo. Marty provides additional time for associates who can use that time to better serve customers. Walmart has also rolled out autonomous robots in its stores. DateCheckPro reports that grocers are "bolstering the use of robotic cleaning mechanisms to keep employees safer, increase social distancing and reduce the number of staff that have to physically come to work." Walmart relies on its robotic force to scrub floors, finding that automated cleaning enables the company to more consistently meet ever-more-stringent compliance standards on top of additional benefits.

AI-robots are also being tested for other uses within grocery stores. Other than inventory and warehousing tasks as previously mentioned, some grocers are testing robots in the area of food preparation. During the COVID-19 Pandemic, DateCheckPro reports that Heine's rolled out "Sally," a salad-making robot to see if AI-powered technology could replace concepts like the self-serve salad bar, because of questionable sanitary concerns. Walmart tested kiosks known as "Blendid" in its stores, an AI-powered station that can receive mobile orders from an app and select and blend ingredients for a smoothie in approximately three minutes, reports DateCheckPro. DateCheckPro reports that "these types of technologies will continue to flourish in a market calling for higher levels of innovation and reduced levels of unnecessary contact."

### *Enhancing the Consumer Experience*

The use of AI technology is also being used in stores to enhance shoppers' experiences during all phases of the trip to the supermarket, from automated check out to smart carts and chef bots. Lind Gao is the CEO of Caper, a technology firm that devised the "Caper Cart," the "world's first AI-powered shopping cart, reports grocery analyst Ashlie D. Stevens. Resembling an ordinary shopping cart, the Cape Cart has the ability to weigh, measure and price items as the shopper places them in the cart. There is a screen attached to the Caper Cart that informs customers of recommendations based on what they have in their basket and alerts them to nearby deals. For example, if a customer puts pizza sauce, mozzarella cheese and pepperoni in the cart, the screen will recommend they travel to the store location that offers pizza dough. The Caper Cart features four high-powered cameras on each of its corners and is equipped with a weighing pad at the bottom of the cart's basket. Customers can also pay for their purchases via the on-camera computer on the Caper Cart. Caper's CEO maintains there are two significant benefits for using the AI-powered Caper Cart: "Number one, you get to bypass the lines and it's just more convenient. Number two, Caper interfaces with customers in-store, giving them tailored recommendations to make their shopping journey a lot smarter. An additional benefit for supermarket owners and management is that the Caper Cart has the ability to extract data from the cart in ways that enable stores to optimize their inventory."

Many of the innovations wrought with AI technologies over the past two years have been driven by consumer changes stemming from the COVID-19 Pandemic. Stevens explains: "The intersection between grocery shopping and artificial intelligence technology is also picking up outside the supermarket aisles, especially as the pandemic inspired home cooks to look for alternatives to in-person shopping." Kroger has leveraged this trend with the development of its Chef Bot in late 2020, an AI-powered Twitter recipe tool that "helps user's pair the groceries in their fridge and reduce food waste by providing mealtime inspiration and personalized recommendations," reports Stevens. People who use Chef Bot merely take a photo of three ingredients that are already in their refrigerator or pantry. They then tweet the photo to @KrogerChefbot. Driven by AI, Chef Bot identifies the three ingredients, before sending the user a list of personalized recommendations for what to cook with them.  Increased shopper personalization is a prized goal of using AI applications in supermarkets.  Stevens reports that Menno Kluin, chief creative officer of 360i, states: "Chef Bot illustrates how marketers can tap into augmented     intelligence to deliver true service and value.  Innovation often happens during times of seismic change.  By leveraging visual AI in a bold new way, Kroger is bringing their promise of 'Fresh for Everyone' to life while addressing pain points and helping shoppers maximize their purchases."

Ongoing innovation in AI will continue to witness an even wider array of applications that grocers can rely on to build customer loyalty and enhance the shopping experience.

## Loss Prevention

The cost of shoplifting is significant for any retailer.  With profit margins so low in the grocery industry, shoplifting losses can be especially painful.  From shoplifting to "sweethearting," supermarkets are vulnerable to losses from theft.  AI Analyst at Emerj Ayn de Jesus explains that sweethearting is "the cashier's act of fake scanning a product at the checkout in collusion with a customer who could be a friend, family member, fellow employee or someone they can call by the endearment."  AI-driven products currently exist to help supermarkets deal with theft prevention.  De Jesus reports that Massachusetts-based StopLift offers a machine vision system that is designed to reduced or eliminate theft and other losses.  StopLift developed an AI-powered vision system known as ScanItAll.  Installed at the checkout line the system detects checkout errors (from items being left under the basket in a grocery cart) to cashiers who engage in sweethearting.  De Jesus describes the AI-powered system: "ScanItAll's computer vision technology works with the grocery store's existing ceiling-installed video cameras and point-of-sale (POS) systems.  Through the camera, the software 'watches' the cashier scan all products at the checkout counter.  Any product that is not scanned at the POS is recognized by the software and considered a loss."  ScanItAll is able to detect a number of behaviors that lead to losses, such as covering bar codes, stacking items on top of one another, and skipping the scanner and putting items directly in bags.  Piggly Wiggly reports its monthly losses from checkout shrinkage, inattentive cashiers or sweethearting dropped from $6,000-$10,000 a month to $1,000 after implementing ScanItAll. U.S. grocer Big Y has also deployed ScanItAll in 35 of its 56 stores to help reduce losses.

## Marketing and Promotions

Marketing and promotions continue to become more personalized and enhanced due to AI-powered applications being specifically designed form grocers.  Daisy Intelligence, an Ontario, Canada-based firm has created AI-powered applications specifically for use by grocers.  The application operates by searching through a minimum of two years' worth of a grocer's data from operations related to point of sale and promotional history.  De Jesus explains the data is processed by "taking into consideration such factors as the relationships between products, cannibalization effects, promotional patterns, forward buying effects, seasonality and competition, and provides weekly promotional recommendations for a variety of marketing channels such as flyers, e-commerce, direct marketing, or mobile app promotions."  The Daisy Intelligence Website explains that the AI-powered application uses this data to determine the following:

- The combination of products to promote weekly in each channel
- The cadence or pattern for promoting specific items
- Product combinations that will bring best results to the bottom line
- The effect a certain promotion has on the bottom line
- The assortment of products per store or region, based on local market conditions

Using this information, the decision then falls to management to determine which promotion to implement.  Results of that particular promotion are then stored in the application, which is used to reference recommendations for future promotions based on machine learning.

De Jesus reports that Daisy claims the application helps improve a grocer's promotional effectiveness, logistics, stock-outs, transaction size, revenue and margin. The company also maintains the application is able to choose the amount of inventory that is required to support product assortment planning, promotion without overstocking and the ability for each store location to meet local demand. Harps Food Stores, Inc., based in Springdale, Arkansas, deployed Daisy Intelligence's application to optimize pricing and promotions decision throughout it 87-store grocery chain. Harps Food Stores' Vice President of Marketing explains: "Daisy's ability to provide us with the associated sales on every item within the individual transactions helps us to promote the items most pertinent to our customers." In this way, the application of such AI-powered apps represents significant benefits for both grocers and customers.

Despite the widely accepted fact that bricks grocers must employ AI to compete successfully in both the online and offline supermarket industry, there are a lot of barriers for grocers to overcome in doing so. The top ten barriers to successful implementation of AI by percentage are listed below:

| AI BARRIER | PERCENTAGE |
| --- | --- |
| Cost of Solution | 35 |
| Lack of Skilled Personnel | 33 |
| Trustworthiness of Data | 28 |
| Unclear Business Cases | 26 |
| Support From Lines of Business | 25 |
| Operationalization of AI Development Tools | 23 |
| Difficulty Selecting Right Algorithms | 22 |
| Lack of Quality Training Data | 22 |
| Lack of Explainability | 21 |
| Unclear Decision Criteria | 21 |

(itrex, 2021)

Itrex advocates that grocers follow these five steps in successfully using AI in their stores:

1. Define your vision for the role you expect this technology to play in

your organization and the returns on investment (Deloitte recommends: Start small, scale fast, and build iteratively).

2.  Find the right talent to fill different expert roles.

3.  Adapt the organization's culture to develop the right attitude towards AI.

4.  Clean up your data.

5.  Gain an ecosystem advantage (Alkhaldi).


### *Talent is Crutial*

Finding the right talent takes more than throwing a pool of data at data scientists and expecting new strategies. Talent should be able to derive, transform and sustain value in the long run. Where culture is concerned, many managers and other employees fear AI. Instead, hese individuals must be taught to view AI as supporting human beings in making better decisions. In direct relation to the previous section, Big Data, AI is able to use larg amounts of data that is being pulled from video, social media, geo-location apps and devices. Big Data is also growing in complexity. Brian Kilcourse, Managing Partner at Retail Systems Research, argues the significance of clean data in the successful adoption of AI: "The top challenge is dirty data (it's the elephant in the room). Models are only as good as the data that creates them. One recent study estimated that over 80% of the effort of implementing AI relates to data cleansing." Teaming up with a predictive analytics company is one example of how to gain an ecosystem advantage.

Implementing AI in retail grocery is not a one-time event. It is a lengthy process that demands changes to a grocer's internal processes and culture. Sanjeev Sularia, CEO of Intelligence Node explains: "Retail organizations often get deterred by the costs of building the infrastructure and data processing capabilities needed for AI adoption. However, flexible businesses have successfully integrated AI across all business functions and upskilled their people to efficiently reorient to a data-driven mindset without trying to build everything from scratch."

It is clear that ongoing advances in automation and AI will continue to impact all aspects of the grocery supply chain. DateCheckPro argues: "Mobilizing the power of AI, automated machines, and data has become a must as customers shift between in-store shopping to e-commerce and expect stores to maintain a personalized and frictionless experience." Bricks grocers who hope to retain competitive advantage will need to determine how best to employ AI technologies to improve the grocery experience from warehouse to in-store to shoppers.

# ANOTHER SILENT KILLER EMERGES: **COVID-19**

W HEN THE COVID-19 PANDEMIC BECAME A REALITY IN 2020, NO
one could have predicted how far-reaching its impact would be.
In addition to COVID-19's tragic human toll, the outbreak has touched
nearly every facet of life — including consumer behavior. As a result,
retailers have been scrambling to accommodate consumers' new priorities,
beginning with the ability to shop safely. This certainly has been true
in the grocery industry: Since the spread of the global pandemic in the
U.S., online grocery sales, delivery and curbside pickup have experienced
enormous growth among consumers, intent on limiting their risk of
catching and spreading COVID-19.

## *A Tsunami of Online Grocery Shopping*
Before the COVID-19 outbreak, the online share of grocery sales in
the U.S. was 5% and projected to reach close to 6% by the end of 2020,
according to business consultancy Fabric Ltd. Within months of the
COVID-19 virus impacting Americans, online grocery sales penetration was "on track to approach and even exceed 10%" by the end
of 2020, according to Fabric's report, "The Impact of COVID-19 on
Online Grocery."

Barely a month after news of the virus being present in the U.S.,
numbers for online grocery shopping and delivery apps, online grocery

orders and online grocery site visitors skyrocketed. App intelligence provider, *Apptopia*, comparing daily downloads in February to mid-March 2020, found that Instacart, Walmart Grocery and Shipt saw increases of 218%, 160% and 124%, respectively. During the same time, Instacart grocery orders were 10 times higher than average and as high as 20 times in states heavily hit by the virus, including New York and California. *Fabric* also reported that during the first 20 days of March, average daily traffic on Walmart's online grocery site reached 1.1 million, a 55% increase in the average number of daily visitors over the previous two months, according to *SimilarWeb*.

The pandemic and the fear the pandemic generated also prompted a huge increase in first-time online grocery buyers. A 2020 *Fabric* survey revealed that 52% of responding consumers were purchasing groceries online due to the virus, and 20% of them were new to online grocery shopping. *Fabric* found this increase was evenly distributed across all age groups, revealing that online grocery shopping is not just something Millennials, big-city shoppers and early adopters were doing.

"COVID-19 is a force majeure that's propelling a new cohort of consumers towards online grocery shopping much faster than would have happened otherwise," *Fabric* said at the time.

The *Fabric* survey suggested an even bigger wave of online grocery shopping would occur. Approximately 70% of the responding consumers said they were more likely to purchase groceries online, due to the virus, while 51% of shoppers who never ordered groceries online said they were planning to start because of the virus.

## *Bricks' New Reality*

The staggering growth of online grocery purchasing does not mean the end for bricks grocers. Nevertheless, the pandemic has wrought a new reality for them.

"We expect COVID-19 to usher in a new era of 'Grocery 2.0' where retailers will be expected to offer a truly omnichannel experience for consumers that consists of experiential in-store grocery shopping in addition to a robust e-commerce presence," *Fabric* wrote in 2020.

I agree: The huge increase in online grocery orders, delivery and curbside pickup puts even more pressure on bricks grocers to be able to offer rapid fulfillment. Online grocery orders will be fulfilled through a combination of micro-fulfillment centers, providers like Instacart, retailer direct delivery like Walmart provides, and curbside pickup. The experience during COVID-19 might be a pivotal point for online commerce when it comes to the grocery retail sector. Now that millions more Americans are ordering groceries online for delivery or pickup, once the pandemic is over, people may continue to order their groceries in this way. This could be a serious blow to some bricks grocers who are not able to compete well online or when it comes to rapid fulfillment. To excel, bricks grocers must become local distribution centers for clicks customers who want to pick up their orders and serve as bases for home delivery. Bricks grocers need to innovate and even partner with technology companies to accelerate innovation.

Some grocers have already started adapting to the staggering increase in demand for online ordering, delivery and pickup of groceries. In fact, I observed some significant responses as soon as March 2020. Around that time, H-E-B began waiving its fees for next-day grocery pickup and pharmacy delivery and initiated a dedicated grocery delivery service, powered by Favor, for customers aged 60 and older all across Texas. Kroger converted a Cincinnati store into a "dark store" to focus solely on fulfilling pick-up-only orders. Walmart announced it would hire an additional 150,000 associates in the same month, while Amazon announced it was hiring 100,000 warehouse and delivery workers to help meet the enormous demand created because of the virus. *Grocery Dive* reported that also in March, Hy-Vee switched to fulfilling all grocery deliveries by third-party providers such as Shipt and DoorDash, so in-store employees could work solely on fulfilling pick-up orders. Grocers took unprecedented steps to meet demand in the wake of the virus, and they will likely continue to offer new services moving forward.

The impact of COVID-19 extends to other areas of grocery retail as well, from the opportunity to win private label-brand customers to reducing consumers' fears of catching the virus from grocery shopping.

*H-E-B initiated a dedicated grocery delivery service, powered by Favor, for customers aged 60 and older all across Texas.*

## Private Labels in the COVID Era

The COVID-19 pandemic has resulted in private label brand opportunities for grocery retailers. Retail analyst Gina Acosta reports that private brands have won over more than 75 million new fans during the pandemic. This is in addition to significant growth in private label food sales. Chicago-based Information Resources Inc. estimates that private label sales of food and beverages would grow between $10 billion and $12 billion to $95 billion in 2020, fueled by pandemic-related demand. I have already discussed the importance of private label brands as a means for bricks grocers to differentiate themselves from competitors and win customer loyalty. Wes Bean, SVP of Catalina's U.S. retail network, also maintains one-off campaigns will not be enough for grocers to successfully leverage the power of their private label brands.

"The pandemic has created a decade's worth of trial in a few weeks," Bean said. "As the predicted recession sets in, private brands need to start behaving like national brands, leaning into marketing across channels to promote the value of these products and the innovative portfolios they've developed."

During the pandemic, private label brands have shown to be very popular among specific kinds of shoppers, including families with young children, bakers and breakfast makers and natural and organic shoppers. Data from Catalina reveals that many shoppers were attracted to private label brands for the first time during the COVID-19 crisis. Because of this, new grocers should employ new marketing strategies to win these shoppers' loyalty.

"New shopping habits and tighter wallets require closer integration with an investment in marketing communication to drive loyalty with these new private-brand shoppers," Beans said.

Based on information in its Buyer Intelligence Database, Catalina recommends five ways proactive strategies to win the loyalty of new private label brand shoppers:

1. Think strategically about how marketing can improve your business across the store, not just with one-off campaigns for this month's new product.

2. Start building effective one-to-one personalized conversations along the shopping journey. Don't rely solely on promotions and unnecessary discounts when data analytics can identify those willing to pay full price for the value that private brands represent.

3. Remind new buyers of relevant private-brand products throughout a given portfolio. Now price, variety, cost and differentiation can better stand up to buyer demand with value that addresses their unique needs. All of that hard work has already been done.

4. Set specific growth goals for each private brand that goes beyond just sales and sales share. Consider metrics like sales per trip and trips per household. Align marketing efforts to these specific goals.

5.  Seek the why behind the buy: What are the underlying household preferences and behaviors driving potential buyers' interest and repeat participation with attributes of a specific private brand?

The final point about underlying household preferences and behaviors is especially important for bricks grocers.

"As the crisis continues, customers now have more time to form new attitudes and behaviors, which are important guides that point the direction toward the 'normal/reality,'" retail analyst Bill Bishop said. "They also signal what retailers should be thinking about to keep up with their customers."

## Evolving Shopper Needs

Retail Feedback Group's (RFG) "2020 U.S. Online and Instore Grocery Shopping Study, Food Shopping During The COVID-19 Pandemic," illustrates four growing areas of shopper needs.

These are:

1.  Reduce the fear of getting COVID-19 from shopping at the store.
2.  Make it quicker and more pleasant to do regular grocery shopping.
3.  Ensure essential product will be on the shelf.
4.  Offer "greater value for money."

The RFG report also provides potential responses to each of these emerging areas of shopper needs. The study found that 67% of shoppers were somewhat or not at all confident that it was safe to shop in a supermarket. RFG maintains it is unrealistic to create a zero-risk store, but customers in the study reported they were appreciative when grocers maintain social distancing and provide/require masks for workers and shoppers. Shoppers in the report said the safety measures they considered most important were providing disinfecting wipes with carts and encouraging employees to stay home if they feel unwell.

The RFG report also showed declining satisfaction with shopping in supermarkets during the pandemic. RFG recommends a couple of strategies for grocers to make it quicker and more pleasant to do regular grocery shopping. These include encouraging shoppers to shop online and in-store and making it easier to find products while in-store with navigation tools. The former helps build shopper loyalty and cultivates dual shoppers who spend more than those who shop only online or only in-store. The navigation tools can be achieved through app enhancements.

One strategy recommended by RFG to improve shelf availability of popular products is to develop store-specific planograms that reflect customer spending patterns in shelf inventory. A shelf reset helps ensure the products customers want the most are more likely to be available in-store.

Offering "great value for money" can be done by explaining to customers the heightened value they are getting during the pandemic in ways they are willing to pay for.

"There is a marketing opportunity to be built around describing how hard the store and its employees are working to offset the risk of COVID-19, and how the friction caused by safety measures is impacting prices because it is not time to take shortcuts. That's something some customer is willing to pay for."

## Fluid Situation

It seems as I near the finish of this book that changes in consumer needs and the grocery retail industry change nearly daily as a result of the pandemic. *Brick Meets Click* reported in August 2020 that the online grocery market is rebalancing after the spike due to COVID. U.S. grocery delivery and pickup sales for August 2020 totaled $5.7 billion, down from June's peak. Even so, other performance indicators revealed strength in a market that still was five times bigger than it was a year ago, at a total of $1.2 billion. *Brick Meets Click* in August described a "large base of committed shoppers, which shows signs that the online grocery pickup and delivery market is substantial and can be expected to strengthen."

In March 2021, however, *Brics Meets Click* reported that online sales in February had dropped 14% from January, according to a joint survey it conducted with grocery e-commerce platform Mercatus. What's more, while more than 40% of the first-time delivery service users who responded to the survey reported they were likely to use the same service again, less than 30% of first-time pickup service users said the same. This trend suggests that bricks grocers have more work to do to keep pickup customers satisfied.

"For many regional grocery chains, the online shopping battleground has shifted from delivery to curbside," Mercatus President and CEO Sylvain Perrier said. "Lower repeat intent rates for first-time pickup customers puts the spotlight squarely on customer service. Implementing a frictionless curbside fulfillment experience that wins the customer the first time, every time, will help grocers defend against mass merchants' low-price advantage. Enhanced pickup services combined with retailer branded marketing strategies to win back lapsed and lost customers can help increase monthly order frequency, and contribute to a healthy contribution margin from online shopping."

While the impact of COVID-19 is still changing, grocery retailers still need to respond to changes in consumer attitudes, behaviors, and needs to remain successful and gain a competitive advantage.

# AMAZON THE GOLIATH AND
# REINVENTING GROCERY SHOPPING

A MAZON IS THE GOLIATH OF THE CLICKS UNIVERSE. IF THE BRICKS grocery industry is facing a threat in the form of clicks grocery retailers, then Amazon is the most powerful behemoth of the lot. It is also the most effective. While discussed throughout this book, Amazon is such a driving force of online grocery sales it merits its own chapter. In fact, as I've been writing, Amazon opened its new brand of bricks, full-scale grocery stores: Amazon Fresh. Company founder Jeff Bezos has built Amazon to last in an evolving economy. More than any other online company, Amazon is not content with only being an online presence, especially where groceries and other essential items are concerned. In addition to selling grocery items on its own website, Amazon has been competing directly with bricks grocery retailers since acquiring Whole Foods in 2017 and launching Amazon Go grocery stores in 2018. Amazon Go's technology has revolutionized the grocery shopping experience: Customers enter the store with a swipe of their app, pick up whatever they want from the shelves, then walk out the door. Sophisticated cameras monitor what shoppers gather and automatically charges the totals to their already existing Amazon accounts.

Now Amazon is taking its bricks grocery competition up a notch: In August 2020, Amazon opened its first full-scale Amazon Fresh

*No longer content with only being an online presence, Amazon opened its new brand of bricks, full-scale grocery stores: Amazon Fresh.*

supermarket in Woodland Hills, California. Amazon Fresh offers a broad selection of grocery products, including 365 by Whole Foods Market organics, national brands like Coca-Cola and Kraft Mac and Cheese, local brands and regional favorites, along with newly created Amazon brands like Fresh (meats, seafood, and bakery items) and Cursive (wines).

And like Amazon Go, Amazon Fresh features new technologies that enhance customers' overall shopping experience and convenience. For example, Amazon Echo Show devices and an Alexa kiosk are available for customer support. Dash Carts, also known as Smart Carts, feature built-in screens and automatically scan the items shoppers put in their cart. Shoppers sign into the Dash Cart with a QR code on the Amazon app. The cart uses a combination of computer vision algorithms and sensor fusion to identify merchandise in the cart. The cart's technology also removes items from the customer's Alexa-enabled shopping list as items are placed in the cart. And, the Dash Carts help customers quickly locate items in the store.

"While there are many features of Amazon Fresh that customers like, it comes as no surprise that Dash Cart is near the top of many of the lists," retail analyst Bill Bishop said. "This provides clear direction for retailers who want to reduce friction and encourage more frequent visits to their stores."

As with Amazon Go, Amazon Fresh checkout is seamless and automatic. The Dash Cart makes bypassing the checkout line possible, though for now, the stores are also making traditional cashier lanes available. Traditional bricks grocery retailers should pay attention to the way technology is impacting Amazon Fresh customers' in-store shopping experience.

"With this new store, we've taken our decades of operations experience at Amazon to deliver consistently low prices for everyone and free same-day grocery delivery for Prime members," Amazon Fresh Vice President Jeff Helbling said.

Amazon is growing its new bricks chain quickly: The first Amazon Fresh has been followed by additional locations in California, along with Illinois, Virginia and Washington. A number of locations that have opened as Amazon Fresh stores previously were used as dark stores by Amazon for online order fulfillment. This model makes Amazon even more competitive with traditional bricks grocers, according to Bishop.

The "low capital cost investment of redeveloping existing stores creates a low cost of occupancy that translates into a low break-even sales volume, especially with Amazon Fresh stores being somewhat smaller (30,000-35,000 square feet) than major national bricks grocers," Bishop said. "As competition increases (as it inevitably will) and margins are pushed down, many competitive stores will no longer be economically viable and eventually need to close."

As I mentioned earlier, grocery retailers who fail to see the writing on the wall and take swift action to compete against Amazon, and its bricks operations, will more than likely struggle to remain competitive.

### Reinventing Grocery Shopping

I would say that the new Amazon Fresh stores represent far more than another grocery competitor. In fact, retail analyst Chris Walton said

Amazon Fresh offers consumers four things that will change grocery shopping forever. First of all, the stores also serve as Amazon package pick-up locations. Fulfillment is currently done manually at the Woodland Hills location, but Amazon has plans to implement an onsite Dematic-automated micro-fulfillment center on-site to fill online orders. This will result in even lower labor costs — and even greater savings that Amazon Fresh can pass on to customers.

Even though many bricks grocers offer their own online ordering, delivery, and curbside pickup, fulfillment is a challenge. Rather, it stems from a lack of fulfillment space or the high cost of traditional labor fulfillment, which forces many grocers to scramble to keep up with increasing consumer demand for same-day delivery and pickup. Amazon's business model, relying on automation for a large percentage of fulfillment, has already helped the online giant bypass these challenges. Analysts consider robotics bricks grocers' best method of succeeding at fulfillment, but Amazon is ahead of the game.

Amazon Fresh stores also serve as a site for Amazon.com order pickup and free "package-less" returns products returns. "Customers don't need a box or shipping label to return an item," Helbling explained. "They just bring the item to the counter, and we'll package it up and ship it back for free."

These services permit Amazon Fresh to serve as a hub for other Amazon customer activities outside of grocery purchases. "Returns and package pickup of wares have nothing to do with grocery stores," Walton said. "Kroger and Safeway cannot do that with their stores. Customers cannot take online electronics back to a Kroger or online apparel back to a Safeway."

Walmart and Target do offer similar services, or have the potential to, but their assortment of offerings is a trifle compared to Amazon's. The bottom line is that if a consumer who needs to pick up or return an Amazon.com item has grocery shopping to do, chances are they will elect to do their grocery shopping at Amazon Fresh where they can do both tasks at the same location. The only means of competing with this for traditional grocers is to let Amazon inside their operations, like Kohls has done, or to contract with third-party retailers to serve as non-Amazon pick-up and return hubs.

The second industry-changer for Amazon Fresh, according to Walton, is what he calls "voice stickiness." Voice technology permeates the customer experience there. Alexa kiosks help customers find items with ease: All a customer needs to do is ask, "Where are the pickles?" and Alexa will tell them where to look. Shoppers at Amazon Fresh can also build a shopping list at home, then access the list via the Amazon app while in-store. A shopper's grocery list can be integrated with the Dash Cart, as well, and it will check items off a customer's shopping list. The Dash Cart can work with Echo Show devices, too. Voice stickiness is a significant competitive advantage.

"No other U.S. grocery retailer has an Alexa within people's homes, and certainly no other retailer has a smart cart already in operation to pair with such a voice assistant, either," Walton said. "If this consumer behavior around voice takes hold, Amazon will be way out in front of everyone on this one."

The third industry game-changer is the ability to bypass the checkout line via Dash Cart technology. Walton warns that "all else being equal, if a grocery store on one corner requires standing in line while the one on the other corner does not, then one can bet his or her bottom dollar on which store will win out in the end." This is one technology that traditional grocers will be forced to invest in going forward, or they will find themselves losing out to competitors that offer check-out-free shopping.

Walton said the fourth Amazon Fresh differentiator is what he calls "omnichannel pricing:" Amazon's strategy for keeping its bricks merchandise competitive with the lower-priced versions that third-party sellers offer on Amazon.com. By deploying in-store price adjustments, Amazon Fresh keeps its pricing fair and transparent. But, Walton said, that's only part of the story.

"Amazon is out learning about any tilts that might come from its model, while the whole rest of the industry, despite its zeal, is still years behind understanding a third-party online marketplace's impact on its core and far more substantial in-store grocery business," Walton said. "One could say Walton sees Amazon Fresh as an experiment, a test of voice shopping, onsite pickups and returns, no lines and omnichannel pricing. And traditional grocery retailers need to get in the lab — or at least pay close attention to Amazon Fresh so they can learn from Amazon's experiment. Then they'll be better prepared.

## The Amazon Experience

Adding to traditional grocers' woes are Amazon's prices, which are difficult to match or beat, and the Amazon Fresh shopping experience. Not only can shoppers find great deals at Amazon Fresh, but they also can earn 5% cash back by using their Amazon Prime Rewards Visa Signature Card or their Amazon Prime Store Card when they pay for their items. In a state like Pennsylvania, where the state sales tax is 6%, such a cash-back incentive effectively eliminates sales tax on grocery items and essential products.

Another component of the Amazon Fresh pricing strategy is micro-merchandising. *Brick Meets Click* contributor Patrick Fisher said he has "found evidence that Amazon Fresh is subtly using price to influence whether a customer buys certain items in-store or online. If this proves to be the case, it opens a new frontier for fine-tuning business performance."

Amazon customers are used to low prices and great selection, but the quality of the Amazon Fresh brand will surprise many.

"Our culinary team offers a wide range of customer favorites made in store every day, from fresh-baked bread and made-to-order pizzas to rotisserie and fried chicken and hot sandwiches," Helbling said.

The Fresh stores also offer a full-service deli and grab-and-go hot and cold items. Retail analyst Russell Redman reports that the Amazon Fresh stores provide customers with terrific values. In 2020, for example, a Fresh-brand natural whole chicken without added hormones retailed for 99 cents per pound; a 3-pound bag of onions ran customers $1.69; and a 10-count box of Quaker Oatmeal cost $2.50 for any flavor available, Redman said. A fresh-baked baguette sold for 89 cents a loaf; a fresh slice of pizza was $1.79; and a whole rotisserie chicken was just $4.97. Such prices coupled with the convenience of Amazon Fresh's technology are enough to have traditional bricks grocers more than concerned.

## Omnichannel Firsts

The launch of Amazon Fresh is a first in another highly significant way: It is the first bricks grocery retailer with a fully integrated melding of online and in-person shopping models. It has achieved the seamless omnichannel shopping experience that traditional grocers are still pursuing. Ironically, Amazon's move into its own bricks' grocery stores probably was driven, in part, by brick grocers' soaring online sales, notes PYMNTS, a business-to-business platform and source of information about payments and e-commerce.

"For instance, Walmart's grocery performance swelled as a result of the COVID-19 pandemic," a PYMNTS article said. "Although Walmart didn't break out specific figures for grocery in its quarterly results, CEO Doug McMillion did say in a call with analysts that grocery performance was a major contributor to the 97% growth the chain saw in e-commerce results (in Q2 2020). He also said that groceries helped spark a 27% increase in average basket size."

Kroger is another competitor with surging online sales that have not gone unnoticed by Amazon. According to PYMNTS, Kroger's online sales shot up 92% in Q1 2020 alone, and the chain expanded its digital offerings with 50,000 additional products. These include international goods, housewares, private label products, specialty items, natural and organic items, and others.

"Our customers are increasingly turning to our e-commerce solutions provided at Kroger.com for their grocery and household essential needs," said Jody Kalmbach, Kroger's group vice president of product experience.

The market for groceries continues to become increasingly competitive and more sophisticated technologically. PYMNTS said the real winners in all of this are consumers, who can take advantage of "the slew of enhanced, multichannel offerings."

Amazon Fresh's seamless integration of both the digital and physical worlds certainly puts the venture in a strong position, added retail analyst Ben Fox-Rubin. This strategy will "help Amazon keep up its revenue growth, build loyalty with weekly food shoppers, and increase its footprint in one of the few areas of retail where it's a tiny player," Fox-Rubin said.

Yes, Amazon Fresh is hoping to provide consistent quality for grocery customers, a tried-and-true focus of many grocery retailers, but it is differentiating itself with its technological prowess.

"It's a very, very well-functioning industry that gives consumers historically low prices, really great redundant selection and a pretty convenient experience," said Amazon's vice president of grocery, Stephenie Landry. "So, in order to make it better, which is what we're really focused on, you have to think differently and have a lot of innovations in the experience."

Landry acknowledges that "even as e-commerce grocery leaped ahead during the pandemic, most consumers now and in the future will prefer a combination of online and in-store shopping."

### Challenging Time

Amazon is developing its bricks grocery presence during a difficult period for the grocery industry, Annie Palmer of CNBC said.

"Amazon is expanding its footprint of physical stores at a time when the coronavirus pandemic has accelerated the collapse of already struggling brick-and-mortar retailers. Many retailers have been hobbled in recent months by declining foot traffic, reduced consumer spending, and a shift to online shopping, putting some at risk of permanent store closures."

Initially, the pandemic caused Amazon to delay some of its Amazon Fresh openings and even use locations intended for Amazon Fresh stores to help meet fulfillment needs during a time of unprecedented increases in online sales, curbside pickup, and delivery due to the virus. But when the virus is contained, online grocery sales are expected to become the norm.

Amazon's foray into bricks grocery stores with the acquisition of Whole Foods has taught the company many lessons it is prepared to leverage in Amazon Fresh stores, including COVID-19 safety measures. At Amazon Fresh, these measures include "daily temperature checks for all employees, face coverings for all employees and customers entering the store, free disposable masks for shoppers who need one, and a 50% customer capacity limit to promote social distancing, among other efforts," Redman said.

Meanwhile, some have wondered how the opening and growth of Amazon Fresh will impact Amazon's Whole Foods chain.

Helbling explained the synergy the company hopes to leverage with Whole Foods and Amazon Fresh. "We do think of these formats as complementing one another and serving different needs," he said. "Whole Foods is a longstanding pioneer and leader in natural, organic, and clean foods. Amazon's Fresh selection is fairly different. We see them operating next to one another, and we're excited to offer customers the choice between the two."

### *Going the Extra Mile*

Some of the biggest challenges for bricks retailers, as noted earlier in this book, are improving efficiency and lowering costs of serving the last mile. Amazon Fresh appears to be leaping those hurdles effortlessly through its use of technology.

Though Amazon's major competitors in the retail grocery market, including H-E-B, Walmart, Target and Kroger, have been working to improve their last-mile delivery of groceries, they have yet to introduce "a new-age, automated grocery store to compete directly against Fresh," retail analyst Ed Scannel said. "When you take a step back, Bezos bought Kiva robotics because he knew that automation was coming to the warehouses. So now he wants to get a head start on the competition in automating grocery stores."

Amazon has announced plans to license out the technological innovations employed at Amazon Fresh stores as well.

Amazon Fresh is also overcoming the challenges of the last mile by locating Amazon Fresh stores in the center of its target market areas — areas where the median income is above average — providing convenient access to customers. Bishop said this gives Amazon Fresh two significant last-mile advantages:

- A shorter average distance between the customer's home and the store, making both pickup and delivery easier.

- A higher density of online orders from the immediate trade area, which can translate into lower delivery costs. The importance of this is shown by Amazon's decision to email thousands of nearby customers during pre-opening.

By hiring a slew of efficiency experts from Lidl, Amazon has been working to find even more ways to appeal to target customers, while also operating at such a low cost that it makes it hard for competing retailers to survive. This has led many retail analysts to speculate that Amazon Fresh is going after Lidle, which has mastered extreme efficiency more than the other retail giant in the industry, Walmart.

The Amazon Fresh strategy, which is intended to appeal to affluent customers, includes "value, flexibility in meeting changing shopper needs, and lower operating costs," Redman said. Despite its resemblance to traditional bricks grocery stores, Amazon Fresh is built to outlast other retailers by continuously modifying these strategies as competition intensifies and consumer needs change. When margins shrink and sales volumes decline, this strategy will enable Amazon Fresh to maintain profitability, a key to survival in the retail grocery industry.

Amazon Fresh has kept a sharp focus on price, convenience, and food selection — in addition to its technological innovations — to hopefully "entice customers to break from their regular grocer and switch to Amazon Fresh," Helbling said.

The new venture also has a coolness factor working in its favor, retail analyst Andrew Lipsman suggested. Many grocers haven't remodeled in years, so a flashy new store with lots of tech innovations will likely appeal to "younger shoppers," who are most open to trying a new place to shop, Lipsman said.

Even if Amazon Fresh isn't profitable right away, it won't be a big problem for Amazon, Lipsman added. "Amazon benefits even if these stores don't make money for years, able to draw from them valuable consumer shopping data it can use for its website and advertising business."

## Overcoming a Crisis of Confidence

Despite the threat of Amazon and its bricks grocery stores, some retail analysts maintain there is reason for optimism among traditional bricks grocers. Bricks grocers worry Amazon is taking market share, but it only has 2-3% of the retail grocery industry market share. Yes, as I write this book, Amazon has 30% of the online market share, but this number is declining as more traditional grocers ramp up their online presence and offerings.

Retail analyst Andrew Blatherwick said part of the problem is a crisis of confidence among traditional grocers when it comes to their capacity to compete against Amazon. "Amazon certainly isn't the only business to provide online ordering and delivery of fresh groceries, but its significant investments and assets give the impression of being unbeatable," he said. "Rival grocers, however, have many advantages over Amazon (and often match its offering). They just need the right foundation in place to leverage those advantages."

General Manager of Retail & Consumer Goods Brent Biddulph has predicted who he believes the winners and losers will be as brick grocers face off against the "Death Star" known as Amazon.

> Let's not so easily forget Amazon's epic "grocery" e-commerce failure just a few months ago with Pantry (shutting down) and their utter inability to deliver basic "essentials" up to 4-5 weeks regardless of the Prime promise early in the COVID crisis. Simultaneously, traditional grocery retailers' replenishment response times were far superior both in-store and online, crushing the Death Star with much deeper inventories and replenishment capabilities. Frankly, Amazon still seems puzzled by grocery, having played around the edges (unprofitably) for nearly two decades (yes, nearly 20 years)...Not that Amazon won't figure it out; they most certainly will. But it will most likely be at the expense of mom and pops and weak regionals that will lose. Grocery leaders like Walmart, Kroger, Albertsons, Tesco, Loblaw's, H-E-B, and Wegmans have not been sitting on the sidelines when it comes to investing in data and technologies.

The struggles of Whole Foods under Amazon's leadership provide evidence for the company's inexperience in the physical retail realm. Retail analyst Jeff Wells reports that "Whole Foods is now lagging way behind other grocery retailers in foot traffic with trips down 25% in September 2020," compared to the previous year.

Amazon Fresh may help Amazon compete with physical location grocers, but so far the company has not been a major winner in this category of grocery retail. Retail analyst Jeffrey Dastin reported that in July of 2020, Amazon "posted its biggest quarterly profit ever due to online sales during the coronavirus pandemic," but for the same period, it reported a 13% decline in physical store revenue. Some retail analysts, such as Walter Loeb, predict that Amazon's domination of home food shopping will not last.

This is because competitors like H-E-B, Walmart, Kroger, Costco, and others are adopting strategies to put themselves in a position to compete against Amazon. Walmart has partnered with Instacart for grocery fulfillment and delivery. It has also launched its own version of Amazon Prime, which provides free delivery for members. Dastin said this will "attract and please many loyal customers."

Dastin added that Costco will likely increase market share, too, as it focuses on rapid food delivery and a broader grocery assortment. At the same time, both Kroger and Albertsons have seen sharp increases in online grocery sales during the COVID-19 pandemic, an increase Dastin maintained "will likely remain high into the foreseeable future." Taken together such developments point to a "day of reckoning" coming for Amazon, in Dastin's assessment.

While Amazon has been gaining on competitors like Walmart and Costco where online sales are concerned during the pandemic, this is not the case where retail sales of groceries at physical locations are concerned. Amazon may be dominant in online grocery sales for now, but as other competitors become more adept at counteracting their dominance and adding faster shipment of deliveries, this dominance will more than likely continue to erode moving forward. Walmart is by far the biggest grocer in the U.S. and is fast-encroaching on Amazon's online position.

So, while there may be a significant disturbance in the universe, many bricks grocers are well-positioned to leverage such capabilities and overcome the threat of Amazon, which has, despite significant investment and effort, failed to conquer the retail grocery industry as of yet.

## *Work to be Done*

This is not to say that bricks grocers don't have a lot of work ahead of them.

"Experts have been quick to caution that early stumbles by Amazon shouldn't breed complacency, given the company's near-limitless capital, its track record, and its focus on testing and adjusting," Jeff Wells warns. "A case in point is Amazon's use of proprietary technology that drives innovation. This helps the company offer shoppers at physical locations an advanced shopping experience that is difficult for competitors to match."

I agree: There will not be much reason to celebrate if brick grocers fail to quickly launch proactive and, at times, sweeping measures and changes. They will need to leverage supply chain tools, including omnichannel inventory management, unified commerce platforms, synchronization with suppliers, demand forecasting, AI and ML analytics, and others.

To effectively compete with Amazon, grocers first have to stop thinking of e-commerce as an add-on. Jeff Weidauer, principal of SSR Retail LLC, said, "Online ordering may soon comprise half of sales and will be the growth engine over the next decade in any case. Accepting that reality will change investment strategies and supply chain structure."

For example, grocers trying to place online orders from in-store will never be able to replenish supply quickly enough if they rely only on in-store forecasts. To keep from having a high level of out-of-stocks, which sends shoppers to competitors, bricks grocers need to develop separate, automated, and data-based demand forecasts for each channel and combine them in a supply chain strategy. Remember, online grocery ordering, whether for curbside pickup or home delivery, accelerated because of the COVID-19 pandemic. Many customers have discovered they like shopping for groceries this way, and even when COVID-19 is no longer a threat, many will continue to order groceries online.

Bricks grocers will need to continue adapting to meet their shoppers' evolving needs and consider the premium consumers place on convenience.

"Convenience in the future will almost certainly require a mixture of local physical stores and excellent online purchasing and delivery capabilities," Wunderman Thompson Commerce Marketplace Services

President Frank Kochenash said. "Grocers of the future, whatever their name, will need both, and they will need them to work together seamlessly."

Regional grocers like H-E-B may be better positioned than other bricks stores to take advantage of this strategy since they have in-depth knowledge of their target market and its needs, and H-E-B has more "local" capability where supply chain logistics are concerned. Amazon Fresh's focus on "free," where delivery and Amazon.com returns are concerned, is only one aspect of the game, leaving room for savvy bricks grocers to best them. Doug Garnett is the founder and president of Protonik, a marketing consultancy that works with manufacturers, brands, inventors, and retailers. He said the fact Amazon's reliance on the appeal of "free" puts the company in an incredibly weak position. "If a retailer gets smart and cracks the code on a paid service, Amazon continues to lose vast sums from their 'free' commitments," Garnett said.

The bottom line for bricks retail grocers that want to successfully compete against and stay the course with Amazon grocery retail is they must find innovative ways of thinking, planning, and changing, said Michael La Kier, principal of What Brands Want, LLC.

"The grocery business model has not fundamentally changed in decades and now must handle rapid modernization and rapid change due to COVID-19 and competition," La Kier said. "Amazon has the advantage of technology and white sheet planning. Grocers must fight a battle on two fronts: offering an excellent consumer experience in-store and an excellent user experience online. AI-enabled supply chain planning to better handle demand may help on both fronts."

As I've written, the old business model for retail grocers is no longer adequate or sustainable. The executive director of Global Commerce Education, Gene Detroyer, calls for a total change, one that's dramatically forward-thinking.

"The grocer should tear up the blueprints and also adapt "white sheet planning," he said. "Let's take that blank piece of paper and design the business for 2025. What would we come up with?"

I would suggest going even further: We should be designing our businesses for 2040.

# CLICKS: **KNOWING THE COMPETITION**

WHEN ERIC STEILBERGER'S BELOVED DOG, ANNIE, PASSED AWAY, HE emailed online pet supply retailer Chewy to cancel his no-longer-needed pet food order.

Chewy's response? They sent the heartbroken man flowers.

"I cancel their service, and they send flowers?" Steilberger posted on LinkedIn. "I will tell everyone I can: If they need pet food, they should try Chewy. Annie's sister and everyone else in the house is still grieving, and these made me smile."

Chewy, based in Dania Beach, Florida, has been making a name for itself through above-and-beyond customer service measures like this.

"No wait service, handwritten notes, pet paintings, condolence flowers and donating to shelters in lieu of returns are just a handful of their differentiators," Stan Phelps, author, speaker, and instructor for the ANA School of Marketing and Rutgers Business School, wrote in a blog about the company.

Chewy's actions convey messages that resonate with shoppers. They say, "We care about you. We understand what's important to you, and we share the same values."

And those messages have not gone unnoticed. As of January 31, 2021, the company's sales had risen 47% from January 2020 to $7.1 billion. Because of its aggressive growth strategy, the publicly-traded company was not profitable yet as of June 2021, but business analysts are optimistic about its future.

Not only is Chewy straining at the leash to take more pet product market share from other clicks retailers, but the company also has become a tough competitor for bricks grocers with pet products on their shelves.

Of course, Chewy is far from the only online retailer successfully selling products carried by grocery stores, from diapers and cleaning supplies to pantry staples and even meat and produce. The threat clicks retailers represent to bricks grocers has been a major motivation for writing this book. Though the COVID-19 pandemic and consumers' need to maintain social distancing have elevated interest in online grocery retailers to new heights, many of these clicks businesses likely would be gaining market share anyhow because of the convenience and savings they offer, or other unique differentiators like Chewy's personal touch. That means bricks grocers will need to watch these clicks businesses closely, ascertain what has been contributing to their success, and use that information to develop strategies for their own survival.

To help you achieve these objectives, this chapter provides examples of some of the clicks retailers gaining ground in groceries.

## *Warm Fuzzies and Retail Success*

While bricks grocers certainly can take a cue from Chewy's commitment to injecting a warm, human touch into their interactions with the public, the company's strong example doesn't stop with personal notes and acts of kindness. Chewy also can attribute its success to overall customer service excellence and responsiveness, its popular product subscription model, technological solutions like its telehealth "Connect With a Vet" program, and ongoing order fulfillment improvements. Let's take a look at each of these areas.

Since Ryan Cohen and Michael Day founded Chewy in 2011, excellent customer service was part of their business model.

"When a customer phoned, a representative said hello within six seconds," Anders Melin and Bryan Gruley of Bloomberg Business wrote. "Emails were answered within an hour. Messed-up orders were replaced without question or cost."

*Chewy's Autoship subscription program capitalizes on growing consumer interest in product subscription services and makes up nearly 70% of the online pet supply retailer's total net sales.*

Another important note for bricks grocers: Chewy understands the connection between excellent service and well-trained, empowered employees. The company hires people craving more training and knowledge, and it accommodates them, retail reporter Paula Rosenblum wrote for *Forbes*.

"Employees self-select if they want to advance," Rosenblum said. "They are told from the very beginning of their tenure that the company will help them do that . . . If there's one take-away I would offer to both store-based and online retailers, it's this: The customer always rewards a retailer for having thoughtful, knowledgeable, enthusiastic employees. This is the key to Chewy's success, and it can be the key to yours, too."

Well said.

Chewy also has capitalized on growing consumer interest in product subscription services, which give customers the option of having products delivered regularly, usually at a discount or with free shipping. In the case of Chewy's Autoship subscription program, customers get discounts on pet supplies, and, if their regular orders cost more than $50, shipping is free. Customers seem to like this feature: Autoship sales make up nearly 70% of Chewy's total net sales.

Another perk for Chewy Autoship clients: They get access to the company's "Connect with a Vet," inspired by growing interest in tele-medicine since the COVID-19 pandemic started. Through "Connect with a Vet," customers can ask licensed veterinarians questions about their pets' health. The vets don't diagnose or treat pets' conditions or prescribe medication, but they help owners determine if they need to take their pet to an in-person vet appointment or an emergency service. There's no charge to use the service if you're an Autoship customer.

During the pandemic, "what we recognized was that veterinarian availability was compromised," Chewy CEO Sumit Singh told CO. "There was a bit of friction there because of the lack of availability of veterinarians or reduced hours or the customer not being able to travel during lockdown."

Chewy also has been willing to make significant investments in order-fulfillment technology to increase its operational efficiency. *Supply Chain Dive* reporter Emma Cosgrove wrote in November 2020 that the company had opened its first automated fulfillment center in Archbald, Pennsylvania. Mike Gilbert, Chewy's vice president of operations, told Cosgrove that he expected the cycle time between customer order submissions and boxes with their merchandise landing on a truck to decrease 45%.

"He also expects greater picking accuracy and 30% lower fulfillment costs," Cosgrove wrote.

As bricks grocers explore their automated order-fulfillment options, they may want to note the strategic research and testing Chewy completed before approving an approach that meets its unique needs. Ultimately, Chewy created an amalgam of solutions from multiple vendors. The system includes high-speed sortation systems that send goods to pickers via conveyor belts, robots, and a customized merchandise storage system.

"It can range from small toys and treats all the way up to 50-pound bags of dog food . . . so we've really focused on how we slot the building," Gilbert said. The building will be divided into zones based on SKU velocity, with slightly different technology and systems in each."

## *Others in the Pack*

In 2021, market research firm Packaged Facts named Chewy and Amazon the country's top online pet product retailers in its report, "U.S. Pet Market Outlook 2021-2022." The report also noted that Chewy and Amazon are outpacing brick competitors, including Petco, PetSmart, Tractor Supply, and Costco, in sales.

"E-commerce success with pet food has depended not on eliminating the shipping and handling expenses inevitably involved with heavy and bulky items, but on changing consumers' point of view," the report stated. "Amazon wields the larger context of Amazon Prime and Amazon credit card and reward programs."

Amazon, I would add, also benefits from its huge volume of pet product choices. Tom Elliott, managing director of investment firm Capstone Headwaters, wrote in the company's report, "Pet Humanization Accelerates Through COVID-19," there's no question that Amazon still is running at the head of the pet product pack.

"Amazon has continued its impressive run in the pet space, and with the help of the pandemic, it has achieved 39% of total online pet food and supply market share in 2020," Elliott wrote.

And Chewy and Amazon are far from the only clicks pet product retailers providing competition for bricks grocers. Both Petco and PetSmart, for example, have successful online businesses with large selections and savings opportunities. Target.com and Walmart.com are gaining market share in pet products, too. Walmart.com carries "smart" pet products, including automated feeders and pet cameras, along with basic supplies. Target is known for offering regular "Pet Deals," discounts on its pet products.

What's more, a number of online retailers are finding success in monthly pet box subscription services. BARK, for example, offers several popular options including BarkBox, which offers monthly dog treat-toy-chew packages; Bark Super Chewer, with tougher toys, treats, and chews for "adventure-seeking dogs;" Bark Bright, with health and wellness productions; and Bark Eats, featuring dog meals. A few of the other pet box providers out there include PetTreater, Pooch Perks, and Amazon's Meowbox, The Dapper Dog, and Pawstruck.

In a recent article about dog subscription boxes, *Canine Journal* writer Sally Jones listed the benefits these services offer pet owners, including "items that aren't always available at the local grocery or pet store" along with convenience, affordability, organic options, and fun. It seems like these are areas in which bricks grocery stores can up their game, possibly by offering unique, high-quality store brand pets products at good prices.

A 2021 report by Statista, however, said that while online pet care has a bright future, Americans still rely on physical stores, first big box, followed by grocery stores and chain pet stores, to buy pet products, pet food in particular. Bricks grocers can capitalize on these preferences while offering some of the benefits that clicks provide, from exceptional customer service in the same vein as Chewy to deals on popular products.

## Organic Food Clicks Seeing Healthy Growth

If Chewy is a rising star in online pet products, then Thrive Market is the equivalent in online organic products. In fact, Thrive Market made headlines recently for taking business from Amazon, or in this case, Amazon-owned Whole Foods.

"Thrive Market promises the same natural and organic vibe as Whole Foods, but without the negative 'whole paycheck' connotation, thanks to a Costco-like membership model," speaker, author, and market researcher Pamela N. Danziger wrote for *Forbes*. "And a new guided shopping experience added since the pandemic began allows shoppers to create a personal grocery store customized to their special dietary needs and value preferences."

The thrivemarket.com website boasts that it carries more than 6,000 organic brands, including food, home, and beauty products.

"The online store sells everything on your grocery list (yes, that includes wine), plus vitamins and supplements, bath and beauty products, and even apparel and toys for kids," Donna Currie wrote for *The Spruce Eats*. "The site makes it easy to click on what you're looking for, whether it's organic, dye-free, paleo, raw, or any other wide range of attributes," she wrote. "No need to worry about reading descriptions or labels to make sure you choose the right products."

Members get low prices, gifts and samples, and shipping is free for orders over $49.

Thrive has also found a tangible way to demonstrate that it's a company with a big heart: It devotes a portion of each customers' subscription fee to help sponsor a low-income family's membership.

Other successful presences in the online organic market include Vitacost (purchased by Kroger in 2014), a vitamin and organic foods retailer known for its large selection of flours; NaturalZing, which focuses on raw foods; and Manna Harvest, known for its selection of dry foods.

## Growing Market for Online Perishables: Meats and Seafood

I stand by the comments I've made in this book about customers' preferences to feel and touch certain perishable foods, including produce, meats, and seafood, giving bricks grocers an edge over clicks competitors. But we can't ignore the fact that customers do have online options for purchasing these products, options with their own unique benefits.

When it comes to meats, many of the online retailers seeing success offer gourmet and bulk products that are packed in dry ice and quickly delivered to customers' doors.

"For general groceries, you can go to any number of online grocery delivery services, such as FreshDirect and AmazonFresh," wrote Connie Chen of Insider. "But if you're craving something a little more gourmet, something heartier, there are even more specific delivery services. The magic of meat delivery services . . . is this: They provide curated shopping experiences, they sell high-quality and responsibly raised meat, and they're really convenient because they'll ship fresh products directly to your door."

Rastelli's, for example, is a family-owned New Jersey brick-and-mortar butcher shop augmented by a popular online business.

"If you're looking to stock up on everything from ground beef and chicken to sirloin steak, pork chops, sausage, shrimp, and salmon, Rastelli's has you covered," Currie wrote for *The Spruce Eats*. "All of the products can be stored in your freezer for up to a year, and you can order in bulk or save money on a subscription. Items like the Chicken Drumsticks Box, Steak Craft Burgers Box, and Ground Beef Box come with 12 servings, so there's plenty for the whole family. There are also gift box options that are perfect for holiday or corporate gifting."

Rastelli's also markets the fact that its meat is responsibly sourced and free of antibiotics, steroids, and hormones.

In the area of seafood, Fulton Fish Market is another example of a longtime bricks market adding a successful online operation to its business. Its clicks market, which sells whole fish, fillets, fish steaks, shellfish, and specialty seafood, offers Seafood Bundles based on such themes as Summertime Grilling and Seafood Lovers.

"A large and impressive recipe archive is available on the Fulton Fish Market website as an additional resource for those wanting some inspiration from other chefs or guidance on how to cook what they order at home," Kristy Del Coro wrote for *The Spruce* Eats. "Fulton Fish Market offers transparent sourcing and provides sustainable seafood logos on all sustainable seafood products. Products are also clearly labeled to indicate whether they are wild or farmed."

Though it is difficult to compete with the convenience of food coming right to the door, bricks grocers still have a fighting chance of keeping their meat, seafood, and produce customers. In addition to the fact that customers like to inspect these products before buying, as discussed, grocers can duplicate the fun of themed boxes and recipes like Fulton Seafood Market does. H-E-B, for example, not only shares recipes with customers, but it also provides demonstrations by chefs who can answer customers' questions and give them a taste of the finished product. Clicks retailers can't do that, nor can they entice customers with the aromas of the dishes their chefs are preparing.

## *Fresh Produce and Customer Preferences*

As for produce, consumers have online options here, too, though they have been a bit hesitant to fully embrace them. A recent survey by food and agribusiness consulting service, Breakthrough Solutions, showed that not only are 50% of shoppers purchasing less fresh produce online than during in-store visits, but shoppers are also much less likely to try new products online. While Fernandez described those trends as a challenge for grocery stores with an omnichannel model—which has customers buying from them both in person and online—customers' strong preference to personally inspect the fresh produce they purchase is a promising trend for bricks grocers, especially as more people are vaccinated against COVID-19 and start venturing back into grocery stores.

That said, the success of such bricks fresh produce retailers as Farmbox Direct, The Fruit Guys, and Full Circle Farms shows growing numbers of consumers are willing to, at least, give online fruit and vegetable shopping a try.

Ashley Tyrner, founder of Farmbox Direct, told *Time Magazine* in 2018 that she started her business after struggling to find high-quality greens and vegetables for her daughter near their New York home.

"I never knew when I started my company that it would turn into what it's morphed into today, or, that it would become a vehicle to help alleviate the problem of food deserts, areas that lack access to affordable healthy foods such as produce, whole grains, and low-fat dairy," Tyrner said.

Today, the multi-million dollar business is thriving, and CNET editors recently named Farmbox Direct "Best for Seasonal Fare" in a recent article about online produce retailers.

San Francisco-based The FruitGuys, which delivers fresh, seasonal produce to businesses and schools in addition to homes, also is known for its commitment to community service. According to an article about the health benefits of eating produce in *Medical News Today*, The FruitGuys donates excess fruit and 20% of its annual profits to promote sustainable projects and fight hunger. In June 2021, the company launched a partnership with nonprofit CUESA (Center for Urban Education about Sustainable Agriculture). Together, they're offering Ferry Plaza Farmers Market Delivered for San Francisco-Bay Area residents.

"This past year has been particularly hard on many small farms, which endured restaurant closures and reduced farmers' market foot traffic due to the pandemic," Marian Zboraj wrote for *Progressive Grocer.* "The new direct online sales channel will help farmers by supporting them as they evolve, diversify, and cater to the way consumer shopping behavior has changed during this past year, specifically in regard to the acceleration of online grocery shopping, which isn't showing any signs of slowing down."

Bricks grocers should also keep an eye on fresh-produce clicks that specialize in "ugly" merchandise. Successful retailers in this space include Imperfect Foods, Misfits Market, and Hungry Harvest. These retailers capitalize on consumers' interest in protecting the environment and minimizing food waste by delivering less-than-attractive products.

While large numbers of consumers will continue buying their fresh produce in person, bricks grocers should not be complacent in this area. As this book describes, strategies such as making visits to grocery store produce sections pleasant and forming partnerships with local growers can help bricks grocers compete effectively with online retailers.

## More on Subscription Services

You may have noticed that many of the clicks retailers successfully selling products found at grocery stores have something in common: They offer subscription services. And these services don't stop with pet products, organics, meats, and produce. The list goes on with wines, baby food and diapers, snacks, personal care products, and more — nearly every grocery category imaginable.

The clicks retailer possibly best known for subscription service success is Amazon. Since 2007, its Subscribe & Save program, for example, allows customers to get free shipping and discounts on products they continuously use, from paper towels to coffee. Customers decide how often they want orders to arrive (as frequently as every month). Discounts begin at 5% and increase to 15-20% for auto-orders comprising five or more products.

"The subscription e-commerce market has grown by more than 100% annually since 2013," Ana Franciosi wrote in a 2021 blog for e-commerce consultancy Object Edge. "It's a major source of consistent revenue for sellers and a source of convenience for customers."

Franciosi added that, according to McKinsey research, 15% of online shoppers have signed up for one or more e-commerce subscriptions at some point.

*Brick Meets Click* writer Steve Bishop explored the developing trend of subscription services in 2017, noting their potential to help grocers establish long-term relationships with customers.

"Subscriptions can strengthen loyalty and transform the shopping and buying process from a one-off transaction into an ongoing, dynamic two-way relationship — one in which information flows between the company and the consumer in addition to the exchange of money," Bishop wrote. "Consumers receive valuable subscription content and services (like cooking directions, lifestyle tips, and access to extended product selections), and retailers receive valuable consumer data about the needs, concerns, and preferences of their customers."

As I worked on this book, consumer interest in subscriptions was going strong. Busy consumers like the ability to "set-it-and-forget-it," Jordan Berke, founder of Tomorrow Retail Consulting and a former Walmart executive, said during an interview with *Grocery Dive*.

"I have been very amazed at what I would call the subscription culture that has emerged with consumers, where they prefer a subscription model for experiences that remove friction from their lives," Berke said. "They love to pay to free the mental load."

For bricks grocers, offering subscription services of their own remains a valuable strategy for competing against clicks competitors.

"It's a defensive move because it stops existing loyal shoppers from going and shopping with someone else," consultant James McCann, the former CEO of Ahold USA, told *Grocery Dive*. "The industry is getting pushed in this direction. I think it's going to become a big part of the game plan at all the major grocers."

## *The Behemoths of Online Retail*

In today's competitive retail landscape, bricks grocers also can benefit from observing the giants of click retail. Most carry a wide range of products, including groceries. And some of them, like Amazon, have launched their own brick-and-mortar grocery stores as well.

Here's a look at a few of these online retail titans.

**Amazon:** For bricks grocers, and even other online retailers, Amazon is a force to be reckoned with. A survey by marketing service Epsilon showed that the top reasons consumers shop on Amazon are low prices, free shipping, convenience, and because Amazon carries just about everything, making it a one-stop shop.

Additional benefits for shoppers include:

- Amazon Prime: This paid program offers a long list of benefits, including free deliveries (free same-day deliveries in some areas); free two-hour deliveries on groceries in some areas; and pharmacy and prescription delivery programs, along with Amazon's numerous subscription programs; access to streaming, music, and reading materials; the ability to share memberships with family; and Amazon Prime Day deals.

- Buy Now: Once Amazon has a shopper's preferred payment and shipping information, the shopper can bypass the checkout process by clicking "Buy Now," making shopping quicker and more convenient.

- Amazon Smile: When consumers do their Amazon shopping from this site, they can direct a percentage of their spending to the charity of their choice.

- Alexa: Shoppers with an Amazon Echo device can make verbal orders, taking shopping convenience up another notch.

Add the COVID-19 pandemic and the need for social distancing to the equation, and you have an even larger threat in Amazon.

"Since the start of the coronavirus outbreak, shoppers have relied increasingly on Amazon for delivery of home staples, and the company sees this trend continuing post-pandemic, particularly for groceries," Jeffrey Dastin and Akanksha Rana wrote for Reuters in late spring 2021. "Amazon has now posted four consecutive record quarterly profits, attracted more than 200 million Prime loyalty subscribers, and recruited over 500,000 employees to keep up with surging demand."

**Walmart**: While Walmart is a major presence in brick-and-mortar grocery shopping, it also is the most popular online store in the U.S., second only to Amazon in e-commerce revenue, according to Big Commerce.

"Walmart's online sales are growing at 40% year-over-year," Duran Inci wrote for Big Commerce. "At this pace, you can expect this giant to take away even more Amazon business in the coming years."

Tricia McKinnon wrote about Walmart's strong e-presence for Indigo Digital. Walmart has benefited from the value consumers place on value and their interest in one-stop shopping, McKinnon wrote. The company also positioned itself for success by taking an omnichannel approach to doing business and investing in such e-commerce businesses as Jet.com, Bonobos, Eloquii, and ModCloth to cultivate knowledge, processes, and talent.

But ultimately, McKinnon wrote, the simple fact that Walmart carries groceries has played a surprisingly large role in its success as an online retailer.

"Selling groceries increases the frequency of visits since most consumers shop for groceries on a weekly basis," she wrote. "Amazon has also recognized this dependency, with Amazon's CEO Jeff Bezos saying over a decade ago that for Amazon to become a $200-billion retailer, it has to figure out how to sell food. That is why Amazon purchased Whole Foods and opened a new grocery chain, Amazon Fresh, earlier this year. Core to any e-commerce business is website traffic that returns on a frequent basis."

**eBay Inc.:** The company is a third-party platform used for business-to-consumer and consumer-to-consumer sales. Sellers can invite shoppers to bid on their merchandise via eBay's online auction feature or sell merchandise with eBay's "Buy Now" format.

In 2020, eBay had more than 25 million sellers, and according to digitalcommerce360.com, the gross value of goods sold on eBay's U.S. marketplace grew 22.1% to $37.53 billion in 2020, up from $30.74 billion in 2019. According to StreetSignals, one of eBay's plusses for users is the ability it gives them to provide feedback on products and services.

"Users are able to post comments, send messages, and give ratings to a person that has sold them an item," Josh Wardini wrote for *StreetSignals*.

"This is automatically linked, via the site, to the seller's profile, either making their reputation better or worse. Based on the previous feedback, new buyers are able to decide whether they want to buy from the seller."

Additional eBay benefits include buyer protection, including PayPal payment services, and competitive pricing. The company earns revenue through listing fees, advertising, merchant fee, contractual service, and lead referral fees.

While eBay is not necessarily the first clicks retailer that comes to mind when groceries are mentioned, the company does offer a food and beverage category that includes snacks, cheeses, coffee, tea, wine, beer and beer-making products, sweeteners, candy, sauces, ice-cream supplies, pantry items, gift foods, and seasonings. Shoppers also can go to eBay for pet supplies, health and beauty products, baby items, toilet paper and tissues, and cleaning supplies.

**JD.com or Jingdong:** One of several retail giants in China, JD.com is known for its high-tech delivery system, which incorporates robots, artificial intelligence, and drones. The Beijing-based company has operations in more than 50 cities in China and boasts more than 170 million users.

"JD.com takes a heavy-asset approach like Amazon, building up warehouse centers and keeping its own army of courier staff," Rita Liao wrote for *Tech Crunch*. "As of 2020, JD Logistics had over 246,800 employees working in delivery, warehouse operations among other customer services."

Also, like Amazon, JD.com offers one-stop shopping in such categories as apparel, electronics, home furnishings, fast-moving consumer goods or FMCG (products that are sold quickly at a low cost such as pantry items, beverages, toiletries, and over-the-counter drugs), fresh foods, and home appliances.

"A huge key part of JD.com is its extensive logistics network," the China-based GMA e-commerce agency reported. "Its logistics operation uses JD's advanced technology, which allows them to offer a supply chain that is tough to duplicate. JD.com operates 30 logistics parks, which have been coined as 'Asia n.1.' In fact, they are considered the largest and the most automated smart fulfillment centers in all of Asia."

And, the company is building a significant presence in the grocery space. In 2018, JD.com launched a bricks grocery store chain named 7Fresh that carries live seafood, dairy, meat, and fresh produce. In an article for Tech Crunch, Liao wrote that the first store had a Whole Foods vibe on a more futuristic level.

"The a-ha moment comes when you get to the fruit section, which lets you scan barcodes on meticulously wrapped items," Liao wrote. "Details of the fruit then pop up on a screen above your head, showing where it comes from, how sweet it is, et cetera."

To shop at 7Fresh, consumers must download its app and set up an account. But once consumers have the app, they can buy the store merchandise remotely, and if they're less than three kilometers away, their order will be delivered in 30 minutes.

In addition to creating 7Fresh, JD.com has been partnering with existing bricks grocers, including Walmart, which has a 12% stake in JD.com. The two companies co-invested $500 million in online company Dada-JD Daojia, which ships groceries and daily necessities to consumers in China using local Walmart stores as their fulfillment centers.

"More than 100 of Walmart's stores double as warehouses for JD.com," Franklin Chu wrote for *SmartBrief*. "This model helps Walmart downsize its stores and move more of its inventory online, similar to its newer competitors in the grocery business."

**Alibaba Group Holding LTD**: If JD.com has parallels to Amazon, then Alibaba.com—an e-commerce and technology conglomerate based in Hangzhou, China—is a closer match to eBay. The company, one of the largest retailers in the world, provides a platform for business-to-business sales, business-to-consumer sales, and consumer-to-consumer sales for users in more than 200 countries.

"For all the accolades for U.S.-based internet-technology giants like Amazon.com and Facebook, the real king of the digital hill lies thousands of miles to the east in China—the home of Alibaba," Brian O'Connell wrote for *TheStreet*. "There's really no doubting that sentiment. Alibaba is the largest e-commerce company on earth, with its three primary e-commerce sites — Taobao, Tmall, and Alibaba.com — engaging tens of millions of online users daily."

Alibaba Group makes money through the commissions on sales made through its website as well as advertising fees and fulfillment services. In addition to its online marketplace, Alibaba's business segments include cloud computing and digital media and entertainment.

"Alibaba hit the headlines with the world's biggest IPO in September 2014," Ming Zeng, chairman of the Academic Council of the Alibaba Group and the author of *Smart Business: What Alibaba's Success Reveals About the Future of Strategy*, wrote for *Harvard Business Review*. "Today, the company has a market cap among the global top 10, has surpassed Walmart in global sales, and has expanded into all the major markets in the world. Founder Jack Ma has become a household name."

Analysts cite multiple factors for Alibaba's ongoing success, beginning with the fact its core businesses focus on serving small enterprises.

"All three of Alibaba's core businesses mainly focus on providing services to small enterprises, helping them create value which could not be accomplished by any of them individually (such as cost control)," *Retail News Asia* reported. "The focus on small enterprises also leads to a phenomenon whereby a large variety of goods are available to a large variety of target consumer groups (age, profession, wealth, etc.) on the platform."

*Retail News Asia* also attributes Alibaba's success to its profit model, which charges for marketing and technical support services instead of admission to its platforms; the company's accurate credit model, including the Alipay payment platform, which protects consumers and e-stores; strong customer service for sellers and buyers; and a focus on identifying customer needs to build loyalty.

Alibaba, like Amazon and JD.com, has created its own grocery brand: Hema. The stores double as fulfillment centers for Hema's online grocery orders.

"Hema, whose English name is Freshippo, is a high-tech supermarket designed around your smartphone," Tricia McKinnon wrote for *Indigo Digital*. "Your smartphone is used for everything in the store, from placing items in a digital shopping cart while you shop for groceries, to getting product nutritional information, to paying for your goods."

Here's a closer look at the Hema shopping experience, as covered by *Indigo Digital*.

- Mobile app: Consumers must download the Hema app to shop in Hema. The app allows them to scan QR codes on the items they want to buy and place them in their digital shopping cad. Scanning the code also provides details about the product, including freshness, nutritional information, customer reviews, recipes, and delivery options.

- Personalized shopping recommendations: Using AI, the Hema app notes shopper buying behavior and harnesses machine learning to offer product recommendations.

- Digital price tags: The products' digital price tags can be updated in real-time, which helps make sure prices online match what's in the store.

- Digital payments employing facial recognition: Hema's mobile app is linked to Alipay, founded by Alibaba. The app, which has more than 1 billion monthly active users, is the world's largest online payment platform. At participating Hema stores, customers can pay using facial recognition payment technology.

- "At self-checkouts, a camera embedded in the screen of a kiosk scans the customer's face," McKinnon wrote. "Then facial recognition payment technology is then used to verify the customer's identity. Customers also enter their phone number into the kiosk as a safeguard against fraud."

- 30-minute deliveries: Like 7Fresh offers, Hema provides deliveries within 30 minutes for delivery addresses within three kilometers of a store.

- Stores are delivery hubs for other retailers: Starbucks Delivers Kitchens operates within select Hema stores. "The partnership allows Starbucks to leverage Hema's delivery capabilities to service Starbucks' online orders quickly and efficiently," McKinnon wrote.

- Grocery/restaurant hybrids: Not only can Hema shoppers dine in the store, but they can also choose an item in the store, like fresh seafood, to be prepared for them to eat in the restaurant. Shoppers can dine in 7Fresh, too.

- Restaurant robots: In one of the Hema stores, most of the restaurant dishes are delivered to diners by robots, though human employees are on hand to answer questions.

**Flipkart:** The company, founded by ex-Amazon employees Binny Bansal and Sachin Bansal, got its start as a small online bookseller based in Bangalore, India. Today, Flipkart is considered the largest online retailer in India.

"Presently, the company facilitates over 80 million products across the range of over 80 categories (including) mobile phones and accessories, computers, laptops, books and e-books, home appliances, electronic goods, clothes and accessories, sports and fitness, baby care, games and toys, jewelry, footwear, and so on," Mallika Rangaiah wrote for *Analytic Steps*. "As of 2019, Flipkart had over 160 million registered users and over a million sellers on its electronic commerce platform."

Since 2018, Walmart has held a controlling stake in the business, and in 2021, the company was preparing for an initial public offering (IPO) in 2022.

Flipkart's strengths, Rangaiah wrote, include its vast selection of products, branded products at economical prices, discounts, user perks, a cash-on-delivery feature, a user-friendly refund policy, and strong customer service.

Company leaders have made groceries a key focus area for Flipkart. In March 2021, it offered grocery delivery in more than 50 cities across India. Its grocery line comprises more than 7,000 products across more than 200 categories, from household staples and personal care items to dairy and eggs.

"Grocery continues to be one of the fastest-growing categories, with the increase in demand for quality food and household supplies from users," said Manish Kumar, Senior Vice President of Grocery, General Merchandise and Furniture, Flipkart. "In line with this, we have invested in scaling up our grocery operations across the country, strengthening ecosystem partnerships, thus ensuring a seamless grocery shopping experience through an expansive product selection, robust supply chain, and smooth in-app experience for consumers."

While this chapter provides only a sampling of the vast number of successful clicks retailers on the scene today, it can be a starting point for your research. Retail is constantly evolving, and successful players in this space will have to adapt to survive — just as bricks grocery stores will. I encourage you to continue monitoring your clicks competitors. The strategies that contribute to their successes could be equally valuable to you.

# BRICKS HAVE A BRIGHT FUTURE

THERE IS NO DENYING THAT INCREASED ONLINE GROCERY SHOPPING is forcing bricks grocers to "up their game" to compete, from offering their own online shopping services to same-day delivery and curbside pickup. Even so, even with double-digit growth in online grocery retail and other segments of the marketplace, bricks stores are here to stay for the foreseeable future. Not only that, but they have the potential to thrive.

## *Season of Growth*

Why am I so confident? First of all, grocery is one of the strongest retail sectors in the U.S., with twice as many new stores opening than closing in 2018. JLL Retail reported that new grocery store openings were up an impressive 30% in 2018. With over 17 million square feet of space occupied in the U.S., bricks grocery stores are, in fact, in a renewed period of growth. I'm not alone in this thinking. When Amazon purchased Whole Foods, they demonstrated even they understand the value of brick-and-mortar grocery retail stores. And as this book describes, Amazon is building more bricks grocery stores under its own brand. It's true that Amazon is by far the leading online retailer, but that can change.

As Moody's analyst Charlie O-Shea told *Supply Chain Dive*, "No individual reseller is going to catch Amazon. But that's not the game . . . Without a brick-and-mortar network, Amazon will find limitations to where it's going to be able to grow."

Another good sign for bricks grocery shopping: Hard discounting chains are also increasing their bricks footprint. In this segment of grocery retail, we're seeing new, larger Lidl stores and ALDI making major investments in new and remodeled stores. Bill Bishop has predicted that combined sales for both chains will reach $50 to $65 billion by 2023.

## New Era for Bricks

In many ways, online grocery retail is not supplanting bricks grocery retail. Instead, online retail is enhancing brick and mortar retail stores. Online retail offers an increasingly significant tool that bricks stores can leverage to add greater conveniences for consumers and enhance the overall shopping experience.

"That's where online is going—third-party fulfillment, retailer direct delivery, online ordering with in-store pickup, which all have retail stores as their source, as opposed to pure-play e-commerce grocers," Stern said. This is why Amazon and other online retailers are expanding into bricks shopping channels.

One of the best solutions for bridging the bricks vs. clicks divide technology: Bricks can harness it to create an in-store culture and committed team of employees that, together, deliver flawless experiences. By doing that, bricks grocers entice consumers to regularly shop in-store instead of online. Achieving this takes leadership that is committed to owning the quality of experience in-store. It also takes the willingness to allocate the resources and take the actions necessary to develop a team that delivers flawless experiences for every customer every time they shop.

Trung Nguyen, VP of e-commerce strategies at Albertsons, has offered a positive outlook on the future of brick-and-mortar grocers. Despite changing demands of younger shoppers, Nguyen said brick-and-mortar grocers still have a bright future.

"Brick-and-mortar's never going away," Nguyen said. "People like coming into stores. But the younger generation is used to the convenience. It's them we're preparing for—they want it now, and we want to provide that. But we still have customers who want to walk in, touch and feel, and talk to people."

# FINAL FOOD FOR THOUGHT

THE MAIN POINT BEHIND THIS BOOK IS THAT BRICKS GROCERY RETAIL-ers are facing a crisis. As I wrote, with some strategic planning and investment, there's every reason to believe they'll thrive well into the future. But, if they sit back and do nothing or wait too long to challenge the onslaught of clicks grocery retailers, they will become victims of the threat that is online grocery retailing.

While bricks grocery retail has remained fairly impervious to loss of market share to clicks grocery retailers compared to other types of retailers, this is changing rapidly, and clicks grocery retailers will continue to increase market share.

A report by consulting firm Fabric LTD is titled "All Roads Lead To Online Grocery." This title was chosen for a sound reason. Despite years of clicks grocery sales remaining at or near 2% of the overall grocery retail market, *Fabric* reported clicks penetration more than doubled in 2019, to 4.5%. Deutsche Bank predicted that in five years, this share of penetration by clicks grocery retailers would climb to 12%. But as discussed, COVID-19 accelerated clicks grocery retailers' movement toward greater market share into overdrive. Many retailers that were already losing in the struggle against e-commerce received a deadly one-two punch when COVID-19 erupted. Clearly, no bricks grocery retailer can afford to ignore the increasing numbers of grocery shoppers purchasing groceries online and expect to survive.

In *How The Mighty Fall* by Jim Collins, the highly respected business author described good companies that failed because they refused to innovate and became obsolete. In contrast, he discussed companies that adapted in the face of competition, became great and won the battle.

"A core business that meets a fundamental human need—and one at which you've become best in the world—rarely becomes obsolete," Collins wrote.

Even so, a company needs to reinvent itself over time, keeping only what works well. Collins wrote that "never-ending creative renewal" and "continuously experimenting with new ideas" are the keys to driving progress and gaining insurance against an uncertain future.

This brings me back to my main point: Unless bricks grocery retailers are willing to suffer the same fate of once-untouchable department stores, they must adapt rapidly to the reality of online grocery retailers.

"Though online grocery is still in its nascency, the industry had undergone a dramatic shift in just two short years and, in fact, has already passed the tipping point," *Fabric* CCO Steven Hornyak said. "Online grocery is no longer a question of 'if,' but 'how fast.'"

As I've said, history is littered with the refuse of companies once considered invulnerable to competition.

"Every institution is vulnerable, no matter how great," Jim Collins wrote. "No matter how much you've achieved, no matter how far you've gone, no matter how much power you've garnered, you are vulnerable to decline. There is no law of nature that the most powerful will inevitably remain at the top. Anyone can fall, and most eventually do."

The reality is that many retailers have been asleep at the wheel while online retailers are penetrating and consuming their businesses. Other retailers fail to acknowledge they are losing business to online retail or lack the resources necessary to adopt strategies to compete against online penetration.

Surviving, and thriving, is possible, but it will require work. I believe the strategies outlined in this book can help.

To bring this work to a close, food may be the most universal, unifying, and yet comfortingly diverse thing on the planet. It is also the primary thing we need, aside from water, to survive and ultimately thrive. Food is a part of the cultural lexicon in so many ways, such as the saying, "something to chew on." Food is a part of numerous traditions, from the sustenance offered by the Communion wafer dipped in wine to the solace of food brought to those suffering the loss of a relative or loved one. As you savor your food, remember the lessons provided in this book to keep your bricks grocery store nourished and thriving.

And remember to visit your local grocery retailer soon!

Thank you for reading *Silent Retail Killer*! Please leave an honest review online about what you liked or learned.

# BIBLIOGRAPHY

Abel, Carol. "The Small, But Mighty, Micro-Fulfillment Center." *Food Marketing Institute*. Retrieved from https://www.fmi.org/blog/view/fmi-blog/2019/08/09/the-small-but-mighty-micro-fulfillment-center, Aug 9, 2019.

Acosta, Gina. "A New Era For Whole Foods Market." *Progressive Grocer*. Retrieved from https://progressivegrocer.com/new-era-whole-foods-market, Dec 18, 2019.

Acosta, Gina. "How Lidl Elevates Private Brands." *Storebrands*. Retrieved from https://storebrands.com/how-lidl-elevates-private-brands, Apr 10, 2019.

Acosta, Gina. "Inside The New Stew Leonard's. Master Of Fresh." *Progressive Grocer*. Retrieved from https://progressivegrocer.com/inside-new-stew-leonards-master-fresh, Jan 6, 2020.

Acosta, Gina. "The Pandemic Private-Brand Opportunity." *Progressive Grocer*. Retrieved from https://progressivegrocer.com/pandemic-private-brand-opportunity, Jul 16, 2020.

Acosta, Gina. "Walmart Looking To Private Label For Growth." *Storebrands*. Retrieved from https://storebrands.com/walmart-looking-private-label-growth, Aug 12, 2019.

"A Fresh Approach To Grocery Order Fulfillment." *DEMATIC*. Retrieved from https://www.dematic.com/en-us/industries/industries-overview/grocery/, 2020.

Albrecht, Chris. "Online Grocery Demand Up 80-100 Percent At Takeoff's Robot Fulfillment Centers." *The Spoon*. Retrieved from https://thespoon.tech/online-grocery-demand-up-80-100-percent-at-takeoffs-robot-fulfilment-centers/, Apr 27, 2020.

"Aldi and Trader Joe's: Are they related?" *Produce Blue Book*. Retrieved from https://www.producebluebook.com/2019/07/19/aldi-and-trader-joes-are-they-related/#, Dec. 28, 2020.

"Aldi: Incorporating Aldi Nord And Aldi Sud." *Omnichannel Retailer Report*. Retrieved from https://lp.planetretail.net/rs/895-ENN-359/images/Aldi%20Omnichannel%20Retailer%20Report%20Oct%202018.pdf?mkt_tok=eyJpIjoiWm1VNE16bG1NamRrWmpneCIsInQiOiJqeTdodnI5Q3lZd0hqMGU4bU5nbHU4VVZmRWRJTWsxVHp3a0s1YmNSYTlEVXprcWVvMGRqMFptNjl2N3JVM1V3bmZKRWZYUjlcLzB0dGZYYTBEYmtiUEN4ejREVlwvSzZGSHRUSjdzelwvZHFhZXR0UnZSTHJNVnZDK3N1ejlIRU5mNSJ9, Oct 2018.

Aldrich, Elizabeth. "Is Amazon Helping Or Hurting Small Business?" *Lendio*. Retrieved from https://www.lendio.com/news/small-business-outlook/amazon-small-business/, Mar 29, 2019.

Ali, Fareeha. "eBay's US sales grow 22% in 2020." *Digital Commerce 360*. Retrieved from https://www.digitalcommerce360.com/article/ebays-sales, June 8, 2021.

Ali, Fareeha. "US e-commerce grows 44.0% in 2020." *Digital Commerce 360.* Retrieved from https://www.digitalcommerce360.com/article/us-e-commerce-sales. April 28, 2021.

"Alibaba and the Future of Business." Harvard Business Review. Retrieved from https://hbr.org/2018/09/alibaba-and-the-future-of-business, June 7, 2021.

"Alibaba vs. JD.Com: Which Of These Is The Amazon Of China?" *Digital Crew.* Retrieved from https://www.digitalcrew.agency/alibaba-vs-jd-com-which-of-these-is-the-amazon-of-china, June 8, 2021.

AlphaSense Staff. "Amazon Go, Whole Foods, And The Future Of Grocery." *AlphaSense.* Retrieved from https://www.alpha-sense.com/insights/grocery-trends-retail, 2019.

Apptopia. "Instacart And Grocery Delivery Apps Set Consecutive Days Of Record Downloads." March 16, 2020.

Amato-McCoy, Deena M. "H-E-B Retailer Buys On-Demand Delivery Start-Up." *Chain Store Age.* Retrieved from https://chainstoreage.com/operations/h-e-b-retailer-buys-demand-delivery-start, Feb 15, 2018.

"Amazon Ups Its Grocery Retail Game By Hiring Efficiency Experts From Lidl." *Brick Meets Click.* Retrieved from https://www.brickmeetsclick.com/amazon-ups-its-grocery-retail-game-by-hiring-efficiency-experts-from-lidl, Aug 17, 2020.

"Amazon Private Label Brands." *Marketplace Pulse.* Retrieved from https://www.marketplacepulse.com/amazon-private-label-brands, 2020.

"Amazon Versus Walmart: Omnichannel Showdown." *Wharton Magazine.* Retrieved from https://magazine.wharton.upenn.edu/issues/fall-winter-2017/amazon-versus-walmart-omnichannel-retail-showdown/, Fall/Winter 2017.

Anderson, George. "What Makes Consumers So Loyal To Publix, Wegmans, Trader Joe's And H-E-B?" *RetailWire.* Retrieved from https://retailwire.com/discussion/what-makes-consumers-so-loyal-to-publix-wegmans-trader-joes-and-h-e-b, 2017.

Angrabright, Jim. "Piggly Wiggly celebrates 100 while we select a CSA." *OurUrbanTimes.* Retrieved from http://oururbantimes.com/food/piggly-wiggly-celebrates-100-while-we-select-csa, April 9, 2021.

"August 2020 Scorecard: Online Grocery Market Rebalancing After COVID Spike." *Brick Meets Click.* Retrieved from https://www.brickmeetsclick.com/august-2020-scorecard--online-grocery-market-rebalancing-after-covid-spike, Sep 10, 2020.

Aylward, Lawrence. "H-E-B And The Human Touch." *Store Brands.* Retrieved from https://storebrands.com/h-e-b-and-human-touch, May 28, 2019.

*Backyard Farms.* "5 Things We Learned At The Whole Foods All Access Staff Training Event." Blog. Retrieved from https://www.backyardfarms.com/blog/2016/06/5-things-we-learned-at-the-whole-foods-all-access-staff-training-event, Jun 24, 2016.

Barron, Brittany. "Brand Loyalty For Retailers: The Rising Power Of Private Label." *Bazaarvoice Blog.* Retrieved from https://www.bazaarvoice.com/blog/the-rising-power-of-private-label/, Oct 31, 2019.

Berthene, April. "Walmart, Target And Home Depot Win At Omnichannel Retailing." *Digital Commerce 360.* Retrieved from https://www.digitalcommerce360.com/2019/02/19/walmart-target-and-home-depot-win-at-omnichannel-retailing/, Feb 19, 2019.

Bishop, Bill. "Amazon Fresh Grocery Stores: Don't Discount Them As Too Conventional – Here's Why." *Brick Meets Click*. Retrieved from https://www.brickmeetsclick.com/amazon-fresh-grocery-stores--don-t-discount-them-as-too-conventional--here-s-why, Sep 18, 2020.

Bishop, Bill. "Competing With Online Grocery Retailers: Five Ways Grocers Can Win More Sales." *Brick Meets Click*. Retrieved from https://www.brickmeetsclick.com/competing-with-online-grocery-retailers--five-ways-grocers-can-win-more-sales, May 6, 2019.

Bishop, Bill. "Don't Count Lidl Out In The US – Here's Why." *Brick Meets Click*. Retrieved from https://www.brickmeetsclick.com/don-t-count-lidl-out-in-the-us--here-s-why, Jun 10, 2019.

Bishop, Bill. "How COVID-19 Has Changed The Way Consumers Shop For Groceries: 4 Ways Retailers Can Up Their Game." *Brick Meets Click*. Retrieved from https://www.brickmeetsclick.com/how-covid-19-has-changed-the-way-consumers-shop-for-groceries--4-ways-retailers-can-up-their-game, Jul 13, 2020.

Bishop, Bill. "Retail expert Bill Bishop on what to expect next from Walmart." *Supermarket News*. Retrieved from https://www.supermarketnews.com/issues-trends/retail-expert-bill-bishop-what-expect-next-walmart, July 1, 2021.

Bishop, Bill. "What Will The Grocery Business Look Like In 5 Years." *Brick Meets Click*. Retrieved from https://www.brickmeetsclick.com/what-will-the-grocery-business-look-like-in-5-years-, Jun 26, 2017.

Bishop, Steve. "Where and how subscriptions can make dollars (and sense) for grocery retail." *Brick Meets Click*. Retrieved from https://www.brickmeetsclick.com/where-and-how-subscriptions-can-make-dollars--and-sense--for-grocery-retail, June 7, 2021.

Biswas, Abhishek. "Amazon Monopoly: The Rise Of Amazon Private Label Brands In 2019." *Hackernoon*. Retrieved from https://hackernoon.com/why-there-is-a-rise-of-amazon-private-label-brands-in-2019-c31b3zhg, Jan 17, 2020.

Blatherwick, Andrew. "Grocers Are Primed To Compete With Amazon's Free Grocery Delivery." *Retail Wire*. Retrieved from https://retailwire.com/discussion/grocers-are-primed-to-compete-with-amazons-free-grocery-delivery/, Sep 22, 2020.

Boss, Donna. "Amazon Tallies $10M In Whole Foods 365 Private Label Sales." *Supermarket News*. Retrieved from https://www.supermarketnews.com/private-label/amazon-tallies-10m-whole-foods-365-private-label-sales, Dec 21, 2017.

Browne, Michael. "Retailers Dig Deep For Community Outreach During Coronavirus Pandemic." *Supermarket News*. Retrieved from https://www.supermarketnews.com/issues-trends/retailers-dig-deep-community-outreach-during-coronavirus-pandemic, Mar 23, 2020.

Brumley, James. "The Kirkland Brand Is Costco's Secret Weapon When It Matters Most." *The Motley Fool*. Retrieved from https://www.fool.com/investing/2019/11/19/the-kirkland-brand-is-costcos-secret-weapon-when-i.aspx, Nov 19, 2019.

Burkus, David. "Why Whole Foods Builds Its Entire Business On Teams." *Forbes*. Retrieve from https://www.forbes.com/sites/davidburkus/2016/06/08/why-whole-foods-build-their-entire-business-on-teams/#75ba14543fa1, Jun 8, 2016.

Butler, Renee Ann. "4 Problems With Costco's Business Model." *Investopedia*. Retrieved from https://www.investopedia.com/articles/markets/011216/4-problems-costcos-business-model-cost.asp, Nov 3, 2019.

Campbell-Schmitt, Adam. "Amazon Opens Its First Full-Size Grocery Store." *Food & Wine*. Retrieved from https://www.foodandwine.com/news/amazon-grocery-store-woodland-hills-ca, Aug 27, 2020.

Castenando, Joseph. "Why Does Walmart Have The Worst Customer Service?" *Quora*. Retrieved from https://www.quora.com/Why-does-Walmart-have-the-worst-customer-service, 2019.

Chen, Connie. "Rastelli's sells top-quality meat and seafood to restaurants around the world—you can now order it online and have it delivered." *Insider*. Retrieved from https://www.businessinsider.com/rastellis-meat-delivery-review, June 2, 2021.

"Chewy and Amazon Continue to Beat Petco and PetSmart Online." *Pet Product News*. Retrieved from https://www.petproductnews.com/news/chewy-and-amazon-continue-to-beat-petco-and-petsmart-online/article_19b281e6-bf06-11eb-b014-bbc7107cda4e.html, June 5, 2021.

Chu, Franklin. "Omnichannel Lessons From Global E-Commerce Leaders." *SmartBrief*. Retrieved from https://www.smartbrief.com/original/2019/07/omnichannel-lessons-global-e-commerce-leaders, Jul 1, 2019.

Cimino, Adria. "Why Is Everyone Talking About Chewy Stock?" *The Motley Fool*. Retrieved from https://www.fool.com/investing/2021/04/20/why-is-everyone-talking-about-chewy-stock, May 26, 2021.

Clabaugh, Jeff. "For autism awareness, Va. teen gets his picture on Lidl peanut butter jars." *WTOP News*. Retrieved from https://wtop.com/business-finance/2019/04/woodbridge-teen-gets-his-picture-on-lidl-peanut-butter-jars, Jan. 20, 2021.

Collins, Jim. *How The Mighty Fall: And Why Some Companies Never Give In (Good To Great)*. New York: HarperCollins, 2009.

Cosgrove, Emma. "Inside Chewy's first automated fulfillment center." *Supply Chain Dive*. Retrieved from https://www.supplychaindive.com/news/chewy-automated-fulfilment-warehouse-goods-to-person/588176, May 19, 2021.

"Costco Food Court Menu & Prices 2021." *Fast Food Menu Prices*. Retrieved from https://www.fastfoodmenuprices.com/costco-food-court-menu-prices, June 19, 2021.

Criteo. "The Quick Guide To Omnichannel Marketing Success." Retrieved from https://go.criteo.com/get-started-with-the-criteo-ad-platform-13/?utm_source=leadgen&utm_medium=googlesearch&utm_campaign=LAD-omnichannel&gclid=Cj0KCQiArozwBRDOARIsAHo2s7tVsOaLPArxyQ8o4iBQjulRFMarbrn1vbNCnmYKh7EQvkXMgc9oIp8aAg27EALw_wcB, 2019.

Currie, Donna. "Best Online Health Food Stores: Purchase a variety of healthy products without ever leaving home." *The Spruce Eats*. Retrieved from https://www.thespruceeats.com/best-online-health-food-stores-4165675, May 3, 2021.

Currie, Donna. "The Best Places to Order Meat Online From the everyday to the unusual, these specialty retailers have what you need." *The Spruce Eats*. Retrieved from https://www.thespruceeats.com/best-places-to-order-meat-online-4165653, April 19, 2021.

D'Angelo, Matt. "How Small Businesses Must Adapt To The Amazon Effect." *Business News Daily*. Retrieved from https://www.businessnewsdaily.com/11161-amazon-changing-small-business.html, Nov 21, 2018.

Danziger, Pamela N. "Why Online Grocer Thrive Market Is Booming During The Pandemic With Sales Up 90%." *Forbes*. Retrieved from https://www.forbes.com/sites/pamdanziger/2020/09/16/thrive-market-is-thriving-in-the-pandemic-with-sales-up-90-thanks-to-these-4-trends/?sh=1163e45e5617, April 19.

Dastin, Jeffrey. "Amazon's Latest Grocery Store Concept Opens, With High-Tech Carts." *Reuters*. Retrieved from https://www.reuters.com/article/us-amazon-com-store/amazons-latest-grocery-store-concept-opens-with-high-tech-carts-idUSKBN25N0QF, Aug 27, 2020.

Dastin, Jeffrey and Rana, Akanksha. "Amazon's sales and profit rise as retailer rides wave of pandemic shopping." *Reuters*. Retrieved from https://www.reuters.com/technology/amazon-first-quarter-sales-beat-expectations-2021-04-29, June 8, 2021.

Davis, Brent. "Alibaba Competitors and Alternatives: Who Stacks Up Against this E-Commerce Giant?" The Stock Dork. Retrieved from https://www.thestockdork.com/alibaba-competitors-and-alternatives, June 8, 2021.

Day, Nellie. "Grocers Go Digital In The Age Of Omnichannel." *Shopping Center Business*. Retrieved from https://shoppingcenterbusiness.com/grocers-go-digital-in-the-age-of-omnichannel/, Feb 26, 2019.

Del Coro, Kristy. "Best Places to Buy Seafood Online: Get fresh fish sent to you on demand." Retrieved from https://www.thespruceeats.com/places-to-buy-fresh-seafood-online-1666076, April 19, 2021.

Del Rey, Jason. "Amazon Is Opening A Supermarket With No Cashiers. Is Whole Foods Next." *Vox*. Retrieved from https://www.vox.com/recode/2020/2/25/21151289/new-amazon-go-grocery-store-supermarket-cashiers-whole-foods-seattle, Feb 25, 2020.

Denning, Steve. "Whole Foods And The Triumph Of Customer Capitalism." *Forbes*. Retrieved from https://www.forbes.com/sites/stevedenning/2012/09/03/whole-foods-and-the-triumph-of-customer-capitalism/#3c6f3d1b4d83, 2012.

Dennis, Steve. "E-Commerce May Be Only 10% Of Retail, But That Doesn't Tell The Whole Story." *Forbes*. Retrieved from https://www.forbes.com/sites/stevendennis/2018/04/09/e-commerce-fake-news-the-only-10-fallacy/#cd09ac939b4f, Apr 9, 2018.

Demaitre, Eugene. "Online Grocery Orders Spike During Pandemic, To Drive Surge In Automation, Finds Fabric." *The Robot Report*. Retrieved from https://www.therobotreport.com/online-grocery-orders-spike-during-pandemic-to-drive-surge-in-automation-finds-fabric/, June 12, 2020.

Droesch, Blake. "US E-commerce by Category 2021. How the Pandemic Reshaped the E-commerce Landscape—and What that Means for 2021." eMarketer. Retrieved from https://www.emarketer.com/content/us-e-commerce-by-category-2021, July 2, 2021.

Dua, Taylor. "Kroger Aims To Become An Omnichannel Retailers Through DDB NY Appointment." *The Drum*. Retrieved from https://www.thedrum.com/news/2019/07/22/kroger-aims-become-omnichannel-retailer-through-ddb-ny-appointment, Jul 22, 2019.

Dudlicek, Jim. "Digital-First Grocery: A Look Inside Micro Fulfillment at Albertsons." *Progressive Grocer*. Retrieved from https://progressivegrocer.com/digital-first-grocery-look-inside-micro-fulfillment-albertsons, Mar 17, 2020.

Dudlicek, Jim. "Giant Food's New Ground-Up Format Focuses On Fresh." *Progressive Grocer*. Retrieved from https://progressivegrocer.com/video-tour-giant-foods-new-ground-format-focuses-fresh, Jan 28, 2020.

Duhigg, Charles. "Is Amazon Unstoppable?" *The New Yorker*. Retrieved from https://www.newyorker.com/magazine/2019/10/21/is-amazon-unstoppable, Oct 10, 2019.

Dumont, Jessica. "Supermarkets Won't Beat Aldi And Lidl On Price Alone." *Grocery Drive*. Retrieved from https://www.grocerydive.com/news/supermarkets-wont-beat-aldi-and-lidl-on-price-alone/550854/, Mar 20, 2019.

Dumont, Jessica. "Whole Foods Is Updating Its 365 Private Label Branding." *Grocery Drive*. Retrieved from https://www.grocerydive.com/news/whole-foods-is-updating-its-365-private-label-branding/570526/, Jan 16, 2020.

Dunnhumby. "Retailer Preference Index: U.S. Grocery Channel Edition." Dunnhumby. Retrieved from http://images.science.dunnhumby.com/Web/DunnHumbyLtd/%7Baff00645-9708-4856-b294-69119c5335a6%7D_2020_dunnhumby_Retailer_Preference_Index_Grocery_Edition.pdf, 2020.

Dwyer, Kate. "Kroger Is Upping Its Advertising Game." *Fortune*. Retrieved from https://fortune.com/2019/08/02/kroger-names-ddb-advertising-agency-of-record-omnichannel-grocery-strategy/, Aug 2, 2019.

Elejalde-Ruiz, Alexia. "Amazon Fresh To Open Thursday In Naperville. Here's What To Expect From The High-Tech Grocery Store." Retrieved from https://www.chicagotribune.com/business/ct-biz-amazon-fresh-naperville-opening-20201204-dgdnkyrv7ra5lk33psfgktuwcu-story.html, Dec 4, 2020.

Ellsworth, Kate Tully. "The 6 best places to order pet supplies online." *USA Today*. Retrieved from https://www.usatoday.com/story/tech/reviewedcom/2020/04/10/how-order-pet-supplies-online/5130133002, June 2, 2021.

Fabric, LTD. "All Roads Lead To Online Grocery." Fabric LTD. Retrieved from file:///C:/Users/TWK/Downloads/All-Roads-Lead-to-Online-Grocery-Fabric-2019-Online-Grocery-Report.pdf, Jan 2020.

Fabric, LTD. "The Impact Of Covid-19 On Online Grocery." Fabric LTD. Retrieved from file:///C:/Users/TWK/Downloads/The-impact-of-Covid-19-on-online-grocery-Fabric-report.pdf, Apr 2020.

FiELD AGENT. "Will Kohl's-Aldi Shopping Areas Really Appeal To Shoppers?" *FiELD AGENT*. Retrieved from https://blog.fieldagent.net/kohls-aldi-partnership-appeal-to-shoppers-photos-analysis?hs_amp=true, Apr 4, 2019.

Fitzell, Phil. "H-E-B Labels Build On Own-Brand Power." *Supermarket News*. Retrieved from https://www.supermarketnews.com/archive/h-e-b-labels-build-own-brand-power, Mar 6, 1995.

"Flipkart Ramps Up Its Grocery Operations; Expands Reach To 50+ Cities Across India." *The Flipkart Group*. Retrieved from https://storiesflistgv2.blob.core.windows.net/stories/2021/03/603dd34923e3f-603dd34923e42Press-Release-ENG_-Flipkart-expands-its-grocery-service-to-50-cities-across-India_March-2-2021.pdf.pdf, June 8, 2021.

Forde, Morgan. "How Online Order Fulfillment Is Changing Grocery In 3 Charts." *Supply Chain Drive*. Retrieved from https://www.supplychaindive.com/news/online-order-fulfillment-grocery-charts-survey-fabric/571811/, Feb 6, 2020.

Fox, Megan. "With Award-Winning Customer Service, Quality, Selection, And Low Prices, Wegmans Lancaster Opens At 7 a.m. On Sunday, Sept. 23." *Wegmans*. Retrieved from https://www.wegmans.com/news-media/press-releases/with-award-winning-customer-service-quality-selection-and-low-prices-wegmans-lancaster-opens-at-7-a-m-on-sunday-sept-23/, 2018.

Fox-Rubin, Ben. "Amazon Fresh Brings Smart Grocery Carts And Alexa To An LA Supermarket." *CNet*. Retrieved from https://www.cnet.com/news/amazon-fresh-brings-smart-grocery-carts-and-alexa-to-an-la-supermarket/, Aug 27, 2020.

Franciosi, Ana. "Subscriptions for e-commerce." *ObjectEdge*. Retrieved from https://www.objectedge.com/blog/subscriptions-for-e-commerce, May 19, 2021.

Garofalo, David. *David vs. Goliath: How To Compete, And Beat, The On-Line Giant: 100 Proven Promotions For Brick & Mortar Retailers.* BookBaby, 2019.

George, Jim. "Wegmans: Market Savvy And Co-Packing Lift Private Label." *Packaging World*. Retrieved from https://www.packworld.com/machinery/primary-packaging/article/13346074/wegmans-market-savvy-and-copacking-lift-private-label, Jan 7, 2010.

Gerace, Robert. *The Brick & Mortar Survival Guide: How To Use Technology To Create A Culture Of Retail Greatness And Thrive In An Increasingly On-Line Buying World.* Amazon Digital Services, 2017.

"Global grocery retail to generate an additional $440bn in sales by 2022." *Institute of Grocery Distribution*. Retrieved from https://www.igd.com/articles/article-viewer/t/global-grocery-retail-to-generate-an-additional-440bn-in-sales-by-2022/i/27776, July 1, 2021.

Goldberg, Jason. "The Race To Reinvent Grocery: How Amazon, Walmart And More Are Trying To Conquer The Space." *Forbes*. Retrieved from https://www.forbes.com/sites/jasongoldberg/2020/03/01/the-race-to-reinvent-grocery-how-amazon-walmart-and-more-are-trying-to-conquer-the-space/#6cc74ebe6138, Mar 1, 2020.

Green, Dennis. "Amazon Says Its Private Labels Are Only 1% Of Its Business, But New Data Shows Some Are Seeing Huge Growth." *Business Insider*. Retrieved from https://www.businessinsider.com/amazon-private-labels-some-grow-quickly-data-shows-2019-4, Apr 24, 2019.

Griffith, Eric. "22 Tips Every Amazon Addict Should Know." *PC Magazine*. Retrieved from https://www.pcmag.com/how-to/amazon-prime-tips-tricks, June 7, 2021.

Guarino, Raquel. "3 Reasons Why HEB Is One Of The Best Grocery Stores In The Country." Help.com. Retrieve from https://www.help.com/portfolio/3-reasons-why-heb-is-one-of-the-best-grocery-stores-in-the-country/, 2019.

Hamstra, Mark. "Chewy's CEO Explains How the Pet Products Disruptor Has Set the Stage for Ongoing Growth." *U.S. Chamber of Commerce*. Retrieved from https://www.uschamber.com/co/good-company/the-leap/chewy-repositions-for-growth, May 26, 2021.

"Harms Of Big Box Retail." *Good Jobs First*. Retrieved from https://www.goodjobsfirst.org/smart-growth-working-families/harms-big-box-retail, 2019.

Haroun, Chris. "Why The Best Companies Always Have The Best Customer Service." *Inc*. Retrieved from https://www.inc.com/chris-haroun/why-companies-like-apple-and-amazon-always-have-the-best-customer-service.html, 2018.

Hartman Group. "Walmart And Aldi And Lidl, Oh My!" *Forbes*. Retrieved from https://www.forbes.com/sites/thehartmangroup/2017/06/30/walmart-and-aldi-and-lidl-oh-my/#28a70fa4420b, Jun 30, 2017.

Hearn, Bradley. "What's In Store For Walmart Private Label Brands?" *ChannelAdvisor*. Retrieved from https://www.channeladvisor.com/blog/marketplaces/whats-in-store-for-walmart-private-label-brands/, Sep 26, 2019.

H-E-B. "H-E-B Expands Leadership Team, Reflecting Growing Importance of Digital." *Press Release*. Retrieved from https://newsroom.heb.com/h-e-b-expands-leadership-team-reflecting-growing-importance-of-digital/, May 15, 2018.

"H-E-B Dethrones Trader Joe's As Top U.S. Grocery Retailer In The 2020 Dunnhumby Retailer Preference Index." *Business Wire*. Retrieved from https://finance.yahoo.com/news/h-e-b-dethrones-trader-130000060.html, Jan 8, 2020.

"H-E-B Has Texas-Sized Digital Aspirations." *Retail Leader*. Retrieved from https://retailleader.com/h-e-b-has-texas-sized-digital-aspirations-0, Sep 7, 2018.

"H-E-B Is Top Retailer For Customer Experience Excellence." *Store Brands*. Retrieved from https://storebrands.com/h-e-b-top-retailer-customer-experience-excellence, 2019.

"H-E-B ranks highly on 2021 list of 100 best places to work." *ABC 13 Eyewitness News*. Retrieved from https://abc13.com/heb-work-at-h-e-b-best-places-to-glassdoor/9687968, June 18, 2021.

"H-E-B To Test Autonomous Delivery Later This Year." *Food Logistics*. Retrieved from https://www.foodlogistics.com/transportation/news/21077884/heb-to-test-autonomous-delivery-later-this-year, Jul 12, 2019.

"Here's Why People Shop on Amazon – And Why They'd Shop Elsewhere Too." *Marketing Charts*. Retrieved from https://www.marketingcharts.com/industries/retail-and-e-commerce-82536, June 7, 2020.

Hickman, Kiersten. "13 Reasons Why Aldi's Groceries Are So Cheap." *Taste of Home*. Retrieved from https://www.tasteofhome.com/collection/reason-aldis-groceries-are-so-cheap/, 2020.

Hoogeveen, Blake. "How Chick-Fil-A Exceeds At Customer Service." *MindSet*. Retrieved from https://blog.gomindset.com/chick-fil-as-secret-sauce, June 18, 2021.

Hornyak, Steven. "2019 Was A Crazy Year For Online Grocery, According To Our New Report." Retrieved from https://www.linkedin.com/pulse/2019-crazy-year-online-grocery-according-our-new-report-hornyak?trk=related_artice_, Jan 30, 2020.

Hornyak, Steven. "Expert Insight: Why COVID-Era Dark Stores Aren't Here To Stay." *Chain Store Age*. Retrieved from https://chainstoreage.com/expert-insight-why-covid-era-dark-stores-arent-here-stay, Jul 14, 2020.

Hornyak, Steven. "Micro-Fulfillment Can Save Retailers From The Online Grocery Money Pit." Retrieved from https://www.linkedin.com/pulse/micro-fulfillment-can-save-retailers-from-online-grocery-hornyak/?, Mar 11, 2020.

Hornyak, Steven. "The 'Click And Have It Now' Inferno That Has Sparked An Online Grocery Revolution." Retrieved from https://www.linkedin.com/pulse/click-have-now-inferno-has-sparked-online-grocery-steven-hornyak?trk=related_artice, Feb 21, 2020.

"How Aldi And Lidl Are Making The Difference." *Engage Business Media*. Retrieved from https://engagecustomer.com/how-aldi-and-lidl-are-making-the-difference/, Nov 14, 2019.

"How Will Micro-Fulfillment Centers Change The Retail Industry?" *I Am Robotics*. Retrieved from https://www.iamrobotics.com/how-will-micro-fulfillment-centers-change-the-retail-industry/, 2020.

Howland, Daphne. "Private Label Sales Growing Four Times Faster Than National Brands." *Retail Dive*. Retrieved from https://www.retaildive.com/news/private-label-sales-growing-four-times-faster-than-national-brands/564568/, Oct 2, 2019.

Howland, Daphne. "With Private Brands, Amazon Plays The Long Game." *Retail Dive*. Retrieved from https://www.retaildive.com/news/with-private-brands-amazon-plays-the-long-game/550790/, Mar 19, 2019.

Hunersen, Chelsea. "Why Amazon Is A Leader In Customer Experience." *Qualtrics*. Retrieved from https://www.qualtrics.com/blog/amazon-customer-experience-leader/, Jul 15, 2019.

Hyken, Shep. "Walmart Creates Training Academies To Improve Customer Service." *Forbes*. Retrieved from https://www.forbes.com/sites/shephyken/2016/03/12/walmart-creates-training-academies-to-improve-customer-service/#5982a35e2c57, 2016.

Inci, Duran. "Competing With Amazon: How Amazon's Top E-commerce Competitors Survive and Thrive." *Big Commerce*. Retrieved from https://www.bigcommerce.com/blog/amazon-competitors/#top-e-commerce-competitors-for-amazon, June 8, 2021.

Jacobsen, Tara, and Welch, Rebekah. *Retail Marketing Strategies For Brick & Mortar Businesses*. M&M Monsters, 2014.

Jagielski, David. "Why The Grocery Business Could Be A Big Part Of Amazon's Future Growth: Amazon Is Planning To Launch A New Grocery Store In Los Angeles." *The Motley Fool*. Retrieved from https://www.fool.com/investing/2019/11/24/why-the-grocery-business-could-be-a-big-part-of-am.aspx, Nov 24, 2019.

"JD growth trends in 2021." *GMA*. Retrieved from https://e-commercechinaagency.com/jd-growth-trends-in-2021, June 8, 2021.

Johnstone, Simon. "Aldi And Lidl: A Journey From Hard Discounters To Multichannel Retailers." *EssentialRetail*. Retrieved from https://www.essentialretail.com/analysis/58c806d412122-aldi-and-lidl-a-journey-from-hard-discounters-to-multichannel-retailers/, Mar 14, 2017.

Jones, Sally. "Best Dog Subscription Box 2021: Pet Treater vs. BarkBox vs. PupBox vs. PupJoy vs. Bullymake & More." *Canine Journal*. Retrieved from https://www.caninejournal.com/petbox-vs-barkbox-vs-pawpack, May 27, 2021.

Kaiser, Tom. "Brick Meets Click: Online Grocery Sales Dip 14 Percent." *Food On Demand*. Retrieved from https://foodondemandnews.com/03182021/brick-meets-click-online-grocery-sales-dip-14-percent, April 5, 2021.

Kang, Jaewon. "Kroger And Walmart Focus On Produce As Sales Soar." *MarketWatch*. Retrieved from https://www.marketwatch.com/story/kroger-walmart-focus-on-produce-as-sales-soar-2019-12-26, Dec 26, 2019.

Karlson, Eric, and Kahner, Erich. "Hospitality Will Make Or Break A Company Dealing With A Online Competitor." *Winsight Grocery Business*. Retrieved from https://www.winsightgrocerybusiness.com/retail-foodservice/3-strategic-paths-success-grocery, 2019.

Kelly, Debra. "The Untold Truth About Aldi." *Mashed*. Retrieved from https://www.mashed.com/79564/untold-truth-aldi/?utm_campaign=clip, 2019.

Keyes, Daniel. "Here's Why Costco's E-commerce Is Growing." *Business Insider*. Retrieved from https://www.businessinsider.com/costco-e-commerce-growing-2018-3, Mar 9, 2018.

Kim, Yujin. "Tracking Micro-Fulfillment In The Grocery Industry." *Grocery Dive*. Retrieved from https://www.grocerydive.com/news/tracking-micro-fulfillment-in-the-grocery-industry/569779/, Jan 8, 2020.

Kleckler, Abby. "Aldi Curbside Rolls Out To 35 Stores." *Progressive Grocer*. Retrieved from https://progressivegrocer.com/aldi-curbside-rolls-out-35-states, May 28, 2020.

Kleckler, Abby. "No Ceiling In Sight For Grocery Pickup, Deliver?" *Progressive Grocer*. Retrieved from https://progressivegrocer.com/no-ceiling-sight-grocery-pickup-delivery, Jul 06, 2020.

Koch, Lucy. "Did 'Clicks' Really Surpass 'Bricks' For Share Of US Retail Sales? Not Exactly. eMarketer. Retrieved from https://www.emarketer.com/content/did-clicks-really-surpass-bricks-for-share-of-us-retail-sales-not-exactly, Apr 17, 2019.

Kowitt, Beth. "Trader Joe's Really Puts The Private In Private Label. Here's How They Do It." *Fortune*. Retrieved from https://fortune.com/2017/08/10/trader-joes-private-label/. Apr 10, 2017.

KPMG LLP. "H-E-B, Public, Wegmans, Amazon Among Best In Customer Service." *Progressive Grocer*. https://progressivegrocer.com/h-e-b-publix-wegmans-amazon-among-best-customer-service-kpmg, 2018.

Krishna, Mrinalini. "The Amazon Effect On The U.S. Economy." *Investopedia*. Retrieved from https://www.investopedia.com/insights/amazon-effect-us-economy/, Jul 29, 2019.

"Kroger Expands Omnichannel Options With Seamless Shopping." *PYMNTS*. Retrieved from https://www.pymnts.com/news/retail/2018/kroger-grocery-earnings-omnicommerce/, Mar 9, 2018.

"Kroger's Simple Truth Brand Hits $2B In Sales." *Progressive Grocer*. Retrieved from https://progressivegrocer.com/krogers-simple-truth-brand-hits-2b-sales, Jan 25, 2018.

"Kroger Touts Omnichannel Moves As Investors Lose Patience." *PYMNTS*. Retrieve from https://www.pymnts.com/earnings/2019/kroger-omnichannel-investors-q4/, Mar 7, 2019.

L., Sean. "Walmart: A Surprising Winner In Omnichannel Retail." *Digital Innovation And Transformation*. Retrieved from https://digital.hbs.edu/platform-digit/submission/walmart-a-surprising-winner-in-omnichannel-retail/, Oct 19, 2015.

Ladd, Brittain. "Grocery Retailers Are Embracing Micro-Fulfillment – But Is That Enough?" *Forbes*. Retrieved from https://www.forbes.com/sites/brittainladd/2019/02/01/crossing-the-rubicon-why-2018-was-the-point-of-no-return-for-online-grocery/#30588de14467, Feb 1, 2019.

Lagroue, Mary Claire. "The Best Sites To Buy Groceries Online In 2020." *All Recipes*. Retrieved from https://www.allrecipes.com/article/best-online-grocery-shopping/, Jan 16, 2020.

Lal, Rajiv, Alvarez, Jose, and Greenberg, Dan. *Retail Revolution: Will Your Brick-And-Mortar Store Survive?* Rajiv Lal, 2015.

Lancefield, Neil. "Aldi And Lidl Top Customer Satisfaction Survey." *Independent*. Retrieved from https://www.independent.co.uk/news/business/news/aldi-and-lidl-top-customer-satisfaction-survey-6277182.html, 2011.

Lauchlan, Stuart. "Costco's Dilemma: E-commerce Is The Future, But The Business Model Is About The Warehouses." *Diginomica*. Retrieved from https://diginomica.com/costcos-dilemma-e-commerce-is-the-future-but-the-business-model-is-about-the-warehouses, Oct 7, 2018.

Lee Yohn, Denise. "H-E-B Goes Beyond Products And Pricing To Connect With Customers," (Excerpt). *Extraordinary Experiences: What Great Retail and Restaurant Brands Do*. Retrieved from https://deniseleeyohn.com/extraordinary-experiences/, 2019.

Lee Yohn, Denise. "Six Surprising Facts That Explain Trader Joe's Secrets To Success." *Forbes*. Retrieved from https://www.forbes.com/sites/deniselyohn/2018/06/13/six-surprising-facts-that-explain-trader-joes-secrets-to-success/#613b0b641601, Jun 13, 2018.

Lempert, Phil. "Inside Aldi's $5 Billion Plan To Become The Third-Largest Grocer In The U.S." *Forbes*. Retrieved from https://www.forbes.com/sites/phillempert/2018/08/09/aldi-is-focused-on-keeping-it-simple-and-high-quality/#1551d0ce427b, Aug 9, 2018.

Liao, Rita. "Alibaba and Amazon move over, we visited JD's connected grocery store in China." *TechCrunch*. Retrieved from https://techcrunch.com/2018/11/15/jd-7fresh-supermarket, June 8, 2021.

"Lidl 2019: Going Omnichannel, Disrupting Itself Before Others Do It, Vertical Integration, Digitalization And US Expansion." *Business Wire*. Retrieved from https://finance.yahoo.com/news/lidl-2019-going-omni-channel-184000784.html, Nov 14, 2019.

"Lidl Private Label." *Numerator*. Retrieved from https://www.numerator.com/resources/blog/lidl-private-label, Oct 24, 2017.

Lincicome, Elizabeth. "Competition among grocery chains heats up across NC." *The North State Journal*. Retrieved from https://nsjonline.com/article/2021/05/competition-among-grocery-chains-heats-up-across-nc, June 18, 2021.

Loeb, Walter. "Why Amazon's Domination Of Home Food Shopping Will Not Last." *Forbes*. Retrieved from https://www.forbes.com/sites/walterloeb/2020/08/31/why-amazons-domination-of-home-food-shopping-will-not-last/?sh=757635985eba, Aug 31, 2020.

Loria, Keith. "H-E-B Turns To Vertical Farming To Freshen Up Its Store-Grown Produce." *Grocery Dive*. Retrieved from https://www.grocerydive.com/news/grocery--h-e-b-turns-to-vertical-farming-to-freshen-up-its-store-grown-produce/535218/, Apr 17, 2020.

Lowrey, Tina M., ed. *Brick & Mortar Shopping In The 21st Century*. Psychology Press, 2007.

Ludwig, Frank. "The Lidl Shop Of Horrors." Retrieved from http://franklludwig.com/lidl.html, 2019.

Lusk, Mark. "Costco Shines As A Model Of Consistent Customer Service." *Label & Narrow Web*. Retrieved from https://www.labelandnarrowweb.com/issues/2017-04-01/view_customer-service/costco-shines-as-a-model-of-consistent-customer-service/, 2017.

Lutz, Ashley, and Hanbury, Mary. "Here's Why H-E-B Is The Best Grocery Store In The US." *Business Insider*. Retrieved from https://www.businessinsider.com/h-e-b-is-americas-best-grocery-store-2014-3, 2018.

M, Michael. "JD.com Opens Six 7Fresh Markets in Two Weeks." *Produce Report*. Retrieved from https://www.producereport.com/article/jdcom-opens-six-7fresh-markets-two-weeks, June 8, 2021.

Marino-Nachison, David. "Costco: Signs That Its Digital Strategy Is Working." *Barron's*. Retrieved from https://www.barrons.com/articles/costco-signs-that-its-digital-strategy-is-working-1535036857, Aug 23, 2018.

Martino, Victor. "Despite Headlines To The Contrary, Grocery Stores Are Alive And Well." *CO*. US Chamber of Commerce. Retrieved from https://www.uschamber.com/co/good-company/launch-pad/grocery-stores-alive-and-well, 2019.

Maxwell, Peter. "Why The Battle Between Sales And Fulfillment Will Redefine The Physical Store." *FRAME*. Retrieved from https://www.frameweb.com/news/fulfilment-centres-bod, Jun 22, 2020.

McGee, Tom. "Amazon And Whole Foods: Prime Time For Omnichannel Commerce." *Forbes*. Retrieved from https://www.forbes.com/sites/tommcgee/2017/06/16/amazon-and-whole-foods-prime-time-for-omnichannel-commerce/#4343de3a7919, Jun 16, 2017.

McKinnon, Tricia. "5 Reasons Walmart's e-commerce Strategy is Winning." *Indigo Digital.* Retrieved from https://www.indigo9digital.com/blog/4-secrets-to-walmarts-e-commerce-sucess, June 8, 2021.

McKinnon, Tricia. "The Future of Retail: 9 Ways Alibaba is Redefining Retail Stores." *Indigo Digital.* Retrieved from https://www.indigo9digital.com/blog/futureofretailalibaba,June 8, 2021.

McMillon, Doug. "How Walmart Is Transforming To Better Serve Customers." Walmart. Retrieved from https://corporate.walmart.com/newsroom/business/20161006/how-walmart-is-transforming-to-better-serve-customers, 2016.

MCORP.CX. "8 Customer Service Strategies You Can Steal From Amazon." MCORP.CX. Retrieved from https://www.mcorpcx.com/articles/8-customer-service-strategies-can-steal-amazon, 2019.

Melin, Anders and Gruley, Bryan. "Who's a Very Good Pandemic Business? Chewy Is. Oh, Yes It Is." *Bloomberg.* Retrieved from https://www.bloomberg.com/news/features/2020-11-18/chewy-chwy-is-having-a-great-2020-as-pet-care-surges-in-the-pandemic, May 19, 2021.

Mello, Tommy. "What Amazon Gets About Customers (That You Probably Don't)." *Inc.* Retrieved from https://www.inc.com/tommy-mello/this-5000-friends-strategy-made-amazon-more-successful-than-any-company-in-world.html.

Melton, James. "During the pandemic, Walmart and Target leverage their stores." *Digital Commerce 360.* Retrieved from https://www.digitalcommerce360.com/article/omnichannel-retail-strategies, July 1, 2021.

Melton, James. "Kroger Ramps Up Its Omnichannel Strategy." *Digital Commerce 360.* Retrieved from https://www.digitalcommerce360.com/2017/10/16/kroger-future-data-digital-customers-omnichannel-personalization/, Oct 16, 2017.

Meyer, Danny. *Setting The Table: The Transforming Power Of Hospitality In Business.* Ecco, 2008.

Meyersohn, Nathaniel. "America's Largest Grocer Is Revamping Its Produce Section." *CNN Business.* Retrieved from https://www.cnn.com/2019/11/20/business/walmart-groceries-kroger-aldi/index.html, Nov 20, 2019.

Meyersohn, Nathanial. "How A Cheap, Brutally Efficient Grocery Chain Is Upending America's Supermarkets." *CNN Business.* Retrieved from https://www.cnn.com/interactive/2019/05/business/aldi-walmart-low-food-prices/index.html, May 17, 2019.

Meyersohn, Nathaniel. "How Kirkland Signature Powers Costco's Success. *CNN Business.* Retrieved from https://www.cnn.com/2019/01/10/business/costco-kirkland-signature-brand/index.html, Jan 10, 2019.

Meyersohn, Nathaniel. "How Wegmans and H-E-B Survived Amazon's Onslaught." *CNN Business.* Retrieved from https://www.cnn.com/2019/11/13/business/heb-wegmans-publix-hy-vee-regional-grocery/index.html, Nov 13, 2019.

Milkman, Sam. "The Branding Genius Of Trader Joe's." *Coleman Insights Media Research.* Retrieved from https://colemaninsights.com/coleman-insights-blog/the-branding-genius-of-trader-joes, Apr 3, 2018.

Miller, Carolyn. *Brick & Mortar Franchise Success: Know The Costs Or Pay The Price.* Higher Purpose Publishing, 2017.

Misso, Ryne. "H-E-B's Bricks To Meet Clicks." *Numerator.* Retrieved from https://www.numerator.com/resources/blog/h-e-bs-bricks-meet-clicks, Aug 13, 2018.

Morgan, Blake. "Costco Takes Top Spot In Online Customer Satisfaction Over Amazon." *Forbes*. Retrieved from https://www.forbes.com/sites/blakemorgan/2019/02/27/costco-takes-top-spot-in-online-customer-satisfaction-over-amazon/#1a74ad9549a7, 2019.

Morton, Neal. "Wal-Mart Keeps Growing In Texas." *Houston Chronicle*. Retrieved from https://www.houstonchronicle.com/business/retail/article/Wal-Mart-keeps-growing-in-Texas-5169505.php, Jan 23, 2014.

Nichols, Greg. "A Sector Soars: Online Grocery Shopping Numbers Are Officially Crazy." *Robotics*. Retrieved from https://www.zdnet.com/article/one-sector-booms-online-grocery-shopping-numbers-are-officially-crazy/, Apr 16, 2020.

Nielsen. *The Future Of Grocery: E-Commerce, Digital Technology And Changing Shopping Preferences Around The World*. Nielsen, 2015.

Nisen, Max. "Wegmans Is A Great Grocery Store Because It's A Great Employer." *Quartz*. Retrieved from https://qz.com/404063/new-york-city-is-getting-a-great-grocery-store-in-wegmans-and-an-even-better-employer/, 2015.

Nolan, Hamilton. "A Walmart Worker Explains Why Walmart's Customer Service Is Horrible." *Gawker*. Retrieved from https://gawker.com/a-walmart-worker-explains-why-walmarts-customer-servic-1520609499, 2014.

O'Connell, Brian. "History of Alibaba: Timeline and Facts. TheStreet. Retrieved from https://www.thestreet.com/world/history-of-alibaba-15145103, June 8, 2021.

Ogino, Sean. "The Omni-Channel Tussle Between Sam's Club And Costco." *Annex Cloud*. Retrieved from https://www.annexcloud.com/blog/the-tussle-between-sams-club-and-costco/, 2019.

"Our Business." JD.com. Retrieved from https://corporate.jd.com/ourBusiness, June 8, 2021.

Owen, John. "The Not-So-Secret Secret To Trader Joe's Grocery Success." *Mintel*. Retrieved from https://www.mintel.com/blog/retail-market-news/the-not-so-secret-to-trader-joes-grocery-success, Mar 9, 2020.

Padmanabhan, V. Paddy. "Where Amazon Is Headed With Whole Foods." *INSEAD*. Retrieved from https://knowledge.insead.edu/blog/insead-blog/where-amazon-is-headed-with-whole-foods-8601, Mar 15, 2018.

Pak, Jaron. "You've Been Shopping At Aldi's All Wrong." *Mashed*. Retrieved from https://www.mashed.com/142014/youve-been-shopping-at-aldi-all-wrong/?utm_campaign=clip, 2019.

Palmer, Annie. "Amazon Expands Grocery Business Beyond Whole Foods With First Fresh Store In Los Angeles." *CNBC*. Retrieved from https://www.cnbc.com/2020/08/27/amazon-expands-beyond-whole-foods-with-fresh-grocery-store-chain.html, Aug 27, 2020.

Palmer, Annie. "Amazon Just Opened A Cashierless Supermarket – Here Are All The Ways It's Trying To Upend The Grocery Industry." *CNBC*. Retrieved from https://www.cnbc.com/2020/02/25/how-amazon-is-trying-to-upend-the-grocery-industry.html, Feb 25, 2020.

Parker, Nils. "Why Whole Foods Is America's Angriest Store." *Observer*. Retrieved from https://observer.com/2015/05/americas-angriest-store/, 2015.

Pearson, Bryan. "2018's Best Retail Trends: Learning From Kroger, Walmart, Lidl & Others." *Retail Customer Experience*. Retrieved from https://www.retailcustomerexperience.com/blogs/2018s-best-retail-trends-learning-from-kroger-walmart-lidl-others/, 2019.

Peirano, Julie. "All The Reasons People Are So Obsessed With Wegmans, The Best Grocery Chain In The Northeast." *CheatSheet*. Retrieved from https://www.cheatsheet.com/culture/reasons-people-obsessed-wegmans.html/, 2018.

Petro, Greg. "Walmart Vs. Amazon: The Private Label War." *Forbes*. Retrieved from https://www.forbes.com/sites/gregpetro/2018/07/15/walmart-vs-amazon-the-private-label-war/#1094a57b14c3, Jul 15, 2018.

Phelps, Stan. "The Secret Behind Chewy's Success." *LaptrinX*. Retrieved from https://laptrinhx.com/news/the-secret-behind-chewy-s-success-g3JOwEx, May 3, 2021.

Phillips-Donaldson, Debbie. "Pet food e-commerce 'on steroids' in 2020 and beyond." *Petfood Industry*. Retrieved from https://www.petfoodindustry.com/blogs/7-adventures-in-pet-food/post/9838-pet-food-e-commerce-on-steroids-in-2020-and-beyond, May 27, 2021.

PYMNTS. "What The Amazon Fresh Store Says About The Future Of Grocery Shopping." *PYMNTS*. Retrieved from https://www.pymnts.com/news/retail/2020/what-the-amazon-fresh-store-says-about-the-future-of-grocery-shopping/, Aug 27, 2020.

Rangaiah, Mallika. "The Success Story of Flipkart." AnalyticSteps. Retrieved from https://www.analyticssteps.com/blogs/success-story-flipkart, June 8, 2021.

Rangan, V. Kasturi. "H-E-B Own Brands." *Harvard Business Review*. Feb 5, 2002.

Rawes, Erika. "Walmart vs. Amazon: Which Online Retailer Is Better And Why." *Digital Trends*. Retrieved from https://www.digitaltrends.com/home/walmart-vs-amazon/, May 18, 2019.

Redman, Russell. "Amazon Fresh 'Built To Outlast' Other Grocery Retailers, Says Brick Meets Click." *Supermarket News*. Retrieved from https://www.supermarketnews.com/retail-financial/amazon-fresh-built-outlast-other-grocery-retailers-says-brick-meets-click, Sep 22, 2020.

Redman, Russell. "Amazon's Next Grocery Moves Will Be Data-Driven." *Supermarket News*. Retrieved from https://www.supermarketnews.com/retail-financial/amazon-s-next-grocery-moves-will-be-data-driven, Jan 30, 2020.

Redman, Russell. "Amazon Unveils First Amazon Fresh Grocery Store In Woodland Hills." *Supermarket News*. Retrieved from https://www.supermarketnews.com/retail-financial/amazon-unveils-first-amazon-fresh-grocery-store-woodland-hills, Aug 27, 2020.

Redman, Russell. "Costco Makes Strides With Grocery, Omnichannel Initiatives." *Supermarket News*. Retrieved from https://www.supermarketnews.com/retail-financial/costco-makes-strides-grocery-omnichannel-initiatives, May 31, 2019.

Redman, Russell. "Gap Between Online, Brick-And-Mortar Narrows For Food Shoppers." *Supermarket News*. Retrieved from https://www.supermarketnews.com/consumer-trends/gap-between-online-brick-and-mortar-narrows-food-shoppers, Jun 19, 2019.

Redman, Russell. "Kroger Unveils Simple Truth Plant-Based Food Line." *Supermarket News*. Retrieved from https://www.supermarketnews.com/private-label/kroger-unveils-simple-truth-plant-based-food-line, Sep 5, 2019.

Redman, Russell. "Report: Whole Foods to nix 365 store banner." *Supermarket News*. Retrieved from https://www.supermarketnews.com/retail-financial/report-whole-foods-nix-365-store-banner, Dec. 30, 2020.

Redman, Russell. "Walmart Realigns Organization To Drive Omnichannel." *Supermarket News*. Retrieved from https://www.supermarketnews.com/executive-changes/walmart-realigns-organization-drive-omnichannel, Jul 19, 2019.

Riemenschneider, Pamela. "Amazon Fresh Takes Huge Step In Competition With Walmart's Online Grocery." *Produce Blue Book*. Retrieved from https://www.producebluebook.com/2019/10/29/amazonfresh-takes-huge-step-in-competition-with-walmarts-online-grocery/#, 29 Oct, 2019.

Rice, Xan. "The Aldi Effect: How One Discount Supermarket Transformed The Way Britain Shops." *Guardian*. Retrieved from https://www.theguardian.com/business/2019/mar/05/long-read-aldi-discount-supermarket-changed-britain-shopping, Mar 5, 2019.

Rodionova, Zlata. "What's It Like To Work At Lidl?" *The Sun*. Retrieved from https://www.thesun.co.uk/money/3805045/whats-it-like-to-work-at-lidl/, Jun 15, 2017.

Rohde, David. "The Anti-Walmart: The Secret Sauce Of Wegmans Is People." *The Atlantic*. Retrieved from https://www.theatlantic.com/business/archive/2012/03/the-anti-walmart-the-secret-sauce-of-wegmans-is-people/254994/, 2012.

Rosenblum, Paula. "Chewy Beats Amazon In The Online Pet Supply Business; Customer Service Is The Key." *Forbes*. Retrieved from https://www.forbes.com/sites/paularosenblum/2018/02/26/chewy-beats-amazon-in-the-online-pet-supply-business/?sh=1b210ed27b02, May 19, 2021.

Rossi, Jason. "Here's Why Everyone Loves Costco's Customer Service So Much." *CheatSheet*. Retrieved from https://www.cheatsheet.com/money-career/costco-best-customer-service-america.html/, 2017.

Rooney, Kate. "Online Shopping Overtakes A Major Part Of Retail For The First Time Ever." CNBC. Retrieved from https://www.cnbc.com/2019/04/02/online-shopping-officially-overtakes-brick-and-mortar-retail-for-the-first-time-ever.html, Apr 2, 2019.

Samuely, Alex. "Will Walmart Become World's Largest Omnichannel Retailer With Jet.com Deal?" *Retail Industry Dive*. Retrieved from https://www.retaildive.com/ex/mobile-commercedaily/walmart-could-become-worlds-largest-omnichannel-retailer-with-jet-com-deal, 2019.

Sanchez, Carlos. "H-E-B Draws Up Battle Plans Against Amazon." *Texas Monthly*. Retrieved from https://www.texasmonthly.com/news/h-e-b-leases-austin-warehouse-huge-tech-facility/, Sep 5, 2018.

Scannell, Ed. "New Amazon Grocery Stores Run On Computer Vision, Apps." *TechTarget*. Retrieved from https://searchaws.techtarget.com/feature/New-Amazon-grocery-stores-run-on-computer-vision-apps, Sep 21, 2020.

Seebacher, Noreen. "Grocers Are Connecting Omnichannel Excellence To Better Customer Experience (CX)." *Customer THINK*. Retrieved from https://customerthink.com/grocers-are-connecting-omnichannel-excellence-to-better-cx/, Apr 25, 2018.

Serrano. Stephan. "What Amazon Teaches Us About Omnichannel Strategy In 2019." *Barilliance*. Retrieved from https://www.barilliance.com/amazon-omnichannel-strategy/, Apr 10, 2019.

Sheldon, Edward. "The petcare stocks I'd buy for 2021 and beyond." *The Motley Fool*. Retrieved from https://www.fool.co.uk/investing/2021/05/24/the-petcare-stocks-id-buy-for-2021-and-beyond, June 5, 2021.

"Shoppers More Interested In Trader Joe's Private Label Than Any Other Retailers." *Progressive Grocer.* Retrieved from https://progressivegrocer.com/shoppers-more-interested-trader-joes-private-label-any-other-retailers#:~:text=, Sep 27, 2018.

Shoup, Mary Ellen. "Online Grocery Shopping On The Rise And Should Be A 'Wake-Up' Call For All Brick-And-Mortar Retailers." *Food Navigator.* Retrieved from https://www.foodnavigator-usa.com/News/Markets/Online-grocery-shopping-on-the-rise-and-should-be-a-wake-up-call-for-all-brick-and-mortar-retailers#, Nov 6, 2018.

Silverstein, Sam. "Pandemic Highlights The Limits Of Store-Based Online Fulfillment, Experts Say." *Grocery Dive.* Retrieved from https://www.grocerydive.com/news/pandemic-highlights-the-limits-of-store-based-online-fulfillment-experts-s/575494/, May 6, 2020.

"Small Towns Devastated After Wal-Mart Stores Inc Decimates Mom-And-Pop Shops, Then Packs Up And Leaves: 'They Ruined Our Lives.'" *Financial Post.* Retrieved from https://business.financialpost.com/news/retail-marketing/small-towns-devastated-after-wal-mart-stores-inc-decimates-mom-and-pop-shops-then-packs-up-and-leaves-they-ruined-our-lives, Jan 25, 2016.

Smith, Jeff. "Is Your Online Grocery Strategy Keeping Up With Customer Preferences?" *Progressive Grocer.* Retrieved from https://progressivegrocer.com/your-online-grocery-strategy-keeping-customer-preferences, Aug 8, 2020.

Smith, Jennifer. "Grocery Delivery Goes Small With Micro-Fulfillment Centers." *The Wall Street Journal.* Retrieved from https://www.wsj.com/articles/grocery-delivery-goes-small-with-micro-fulfillment-centers-11580121002, Jan 27, 2020.

Solomon, Dan. "Take An Exclusive Look Inside H-E-B And Favor's New East Austin Tech Hub." *Texas Monthly.* Retrieved from https://www.texasmonthly.com/news/exclusive-look-heb-favor-new-east-austin-tech-hub/, Jun 24, 2019.

Stafford, Diane. "Inside Walmart's New Training Sessions: Trying To Adapt To Retail Landscape Changes." *Kansas City Star.* Retrieved from https://www.kansascity.com/news/business/workplace/article149941032.html, May 11, 2017.

Stice, Joel. "Workers Reveal What It's Really Like To Work At Aldi." *Mashed.* Retrieved from https://www.mashed.com/150935/workers-reveal-what-its-really-like-to-work-at-aldi/, 2019.

Stine, Lauren. "Aldi And Kohl's Set To Benefit From Combined Stores." *Grocery Dive.* Retrieved from https://www.grocerydive.com/news/aldi-and-kohls-set-to-benefit-from-combo-stores-report-says/552925/, Apr 17, 2019.

Strailey, Jennifer. "What's The Future Of Customer Service At Whole Foods?" *Winsight Grocery Business.* Retrieved from https://www.winsightgrocerybusiness.com/retailers/whats-future-customer-service-whole-foods, 2019.

"The Impact Of COVID-19 On Online Grocery." *Fabric.* Retrieved from https://getfabric.com/wp-content/uploads/2020/04/The-impact-of-Covid-19-on-online-grocery-Fabric-report.pdf, April 3, 2021.

"The seven reasons for Alibaba's success; Alibaba's development and framework." *Retail News Asia.* Retrieved from https://www.retailnews.asia/seven-reasons-alibabas-success-alibabas-development-framework, June 8, 2021.

Thomas, Lauren. "As e-commerce sales proliferate, Amazon holds on to top online retail spot." *CNBC.* Retrieved from https://www.cnbc.com/2021/06/18/as-e-commerce-sales-proliferate-amazon-holds-on-to-top-online-retail-spot.html, July 1, 2021.

Turner, Marcia Layton. "What Small Business Owners Can Learn From Wegmans." *Forbes*. Retrieved from https://www.forbes.com/sites/marciaturner/2017/01/31/what-small-business-owners-can-learn-from-wegmans/#5c5655d457fa, Jan 31, 2017.

Tyrner, Ashley. "The Boss: I Went From Relying on Food Stamps to Running a Multimillion-Dollar Company." *Time*. Retrieved from https://time.com/5278308/farmbox-direct-organic-food-ashley-tyrner-success, June 7, 2021.

"U.S. online pet care market - statistics & facts." *Statista*. Retrieved from https://www.statista.com/topics/4405/online-pet-care-market, May 27, 2021.

Vamanan, Dilip. "10 Walmart New Selling Strategies That Can Help Drive More Sales." *Sellerapp*. Retrieved from https://www.sellerapp.com/blog/walmart-selling-strategies/, 2018.

Vercelletto, Christina. "14 subscription boxes that will keep your pet happy all year long." *CNN Underscored*. Retrieved from https://www.cnn.com/2021/03/10/cnn-underscored/best-pet-subscription-boxes/index.html, May 27, 2021.

Waldron, John. "How Walmart Is Leading The Omnichannel Strategy Charge." *eTail*. Retrieved from https://etailwest.wbresearch.com/how-walmart-is-leading-the-omnichannel-charge, 2019.

Walk-Morris, Tatiana. "Profitero: Private labels pushing out CPGs in search results." *Grocery Dive*. Retrieved from https://www.grocerydive.com/news/profitero-private-labels-pushing-out-cpgs-in-search-results/600462, June 19, 2021.

Wallace, Tracey. "Omnichannel Retail Report: Generational Consumer Shopping Behavior Comes Into Focus + Its Importance In E-commerce." BigCommerce. Retrieved from https://www.bigcommerce.com/blog/omni-channel-retail/#developing-your-omni-channel-strategy, 2019.

"Walmart And The Power Of Private Labels." *ScrapeHero*. Retrieved from https://www.scrapehero.com/walmart-and-the-power-of-private-labels/, Jun 12, 2019.

Walton, Chris. "4 Reasons Why Amazon Fresh Will Change Grocery Shopping Forever." *Forbes*. Retrieved from https://www.forbes.com/sites/christopherwalton/2020/09/01/4-ways-amazon-fresh-will-change-grocery-shopping-forever/?sh=1d28d8cc1bde, Sep 1, 2020.

Wardini, Josh. "What Makes eBay So Successful?" StreetSignals. Retrieved from https://streetsignals.com/ebay-successful, June 8, 2021.

"Wegmans: A Celebration Of Food." *Storebrands*. Retrieved from https://storebrands.com/wegmans-celebration-food, Jan 2, 2013.

Weissman, Cale Guthrie. "How Walmart And Target Are Using Private-Label And Physical Stores To Fight Back Against Amazon." *ModernRetail*. Retrieved from https://www.modernretail.co/retailers/how-walmart-and-target-are-using-private-label-and-physical-stores-to-fight-back-against-amazon/, Sep 4, 2019.

Wells, Jeff. "Amazon's Grocery Lead On Navigating A 'Complicated' Industry." *Grocery Dive*. Retrieved from https://www.grocerydive.com/news/amazons-grocery-lead-on-navigating-a-complicated-industry/586668/, Oct 8, 2020.

Wells, Jeff. "Grocers look to online subscriptions to lock in digital demand." *Grocery Dive*. Retrieved from https://www.grocerydive.com/news/grocers-look-to-online-subscriptions-to-lock-in-digital-demand/588581, June 7, 2021.

Wertz, Jia. "5 Trends That Will Redefine Retail In 2019." *Forbes*. Retrieved from https://www.forbes.com/sites/jiawertz/2018/11/28/5-trends-that-will-redefine-retail-in-2019/#6ec546a46526, Nov 28, 2018.

"Will Amazon's New Grocery Stores Feature More Of Its Private Brands?" *Storebrands*. Retrieved from https://storebrands.com/will-amazons-new-grocery-stores-feature-more-its-private-brands, Oct 2, 2019.

Wilson, Jason. *Brick-And-Mortar Isn't Dead: How To Run A Successful Customer-Centric Business From Launch To Expansion*. Lioncrest Publishing, 2018.

Wolf-Mann, Ethan. "The New Way That Walmart Is Ruining America's Small Towns." *Money*. Retrieved from https://www.nydailynews.com/new-york/brooklyn/study-proves-walmart-super-stores-kill-local-small-businesses-article-1.14012, Jan 25, 2016.

Wood, Lauren. "Walmart As Omnichannel Competitor – Usage, Products And Services Initiative And Competitive Trends Report 2018." *Cision*. Retrieved from https://www.prnewswire.com/news-releases/walmart-as-omnichannel-competitor---usage-products-and-services-initiatives-and-competitive-trends-report-2018-300805045.html, Mar 1, 2019.

Wyman, Oliver. "LIDL Is Winning Over Next Generation Of Consumers According To New Oliver Wyman Survey." Oliver Wyman. Retrieved from https://www.oliverwyman.com/media-center/2018/june/lidl-is-winning-over-next-generation-of-consumers-according-to-n.html, 2020.

Zynstra. "The Store Of The Future: The Customer Reality And The Technical Chasm." Retrieved from https://www.zynstra.com/the-store-of-the-future-pre/?utm_expid=.DjEisisRRr-1fuM7m9jhUQ.2&utm_referrer=https%3A%2F%2Fwww.google.com%2F, 2019.

# ABOUT THE AUTHOR

**EDDY W. HOLLEMAN** draws from three decades of experience as a values-driven General Manager of a retail store and an adjunct professor in the business and accounting division. He lives with his wife in Houston, Texas, and has two adult children. Contact the author at eddy.holleman1@gmail.com.

www.ingramcontent.com/pod-product-compliance
Lightning Source LLC
Chambersburg PA
CBHW060458290526
45791CB00001B/165